# THE HINDENBURG

# THE
# HINDENBURG

*Michael Macdonald Mooney*

*Illustrated with photographs*

*Dodd, Mead & Company*
*New York*

Printed in the United States of America

For *Michael, Laird, and Christopher*

"For by Art is created that great Leviathan called a Commonwealth, or State . . . which is but an Artificiall Man . . . and in which, the Soveraignty is an Artificiall Soul, as giving life and motion to the whole body."

—*Leviathan,* THOMAS HOBBES

# CONTENTS

*Illustrations follow pages 84 and 148*

# THE HINDENBURG

# PROLOGUE

Sunday, May 2, 1937. In accordance with the regulations by which navigators and statesmen have calculated the turning of the world, the sun rose in Frankfurt, Germany at 4:36 Greenwich Mean Time, or at 3:04 Central European Time. But such measurements are only for the well informed. Whether it was morning or some other time was a matter of indifference to the sun, its gaze sweeping west as always, never blinking at the turning earth. Neither would the sun have considered whether it was Sunday, or some other day; 1937, or some other year.

Behind the sun's indifferent rays, paths of heat trailed west, clouds would form, rains fell, and now grasses grew on thirsty grounds. Even in lands where no man lived, passages were cleared for storms, and lightning sped on its way.

Well, this much is observable: each May, in the sun's northern fiefdoms, things quicken. It is the season of warming gentle breezes, of sweet scents on earth. So in 1937 as in every year, May was the season again of choices and consequences, of ancient play and new voyages. If old hopes were being buried, new ones might be born. May is always steeped in the dank secret smells of countless possibilities, of flowers bloomed, of growth and increase, of dancing and singing, of bodies' sweat, and of loam.

As always, every branch of every tree would be touched by some cockbird singing the praises of his territory. His conception of that territory might be capricious. He might not always stay. He might sing from still another branch to promise her—well, to promise her protection on the one hand and adventure on the other; to guarantee her perhaps—but not surely—time enough to work out May's permutations. As always, each soaring and alighting would be accompanied by the flutes and woodwinds of some advance or some retreat. Each trill signified some treaty made, some territory won, some defeat suffered. For May has always been the season of joinings and separations, of love and war, of fulfillments yet to come.

It has always been so. Once, when the sun shone in Eden's May garden, on the new displays of subtle green, among the buds of grapes and pomegranates, there on the slashes of scarlet, cuts of orange, mysterious blues, among the birds' song and flash of wing, then too there were apple trees. Their blooms must have been the same pearly, pink-white. If the fruit of one of them was forbidden, it was to avoid certain possibilities. But men began to calculate the probabilities, which are a somewhat different thing.

Precisely because the indifferent sun and pungent May had been working out the possibilities almost continuously, the same apples were in bloom just east of the airfield in Frankfurt, Germany on Sunday, May 2, 1937. It was the Sunday before Ascension Day, which would fall on Thursday, the sixth, and would be a German national holiday. And by Thursday, Joseph Leibrecht, electrician, and a member of the crew of the dirigible *Hindenburg*, calculated he would be in America.

It was not an unreasonable probability.

About an hour after sunrise Joseph Leibrecht bicycled through an orchard of May apple blooms on his way to report to duty. He was leaving the town of Neu Isenburg. As the sun gained on the horizon behind him, it warmed his back. He pedaled after his own shadow.

The apple orchard gave way to a forest of pine and oak from which song birds chattered. A row of beech marked the edge of the road on his right. As each tree filed by, Leibrecht listened to the birds. A chorus of dove took up a chant—their warning song. Leibrecht recited to himself: "Rain within the day, when the dove has his say."

It was just 11 kilometers from Neu Isenburg to the airfield. If it took him no more than a half hour, he would be early at the airfield. In the dew he could smell lilac from time to time, and wild onions. As an established member of the crew of the *Hindenburg* he would eat in

the Zeppelin Corporation's mess hall. All crew members had the right
to eat in the mess hall on the duty day preceding a flight.

His friends would be there, the other members of the crew, the
members of the Zeppelin family. Leibrecht would report to Philip
Lenz, Chief Electrician. So would Ernst Schlapp, the other electrician. Schlapp was a good fellow from Sprendlingen, near Offen-
bach. The three of them together had put every electrical wire into
the ship.

It had been a big job. They had made sure every connection worked
perfectly and was safe. Aboard a Zeppelin, electricity must be made
safe. If some wire should fail, which would be an unlikely possibility,
they knew the ship so well they could easily repair it. On the ground
or in the air. Everyone in the crew knew his duties.

The engineers and mechanics had helped to build the engines. The
steersmen had strung their own cables. The riggers had sewn the skin
and filled the balloons with gas. They would all be there at breakfast
too. Their common work had made a family of them—the Zeppelin
men.

After breakfast they would prepare the *Hindenburg* for its trip to
America. They had already made ten round trips to America in 1936,
which had been great successes. At first they had been welcomed as
heroes. Now the novelty of their transatlantic crossings had begun to
wane. Tomorrow they would sail on the first of 18 trips scheduled for
1937.

Leibrecht liked going to America. He had many friends in New
York City too. He always had a good time there. As he followed his
shadow towards the airport he hummed first this tune, then that, ex-
perimented again by repeating *Wohlauf, die Luft geht frisch und
rein* in a lower register. Aha, he had always thought it true: in the
morning the voice can sound lower by at least two notes, maybe three;
well, two anyway.

Joseph Leibrecht was 33. He was married to a good girl who loved
him because he was so carefree. She was herself not very practical and
sometimes spent more than he could make, which would leave them
with small debts. He would be angry, but only for a little while, and
she would promise to do better. In 1937 insurance was sold for pfen-
nigs at the kiosk along with the romance magazines. She began to buy
it with her subscriptions, not because she believed some accident

might strike her man on a Zeppelin, but because it seemed to be a way she could prove her ability to save. She told him about it, and they were both very pleased and proud of themselves.

They roomed in Neu Isenburg only because the *Hindenburg* sailed from Frankfurt on its transatlantic voyages. The home of the Zeppelins was in the south, in Friedrichshafen on Lake Constance—which Germans called the "Bodensee." Leibrecht's home was Lindau, at the eastern tip of the lake. He could walk a few steps from his house to the railroad station, take the train 20 kilometers west, and he could alight practically at the gates of the great Zeppelin works.

The railroad ran behind his house, went east to Bregenz in Austria, then around the curve of the lake to Liechtenstein and Switzerland. The borders of Switzerland, Austria and Germany all met right out there on the lake.

If you engaged Joseph Leibrecht on the geopolitical history of the lake's borders, he could not have helped you very much. He had heard it said that before the Great War no passports or identification papers were needed at all, but things were different now. In any case, from his bedroom windows he could see the Rhine flowing into the Bodensee. It flowed through the lake, passed Konstanz, then to Basel in the West, then ran just about due north all the way to the North Sea at Holland. He had made the trip himself in the Zeppelins.

Perhaps he did not know all he should about the councils, the wars, the treaties and the dynastic marriages by which borders are drawn, but as boy and man he had looked south across the lake at white topped alps. He could name every peak he could see: there was Hoher Kasten, Churfirsten, there was Saentis. He could look east and do much the same thing—there were the snow fields even in summer of the Arlberg. He did say he got along in life much as other men did—by eating and drinking and sleeping.

Black-haired, blue-eyed, short—he was sturdy. He was a good electrician. He had learned enough theory to be thorough and competent. In his practical combination of shrewdness and patience, electricity was something caught and tamed, much in the same way as a boy he had caught, caged, and then tamed birds. As he pedaled his bike to the airport, he could still identify every bird song the forest held. There was, however, much more opportunity in this modern world for electricians than for bird tamers.

His path to the airfield passed into a forest of high pine. The hangars would be just ahead. He gave up humming. Even for a practical man like himself the airfield with its huge new hangar was exciting. He passed on his left what would soon be the new town of Zeppelinheim. The houses were being built for crewmen and their families. Each house would have a red tile roof. Each house would have space for a good garden. Then he was across the bridge over the autobahn the New Order had built. Then down a slope to the field and he could coast almost to the mess hall.

The great hangar lay ahead now. One of the largest buildings in the world. It ran northeast and southwest nearly 1,000 feet. Its roof was twenty stories high. Leibrecht approached on the road around the landing circle, arriving at the north doors. They were still closed and he could not yet see the great dirigible sheathed inside, but he could feel it. Though the sun was up now, it would still be cool in there, shadowed, damp and still. And in its cave, suspended by the calculations of its technicians, hung the Leviathan. Air temperature, air pressure, the lift of the gas, the weight of the ballast, balanced it. Larger than the largest battleships, the size of the new *Queen Mary*, but made of gossamer and linen, aluminum and mathematics.

Well, they knew what they were doing, those engineers. The mess hall was about a block beyond the main gate, nestled against the hangar's south wall. He could smell coffee and sausage as he parked his bike. Judging by the other bikes in the stand, many of the crew were already there ahead of him.

"Good morning, Leibrecht."

It was Chief Steward Heinrich Kubis, an old-timer in Zeppelins, having served first as a steward aboard the passenger Zeppelin *Sachsen* in 1910. Chief Kubis, his chief assistant Eugen Nunnenmacher, and a new man shifted on the benches at the end of one of the long mess hall tables and made a place for Leibrecht. Kubis introduced the new man, Richard Mueller.

"Mueller is to cook for us under the direction of Chef Maier, so be good to him, electrician, and perhaps you can have three eggs for breakfast everyday."

Leibrecht beamed and went to work on the rolls, jam, eggs and sausage the Corporation had provided. Other members of the crew were arriving, exchanging the morning greetings, filing past the steam tables, finding places with friends.

"Come, Leibrecht, tell our new cook how New York really is," said Kubis. "You must listen, Mueller, for Leibrecht here is an expert at enjoying that city. Last year he stayed so late in the Yorkville bars visiting the pretty maidens, he almost missed the sailing of the ship. Isn't it true, Leibrecht?"

"No, no, I was just singing with friends."

"Yes, oh yes. They sang so late, in fact, our electrician here must drive a car with those friends from New York to Lakehurst at dawn to make the sailing in time. We are about to 'Up Ship' and Leibrecht arrived, escorted by the New Jersey State Police to the gangway. What was the name of this friend, Herr Leibrecht?"

"Felix Halder. His brother Richard is also my friend and lives near me in Lindau."

Kubis, who loved the little dramas of life, now had an audience. From the next table Helmsman Helmut Lau wanted to know: "Were they song birds, these singing friends of yours, Herr Leibrecht?"

"Whatever they were, they made our electrician very sleepy," Kubis continued. "He drove the car into another car in Elizabeth, New Jersey and had to be taken to the hospital. Fortunately many of the police in that state are good Germans too. They let our electrician escape the hospital, and drove him to our ship themselves. He arrived just in time, but all covered with scratches and bruises."

Helmsman Lau led the laughter at Leibrecht: "Automobiles are very dangerous, Leibrecht, you should know that!"

Which, of course, led to a detailed discussion of whether maidens were more dangerous than cars; whether older women gave more serious bruises, even if they were not all as visible; whether song birds could be kept in a cage; and other matters of high import. Meanwhile, they cleared their plates and cups, then moved in twos and threes to their lockers along the wall of the mess hall to don their Zeppelin uniforms.

They were work coveralls. The men had heard that before tomorrow's sailing they would be issued new ones for the flight. Every man's measurements and sizes had already been filed on a form for the purpose. The coveralls were one piece, with a belt at the waist, and of cotton. They had no buttons anywhere, having been specially designed.

Buttons might catch in the intricate wiring and struts of a Zeppelin. In addition, each man was provided with two pairs of specially made shoes with crepe soles and canvas tops. Even the grommets for the shoelaces were of reinforced cloth.

On the metal gangways and in the shafts of a Zeppelin, no spark could be struck by a hobnail; no static charge induced by the friction of wool or steel. Zeppelins were buoyed up by hydrogen. When mixed with oxygen from the air, hydrogen was the most explosive gas known. Consequently, the Zeppelin Corporation had eliminated even the most ridiculous probability. Their designers had seen to every detail, even eliminating the metal banding at the tip of a shoelace.

Once dressed in their coveralls and fitted in their shoes, the men came out the mess hall doors, angled 200 yards to their left towards the corner of the hangar's entrance, towards the huge doors facing northeast.

By silent understanding they were already walking together in command groups. Joseph Leibrecht had joined Ernst Schlapp in Chief Electrician Philip Lenz's party. Behind them came Chief Engineer Sauter, at his side his assistants Eugen Schaeuble and Wilhelm Dimmler. A pace behind were the two mechanics of starboard motor gondola #1, Joseph Schreibmueller and Walter Bahnholzer. Perhaps the other mechanics had gone ahead. Walking with Chief Steward Kubis were Nunnenmacher and Max Schulze, the other stewards having either gone ahead, or still lagging at the mess table. Out ahead was Chief Knorr.

Chief Rigger Ludwig Knorr had the walk of all chief petty officers in all the navies of the world—a rolling gait as if the North Sea were heaving beneath his feet, his hips on ball joints, the legs independently suspended from his carriage the better to absorb unexpected shocks, or adjust to some impossible feat in balance. At his side were the riggers he had personally trained: Hans Freund, from Rotenburg, who might someday be a chief rigger himself; and Ludwig Felber, who had come to Friedrichshafen five years ago for a job in the Zeppelin works. Felber had learned quickly as a rigger on the *Hindenburg*. This year at landing stations he would stand as a rigger, but on the regular watches he would begin his apprenticeship as an elevatorman. Knorr took pride in his students' advancement. Some elevatormen went on to become captains—as had Captain Sammt and Captain Pruss.

If it could be said that Knorr had a favorite, however, it was Eric Spehl. The young man walking at the Chief's left was 25, tall and blond and blue-eyed and handsome. He had been born in Gösch-weiler, a tiny farm village in the upland meadows of the Black Forest region; then had been trained as an upholsterer's apprentice; then gone to work in the Zeppelin works in late 1934, taking a job as an apprentice rigger, working with the needle and sewing machine. He went to work on the new ship then under construction, the *Hindenburg*, and had come under the wing of Chief Rigger Knorr.

Just like an upholsterer, a rigger's work was with his hands. His prime tools were the heavy sailmaker's needle and thread strong enough to stand the strain of gales. The needle was pushed through the fabric with a device called a palm—a leather half glove from which the fingers had been cut off and in which there was a depression filled with carbonized steel the size of a two mark piece. The back end of the needle was triangular and fit into the nest of carbon. The whole hand then could be used to push the needle through its cloth, or through rope, or even threaded through the strands of steel wire.

With his hands a rigger kept the cloth running straight through the sewing machine, and lying flat. With his hands a rigger whipped and seized the ends of lines; spliced line to line, and sometimes linen line to wire cable. A rigger had to be able to climb high into the ship and patch a tear in a gas bag, or repair the linen covering stretched over the frames. Chief Rigger Ludwig Knorr thought Spehl had good hands. Besides he liked the boy.

He had chosen Spehl as one of the two riggers to assist him aboard the *Hindenburg* after it was commissioned in March 1936. He had talked to the boy and learned about his family and life on the farm. He taught the boy how Zeppelins were made and told him the stories of Zeppelins at war. When Spehl's father died in 1936, Knorr made a considerable effort to spend extra time with the boy—on watch and off. The Chief Rigger sensed that here was certainly a potential helmsman, and perhaps also a captain someday too.

After breakfast that Sunday it was Knorr's group of riggers who rounded the corner of the hangar first. The great doors were now drawn back. The snout of the ship loomed high above their heads, the morning light reflected on its silver bow, its tapered streamlined flanks reaching way back into the shadows of its cave.

But strung across the mouth of the gaping hangar face there was a line of Sicherheitsdienst men—the Schutzstaffel Security Service—at parade rest. In the center of the line, directly below the bow of the ship, stood a group of seven or eight S.D. men. Two of them were handling two Alsatian guard dogs. The dogs barked immediately. Eric Spehl stopped dead in his tracks.

"No, no, come along," said Chief Knorr. "They are nothing but tourists, as we shall see." He led his group towards the dogs where he had spotted Zeppelin Captain Anton Wittemann standing with an S.D. lieutenant.

"Good morning, Herr Captain Wittemann. Good morning, Herr Lieutenant. Have we some new orders for the morning?"

Captain Wittemann returned the good mornings to Knorr and to Knorr's men. He introduced the S.D. lieutenant as a Lieutenant Benziger who acknowledged their "Grüss Gotts" with a "Heil Hitler!" The new salutation made the Zeppelin men uncomfortable, but their respectful faces never changed.

Captain Wittemann explained the ship was to have another inspection in preparation for the trip. It was to be inspected from bow to stern, from top to bottom, in every nook and cranny. The execution of this duty was to be done by command groups under the direction of each chief. With each group, the S.D. lieutenant would assign two men. So, for example, two S.D. inspectors to inspect the engine facilities with Chief Engineer Sauter; two to inspect Electrical with Chief Lenz; two to examine all passenger facilities and mess equipment with Chief Steward Kubis; and two to inspect the interior and the gas bags under the direction of Chief Knorr. The inspection was to be exact and complete. The S.D. men had already been equipped with special non-sparking shoes. They had been provided a plan of the ship.

Chief Knorr paused for a moment in wonder. There were the S.D. men in the proper shoes. But if they were not trained Zeppelin men, what in the world would they gain by clambering through the walks and gangways? What foolishness! What did they think they would see?

Of course, he could guess immediately the reasons for such security measures. Near the end of the Great War, in January 1918, five of the

Navy dirigibles, the L 46, 47, 52 and 58 and the SL 20 had been sabo-taged while sitting in their hangars at the Alhorn Naval Base, near Bremen. The saboteurs were Navy men. They "scuttled" their ships. Then just after the war, when the revengeful French had insisted on commandeering the little passenger Zeppelin *Nordstern*, a bomb had been discovered before it exploded. Perhaps a patriotic German thought he might keep the ship from the French. Then in Rio de Janeiro in 1935 a bomb was found in the main dining saloon of the *Graf Zeppelin*.

But Zeppelin men had found these bombs. An S.D. man couldn't find an elephant aboard a Zeppelin, if a Zeppelin man did not show him where it was hidden. The S.D. men would do well enough to see to the security of passengers coming aboard. That's where they should conduct their searches. Surely, no Zeppelin man would put a bomb in a ship in which he himself was going to travel. Such foolishness. There was so much foolishness these days.

But Knorr said nothing. He nodded his assent to Captain Wit-temann. He said to the two S.D. men who stepped forward: "All right then, come along with us. We will begin from our landing sta-tions."

He marched his group under the bow of the silver ship, past the command gondola, towards the gangway at Ring 173, about 300 feet aft of the bow. The gangway would lead them into the ship's interior. The two S.D. men hung close by Chief Knorr's side. In their canvas and crepe shoes their footfalls made no sound on the concrete hangar floor. They felt the disquiet any pagan feels upon entering a temple in which strange rites were celebrated. What was it that held so large a thing in the air? For all their modern sophistication, when actually confronted with such a strange thing, they sensed its mystery. In their blue coveralls, Chief Knorr and his men had the supreme confidence of ordained priests. As it loomed above their heads the S.D. men knew they should be properly reverent, despite the fact it all could probably be explained in perfectly sensible technical formula. When they reached the gangway stairs, Chief Knorr still led the way into the belly of the whale.

# CHAPTER 1

# DEUS EX MACHINA

"The first condition of power is the worship of power."
—JOSEPH GOEBBELS

THE *Hindenburg* was commissioned in March 1936. Assigned builder's number of LZ 129 (Luftschiff Zeppelin 129), it was actually the 118th of the Zeppelin type dirigible built in Germany, other numbers in the series having been assigned in orderly progression to ships laid down on paper but never built.

It was the pride of Germany and the symbol of postwar German commercial expansiveness. What the *Queen Mary* was to Britain and the *Normandie* to France, the *Hindenburg* was to Germany. One American newspaper had said in an editorial:

"The German people are a race of Titans, of admirable energy and astonishing capabilities. Not yet recovered from the effects of the World War, they developed an activity which has enthralled the entire world and which deserves the highest praise. Hail to the fearless conquerors of space."

A *New York Times* editorial was more circumspect, but equally enthusiastic. In 1936, at the end of the *Hindenburg's* first season, *The Times* said: "There can be only acclaim for the convincing manner in which the Deutsche Zeppelin Reederei has concluded the experimental service by airship across the North Atlantic which it began last May. On Monday the *Hindenburg*, largest aircraft constructed by man, docked at her home port of Frankfurt at the end of her tenth round trip with passengers, mail and freight. During the season she has transported more than 1,200 passengers in both directions between the United States and Germany. All have praised her quiet comfort and their own sense of ease and security.

"The huge structure with sleeping accommodations for fifty passengers—a figure increased toward the end of the season to seventy—has come and gone between Frankfurt and Lakehurst with all the regularity of an ocean liner."

The *Hindenburg* was the successor ship to the *Graf Zeppelin* (LZ 127) launched in 1928, the year after Charles Lindbergh had landed in Paris. The *Graf Zeppelin* had an astonishing record of its own. In 1929 it flew around the world, covering 22,000 miles in slightly more than 20 days, carrying 20 passengers, mail and freight. Then a regularly scheduled service was inaugurated between Frankfurt and Rio de Janeiro, non-stop. It took about 100 hours in the air. By ship the trip would require five weeks instead of five days. By May 1937 the *Graf Zeppelin* had made 650 flights, carried more than 18,000 passengers, and won for its German builders and German crew the admiration of the world. The peacetime potentials of airship service were considered almost unlimited.

But from the beginning it had never been clear whether dirigibles had evolved technologically as craft of peace or war. The Graf Ferdinand von Zeppelin, affectionately known as "that crazy old count," for whom the LZ 127 had been named, and for whom all dirigibles came to be called "Zeppelins," had loved war intensely.

Born in 1838 in Konstanz at the eastern tip of the Bodensee, he came from a Prussian family whose fortune came from landholdings, but whose fame was won at war. When the American Civil War started, the 23-year-old Graf had taken ship for New York as soon as he could arrange it. He arrived in Washington with his own horses, and a letter of introduction to President Lincoln.

Secretary of State Seward introduced the Graf to the President. Graf Zeppelin was supposed to have said to Abraham Lincoln that his family "had been counts for generations," by which he meant with some pride, warrior counts. Lincoln replied that no one would object to that as long as he fought well and minded his manners.

Count Zeppelin joined the Union Army as an "observer." Thanks to Lincoln's acceptance, the Graf Zeppelin did not need to use another letter of introduction he also had in his pocket—a letter to General Robert E. Lee. To gain Graf Zeppelin's alliance in war was apparently a matter of first come, first served.

He joined General Hooker's Army of the Potomac as a cavalry officer, taking part in the action at Fredericksburg and Ashby Gap, then bored with the pace of the Union Army and perhaps suspecting that he had chosen the wrong side, he joined an expedition to investigate the sources of the Mississippi River. The party consisted of two Indians, two Russians, and the Graf. They got as far as St. Paul, Minnesota. There the cavalryman took his first ride in a balloon. It seemed to him that if the thing could be steered and propelled somehow, it might make a better scouting device than a platoon of horse.

By 1866 he was back in Europe. He fought for the King of Württemberg on the losing Austrian side against Prussia. Then in the war of 1870 against France he joined the winning side and led the first long-range cavalry scouting party of the war nearly 100 miles behind the French lines. His little troupe of three officers and six men was surprised and surrounded. The two other officers—a Scot named Winston and a young Baron von Wechmar—were wounded and captured. Though also wounded, Graf Zeppelin arrived back at his own camp on the horse of a French Dragoon. He was decorated and won the title of the "Crazy Count." More important, during the siege of Paris he was again impressed by the scouting abilities of balloons. He drew up plans for a dirigible—a balloon that could be steered. But his Army career still absorbed his time.

Then in 1887, while serving as the Ambassador of Württemberg to Prussia, the plain-spoken cavalry officer earned the disfavor of Kaiser Wilhelm. He was prematurely retired as a brigadier general at 52, and he took up residence again in the kingdom of Württemberg on the shores of the Bodensee. By 1894 he applied for and won a patent for a dirigible. Nearby, Gottlieb Daimler was making gasoline powered engines.

Before the turn of the century, the fever to make a powered flight was international. In 1863 Jules Verne had imagined the *Victoria*, a huge balloon manned by the intrepid Dr. Ferguson and his faithful Negro companion, Joe, on a five-week trip across Africa. The press demanded the engineers get to work and make a practical copy. The scientific simulacrum, the *Giant* (with a real Negro boy called Joe aboard), set off from Paris and covered 400 miles on its maiden voyage while its passengers sipped champagne. The trip ended near Hannover in a reasonably spectacular crash.

In 1880 Edison proposed an airplane powered by an engine that would have to weigh only three pounds per horsepower. He tested an engine which was fueled with stock ticker tape spaced with bits of explosive and ignited by electric sparks. His repeater cap pistol almost killed him. He turned his attention to other devices.

Jules Verne, however, was never discouraged by mere technical difficulties. In 1885 he designed a helicopter he named the *Albatross*. It was to have 37 rotors, each with a pair of counterrotating propellers. Two huge four-bladed propellers at bow and stern would give the ship forward speed. He had the hero of his story, a certain Robur, plan to use the "Clipper Ship of the Clouds" to unite the nations of the world into a brotherhood of peace and democracy.

Verne saw that the fantastic vehicles of air travel would arouse people to an enthusiasm for a society shaped according to the laws of reason and mathematics. He feared that with the help of science, unscrupulous dictators might hypnotize mobs into wars of aggression for world conquest. At the end of Verne's story Robur lectures a crowd in bitter tones. Robur promises to reveal the secret of the airplane only when men cease to be wolves. Robur was ignored. Men wanted to fly.

Clement Ader, who had made a fortune installing the Bell Telephone in France, got a monoplane called the *Éole* in the air for 160 feet of powered flight. It couldn't be controlled, however, and crashed. Hiram Maxim, who had made a fortune from his invention of the machine gun, started a 3.5-ton, steam-powered, 145-foot monster down a rather short railroad launching track. It may have got up to 50 m.p.h., but not, alas, in the air. It plowed through the crash barrier at the end of the track. Maxim lived through it.

On May 6, 1896 in the presence of Alexander Graham Bell and several other friends, Professor Samuel P. Langley catapulted a steam-powered monoplane off a houseboat on the Potomac River. It gained 100 feet in altitude and flew 30 miles per hour. There was no one aboard, but when the motor stopped after three quarters of a mile, it landed gracefully in the Potomac without damage. The War Department put up $100,000 and commissioned further work. Three years later, in 1899, the Wright brothers of Dayton, Ohio, wrote to the Smithsonian Institute, asking for references on aeronautics.

At 6:00 P.M. on July 2, 1900, Graf Zeppelin stepped onto a small floating platform on Lake Constance near Friedrichshafen. He took off his white yachting cap and bent his head in prayer. He was 62. His drooping moustache had turned white and the bowed head was a halo of white. Thousands of spectators hushed in respectful silence. They had come to see the flying machine of the Crazy Old Count.

His prayer finished, he replaced his hat and stepped into the open end of a long hangar built on floats riding on the calm Bodensee. A tow rope was fastened from the little steamer *Buchhorn*, and the steamer began pulling the Count's invention from its hangar and into the wind. What looked like a long sausage, 425 feet long, resting on floats, was being dragged from its cocoon. The crowd was amazed.

A large screen covered the steamer's smokestack to keep live sparks from falling onto the sausage bag, which contained thousands of feet of hydrogen gas. Two little gondolas were suspended under the bag. They were connected by a catwalk, from which hung a cable holding a 550-pound weight. To make the airship rise, the cable was supposed to be shoved to the rear; to descend, the cable was run forward. Rudders at bow and stern were supposed to steer the thing. The crowd hushed.

The steamer gathered speed, the tow ropes cast off. The flying machine's two four-cylinder Daimler engines began to fire. Together they developed all of 32 horsepower. The LZ 1 rose to 1,300 feet and began to move steadily over the lake. The crowd cheered: the monster was actually flying!

After 18 minutes the sliding lever broke; then the rudder ropes tangled; and then the ship's hull began to buckle. It came down near Immenstaad, landing most precisely on the only stake in that part of the lake. The stake punctured the gas bags, but that night the *Buchhorn* towed the new wonder back to its hangar.

On October 17 it flew again for 80 minutes, making lazy turns and circles. By mistake an overanxious mechanic poured distilled water into the gas tanks, the engines stopped and again a motorboat towed it back to the hangar. On October 20 it flew one more time for 23 minutes, but it was slow against the wind. The little Daimler engines did not provide enough power. Imperial Army observers were disappointed: the ship was too slow for military purposes. The Army would not advance money to continue. On November 15, 1900 the Company for the Promotion of Aeronautics, which had financed the building of the ship, was dissolved. "An airshipman without an airship," said the Graf Zeppelin, "is like a cavalry officer without a horse."

Curiously, the credit for the first powered and controlled flight did not belong to Graf Zeppelin at all but instead to a remarkable Brazilian, a devotee of Jules Verne and H. G. Wells, Alberto Santos-Dumont.

His father was the richest planter in Brazil. On his son's eighteenth birthday, the planter gave him a check for a fortune and some practical advice: "Go to Paris, the most dangerous of cities for a young fellow. Let us see if you can make a man of yourself."

The young man took up automobiles, mountain climbing and ballooning. On his first balloon trip he took along a luncheon of roast beef, chicken, ice cream, cakes, champagne, hot coffee, and a good Chartreuse. Afterwards he amused the sophisticated aristocrats of the Jockey Club with his descriptions of his meal in the sky. "No dining room is as well decorated."

He designed his own balloon, using Japanese silk instead of the usual heavily treated taffetas. Uninflated he could pack it in his valise and carry it around Paris. He then decided to power a cigar-shaped bag with the 12 h.p. engine of his tricycle. The cigar shape would offer less resistance to the wind. Below the bag he built a long catwalk. By running up and down the catwalk, he could use his own weight to keep the balloon balanced. To steer he designed a large triangular rudder. A bicycle pump was carried to inflate an inner balloonette, as hydrogen was lost inside the main balloon. His theory was that he should build the smallest balloon possible, thereby demanding the least possible horsepower from the engine's propellers.

On September 20, 1898—two years before Graf Zeppelin's flight —the 82-foot dirigible was ready. It stood on a broad field in the Jardin d'Acclimation. Standing by were dandies in frock coats, groups of students and office workers, pretty girls with billowing skirts and parasols, and friends of Santos-Dumont from "le Jockey." His friends attempted to dissuade him: the sparks of the engine would surely explode the hydrogen. A German, Wolfert, had recently been burned to death in the wire cage of his benzine-powered craft; a Russian aluminum designer had been blown to bits in St. Petersburg.

The dapper young Santos-Dumont would not be dissuaded. He was ready. Dressed in a pin-stripe suit, with high collar, derby, kid-gloves and glossy shoes with heels one inch high, he pulled the starter cord himself. The engine coughed and started. He hopped into the wicker car, and in a few seconds the *Santos-Dumont #1* was sailing safely above the trees of Paris.

He sailed in every direction of the compass. More important, he actually drove the ship upwind. He did figures of eight. He climbed to 1,300 feet, started a steep, and daring glide. Something popped over his head. He looked up and saw the cigar had crumpled into a jack-knife shape. The bicycle pump which was supposed to reinflate the inner balloonette—and keep the bag rigid—wasn't working. The bag was limp.

Down he went. He chucked out ballast at the last moment. Three hundred feet from the ground he saw a gang of boys playing with kites. He was trailing a 200-foot guide rope from his launching. He shouted to the boys to grab the rope: "Run into the wind!"

The boys were bright. They grabbed and ran. Just as the basket was about to crash, they had the balloon soaring again like a kite. A few seconds later Santos had landed with only a slight bump. Santos-Dumont was a man and Paris was enchanted.

Henry Deutsch, a fellow member of "le Jockey," organized the Aero Club. Comte Albert de Dion donated land at St. Cloud to be used for aviation. Deutsch and others put up a prize of 100,000 francs for the first man who could fly from the grounds at St. Cloud to the Eiffel Tower and back—a distance of about seven miles—in thirty minutes. Santos would try for the prize.

His second dirigible landed him in a tree. Reporters rushed to the scene to find their hero sitting on a limb. He asked them for a glass of beer. The guide rope of his third tangled in some telegraph wires and ripped the bag. His fourth ship crashed too. In *Santos-Dumont #5* he set off again. This time it took him only nine minutes to turn the Eiffel Tower. Though it was 6:30 in the morning the streets of Paris were jammed with spectators. "Le petit Santos" had become the city's darling. Young men imitated his slicked-down hair, his moustache, his high-heeled shoes, his excited way of talking. If he could turn the tower in nine minutes, surely the prize was won.

But just after he did turn the tower, the balloon began to sag. When he reached the fortifications of Paris a guy wire holding his wooden keel drooped so low it caught in the propeller. Before the ship was chewed to pieces Santos had to stop the motor. The wind drove him over the roofs of Paris. The ship was still dropping. From St. Cloud the judges saw the ship disappear below the ragged skyline. Then they heard the explosion. The crowd screamed. Henry Deutsch burst into tears.

Firemen raced for the Trocadero. When they arrived they found that the falling ship had straddled between the six-story Trocadero Hotel and the roof of the building across the street. Shreds of the burned balloon hung down in streamers. And there perched on the edge of a tiny barred window, hanging on for life, was the tiny Santos. He had jumped from the keel and caught the window's bars. Firemen lowered a rope from the roof and fished him up.

When he reached the streets he was mobbed by hysterical women who smothered him with kisses. Reporters asked how he had escaped almost certain death. He showed them a medal of St. Benedict: "This saved me." With the help of St. Benedict he would try again.

On October 19, 1901, he made the course in exactly thirty minutes with *Santos-Dumont #6* and won the prize—which he promptly gave to charity. He went on to build 14 airships in all. He spent more than $1,000,000 on his experiments, or on stunts and demonstrations. He would delight boulevardiers by dropping down from the sky to have a drink at a bistro in the Champs Elysées. It was all great fun.

In June 1905 the Lebaudy brothers demonstrated a new passenger dirigible—making a flight that lasted three hours at thirty miles an hour. If dirigible flight was going to be so practical, Santos would turn his attention to the heavier-than-air machine. Already other members of the Aero Club were experimenting with gliders, and powered gliders.

He named his first plane *le Cigale enragé*, "The Infuriated Grasshopper," and on October 23, 1906 he flew it 36 feet in a straight line,

at a speed the judges calculated to be 23 miles per hour, at a height of
10 feet. The judges announced: "It is the first time that a motor
driven airplane has taken off on its own power and flown."

In a second trial in November, Santos was clocked over 720 feet in
21.5 seconds at a height of about 20 feet. The Paris editor of *The New
York Herald* called the flight "the first mechanical flight of man."
Santos won the Legion of Honor. And Edison sent him a note: "To
Santos-Dumont, the pioneer of the air—homage from Edison."

For three generations there would be Parisians who believed that
somehow Santos-Dumont had *both* the first dirigible and the first airplane in the air. They just couldn't accept as a fact the uncivilized
Wright brothers' flight at Kitty Hawk on December 17, 1903.

To a certain extent the obscurity of the bicycle mechanics from
Ohio worked to their advantage. They were flying steadily in 1904 and
1905, with no official observers. They bided their time and continued
their experiments. They thought they were the sole possessors of a
successful airplane, with the possibilities of world patent rights, and a
monopoly on the most important invention in the world. In May
1906 United States Patent No. 831,393 was finally granted to them,
but they were still cautious. They knew a lot about pirates, in-
fringements and spies from their bicycle business.

They would let no one see their planes while they conducted correspondence with the United States Army, the French Army, and
others. No army would get to see their models without a cash-and-
carry contract. They plainly saw, just as Graf Zeppelin had seen, that
the armies would be their principal customers.

After his successful flights in 1906, Santos-Dumont was not as sensible. He spent little time in correspondence with armies, preferring to
celebrate his feats in the air at the Opera, or among friends at his
clubs and cafes. Yet the reports of the Santos-Dumont flights in *The
Infuriated Grasshopper* interested the armies anyway. As a result, the
U.S. Army wrote the Wrights in February 1908 offering them $25,000
for an airplane that met Army specifications. The French wrote offering better terms: $100,000 and 50% of all profits if the Wrights
could meet specifications. Orville agreed to the U.S. Army offer; Wilbur left for Paris.

In midsummer Wilbur was ready at Le Mans. There was much cu-
riosity about the "American bluffeur." The French press was infuriated by his preposterous-sounding claims. They called him "Mon-
sieur Wilbug Bright, a man who imagined himself the original
inventor of the airplane." *The Paris Herald* itself said of the Wrights:
"They are, in fact, either flyers or liars."

When questioned by reporters, Wilbur answered: "My contract
says that I must fly, not hop from the ground, or flutter along like a
hen chased by a dog."

And on August 8, he took off, circled his plane twice within a radius of not more than 70 yards, made a right figure of eight over the
grandstand, and landed. The French Army gladly gave permission for
the American to use its military campgrounds at Camp d'Avours.

Day after day he flew. And negotiated. By the end of 1908 Wilbur
Wright had made 104 flights. On his last day he flew through drizzle
for two and a half hours, covering 77 miles, and winning about $7,000
in prizes. The French press was now delighted: "We have all been
beaten. Aviation has just begun— It was the most exciting spectacle
ever presented in the history of applied science."

Back home Orville had a bad crash, broke both legs and killed the
Army lieutenant riding as his observer. Nevertheless, the U.S. Army
paid $30,000 for the first plane and agreed to pay for four more at
$7,500 each. Russia presented a check of $100,000 to build ten Flyers.
Italy offered 500,000 francs and 25% of the profits. With Orville on
crutches, the brothers set up their factory in the south of France at
Pau.

To fulfill their contracts they trained flyers. Statesmen and kings
came to Pau. The brothers made a triumphal tour of Europe. They
were showered with medals and honors, including the medal of the
Society for Universal Peace.

Back home Glenn Curtiss began to build airplanes too. By 1912 he
was the biggest builder of planes in the United States and was also involved in a bitter legal battle with the Wrights. Discouraged, the
Wrights sold out to an investment group, just before the orders for
planes generated by war poured in. They would have made a billion.

In 1912 Wilbur Wright died of typhus. Orville lived on, in a
deepening pessimism. Although he was perfectly willing to sell the
Flyer to the armies of the world, he had hoped their invention would

make further wars too frightful, and that statesmen would have to
find other ways of settling disputes.

While the Wright brothers were astonishing the French at Le
Mans in 1908, H. G. Wells published his *War in the Air*. It began:
"Everybody talked of flying, everybody repeated over and over
again 'Bound to come. . . .' There were these Wright brothers out in
America. They glided. They glided miles and miles. Finally, they
glided off stage. . . they vanished."

Wells explained why they vanished. The armies were developing air
programs in secret. The hero of Wells' story is accidentally carried in
a runaway balloon into the heart of the German Air Armada. Captured, he is escorted into the presence of Nordic supermen with viking
helmets. The story is a tale of hairbreadth escapes.

The Germans leave in the dead of night to attack New York with
Zeppelins. New York must receive a preemptive strike because the
Americans are secretly developing flying machines "of the Wright
model." When the German fleet is over New York, the United States
surrenders under the threat from the sky. But guerrilla warfare breaks
out. Zeppelins rain down bombs that reduce the city to rubble and an
appalling massacre of the population is a result.

The revolt spreads to other cities. War has become a universal guerrilla warfare—population set against population instead of army
against army. City after city is bombed into rubble, but the Americans manage to build a fleet of airplanes to combat the Zeppelins.
There is no end to the escalation.

Whether either the Wright brothers or Graf Zeppelin read Wells
that summer, no one knows. The old man was still at work on his airborne cavalry horse. After the liquidation of the Corporation for the
Advancement of Airship Travel in 1900, the enterprise became the
sole property of the inventor.

In building his first airship, the LZ 1, more than 1 million marks
had been spent. Though the Graf had been decorated for the flights
of the LZ 1 over the Bodensee with the Order of the Red Eagle, First
Class, what he needed was an Army contract. Personnel at "the factory" were reduced to two night watchmen and Engineer-Designer
Ludwig Dürr. He worked secretly at improvements in construction:

an improved and stronger airframe; elevators and rudders based on the researches of a Professor Hergesell at the Meteorological Station in Friedrichshafen. And Dürr thought he could increase the power plant to 170 horsepower.

But to test Dürr's designs, the Count needed money. He got permission from his staunch friend, the King of Württemberg to run a lottery. It netted 124,000 marks. Then the Chancellor of Germany, Count Bülow, contributed 50,000 marks. And 15,000 marks trickled in from 60,000 petitions the Count mailed post-paid. The LZ 2 took to the air on January 17, 1906.

It was so buoyant it shot up to 1,300 feet. The rudder controls jammed. The ship was pitching up and down, which in turn flooded, then starved the new Daimler motors, and they stopped. The ship drifted downwind, floated to a landing between two farmhouses. The crew anchored it to trees and fences. Overnight a violent storm ripped the fabric to shreds. The next morning local workmen had chopped the remains into pieces before the Count could salvage the undamaged parts. But he seemed undismayed. A few months later he was promoting the LZ 3.

He sold his horses and carriages, dismissed his servants, and talked the King of Württemberg into letting him run a new lottery. In October 1906 the test flights were made. The ship steered easily and bucked 25-mile-per-hour winds. Overnight everyone wanted to be associated with the venture, even Kaiser Wilhelm.

"Zeppelin" cigarettes appeared on the market. Pastry cooks made tiny Zeppelins of sugar. Newspaper ads offered "Zeppelin coats to be worn in the air." The Reichstag granted him financial aid for a fourth ship. And finally the Army indicated it would be interested in paying the bills if he could build a ship which could stay in the air for 24 hours. Meanwhile, the LZ 3 would become the first rigid airship in the Prussian Army.

Designer Ludwig Dürr had built a wind tunnel with his own modest funds. The windows for this primitive contraption were taken from the factory. Through them, Dürr saw airships would need stabilizing surfaces—much like the fins of a fish. At about the same time, the Graf invited a journalist who had been highly critical of the Zeppelin designs to take a ride on the LZ 3. Dr. Hugo Eckener was converted by one trip in the air with the ebullient Graf. More important,

DEUS EX MACHINA

23

Dr. Eckener was an expert sailor and understood the vagaries of weather. They began to collaborate.

By August 4, 1908 the LZ 4 was ready for its 24-hour test. It was 446 feet long and 42 feet in diameter. It was lifted by 519,000 cubic feet of hydrogen. Among its most important features was a small vertical shaft which ran from the control car through the sausage up to the top of the frame near the bow where a small platform had been built. Sitting on a folding chair on the platform as the ship sailed through the sky, was a machine-gunner and a Maxim gun. The final answer to the old sabres-drawn cavalry charge would be the Zeppelin.

The ship took off from Friedrichshafen at 7:00 A.M. Designer Dürr was at the elevators; Lau at the helm. Zeppelin stood at the front of the open control gondola giving the orders. Four members of the Imperial Commission came as passengers to report the ship's performance. In the rear gondola, connected by a narrow catwalk, Chief Mechanic Karl Schwarz and two assistants tended two 110-horsepower Daimler motors. Captain Hacker and Baron Bassus—two friends of the Graf—went along as passengers.

The airship flew down the Rhine, passing Basel at 9:30. At every town factories shut down, schools were closed, church bells rang continuously and the people stood in the streets with their faces upturned. News of the trip was being telegraphed to every corner of the world. Back in Friedrichshafen Dr. Eckener telephoned police stations along the course of the ship to confirm its position.

At about 4:30 as the ship passed over Darmstadt, a cogwheel slipped off the forward motor and the engine began to overheat. They landed on a small tributary of the Rhine, near Oppenheim, where a local wine-merchant gave the crew a bottle of fine Niersteiner, which they all shared. Chief Mechanic Schwarz repaired the engine.

At 10:30 at night they took off again, with a helpful tow from a Rhine steamer. But again the forward motor quit—this time a connecting rod was out. They flew on with only one motor until sunrise, reaching Echterdingen, a meadow town near Stuttgart, where they again landed to work on the forward motor.

Years later Chief Mechanic Karl Schwarz would tell the story again and again to the younger men at the building yards in Friedrichshafen.

"We had been on duty for twenty-four hours without any relief and we were dead tired. The clamor of the hundreds of thousands of people in cities and villages, the steamer sirens, the ringing of church bells —all were drowned out by the deafening roar of our motors. And when the first groups of people ran toward us and spoke to us, we couldn't hear a word they said. But they understood we needed help, and they grabbed on with a will. The cable holding the bow of the ship like a bear's nose ring was secured with a heap of earth; and not content with that, we buried a whole farm-wagon and fastened the cable to it. But even that later proved to be insufficient.

"Soldiers arrived from Cannstadt and helped us arrange the ship so that it would be free to swing with the wind. From Untertuerkheim, Daimler sent out a wrecking car with a portable workshop, and the damaged motor was taken out, repaired and reinstalled. Meanwhile, the news of our forced landing caused a veritable migration. By train, in carriages and automobiles, on bicycles and on foot, more than 50,000 people gathered on the field during the course of the forenoon. Graf Zeppelin had gone to rest at the local hostelry at Echterdingen; the other members of the party were having their midday meal in the village. I remained in the aft gondola, the only one—as I thought—on the ship. I did not know that in the forward part of the ship, my comrade Laburda and one of the soldiers were still replenishing the water ballast.

"At two in the afternoon, a storm came up. It was one of those savagely furious storms like the one which caused the fire at Donaueschingen. The force of the wind overturned the ship and tossed it high in the air. The ground crew, fearing to be dragged along with it, released the tow-ropes. I saw somebody (it was a mechanic from the Daimler Works, who had been repairing the motor) leap from the forward gondola, and I ran along the catwalk as fast as I could to get to the forward gondola and pull the gas valves. My only thought was to bring the runaway airship back to earth. The individual valve levers are placed beside each other on the control panel, and I took one in each finger and pulled with all my strength.

"The gas escaped, but the ship continued to drift. The crowd faded away beneath me, and I found myself about half a mile away from the anchorage. I did not know whether the drifting ship had grazed a tree or the earth, but at any rate it seemed to me that I heard a cry of 'Fire!' The airship was on an incline, with the bow sinking down; I leaned over the rail of the gondola. Within the airship envelope there was a suspiciously bright light which seemed to grow and come closer. And suddenly I knew. Fire. The airship was burning. I cannot say that I was either very frightened or prepared to die. Again, I had only one thought, and that was 'watch for your chance to jump!' I released the valve knobs which I had been holding tightly in my hands, and waited for my chance to jump. But the distance to the earth was still too great, and the burning ship was being driven along at a fast speed. Fifteen thousand cubic meters of hydrogen gas were burning, and the balloonettes were bursting with loud reports. The rings, supports, and struts of the metal frame were glowing, bending and breaking; the envelope was being torn apart in blazing shreds; and soon the flames were eating through to the gasoline tanks. The heat was becoming unbearable; it was Hell itself in which I was burning alive.

"If you ask me how long this lasted—I do not know. At such a moment, time has no meaning, and a second is longer than years or decades. There must have been a crash, the ship must have struck a tree; for suddenly I lay outside, flat on my face. Gas cells, the envelope, and the whole net of girders crackled in livid red above me. As well as I could, I protected my head, breathing fire and trying to sit up and look around. Just then another mass caved in upon me. At such moments, one has terrific strength—I pushed the burden high, wound myself like an eel through the bent girders, slipped under the net of cloth covering me like a shroud, and I did not even feel the flames tonguing at me from all sides. I came free, stumbled to my feet and said grimly to myself, 'Now run like hell!'

"My lungs were filled with smoke and I gasped for breath. Falling as much as running, I nevertheless got about a hundred feet away from the ship. When I looked back, the proud giant airship was no more.

"I saw another man lying near the edge of the ruins. It was my comrade Laburda. I stumbled toward him, and with the aid of a soldier dragged him out of danger. Blood was running in two streams from his nose. The impact had thrown him, just as it had me. But Laburda was unfortunate and was knocked unconscious.

"While I was still working over him, an excited crowd of people gathered to stare with dumb horror at the ruins which, only a few minutes before, had been a triumph of human endeavor and the symbol of German aspiration.

"How did I get to Echterdingen? I walked. There weren't as many autos then as there are now. I dined with the Stuttgart Fire Commissioner, Jacobi, an efficient Berliner, who had me bandaged by an intern. I slept in his guest room. On the next morning, the clean new linen on the guest bed was in such a mess from my blisters that I was ashamed to face my hosts. But I couldn't help it. I looked frightful; the blisters had swelled so much that I couldn't recognize myself when I looked into a mirror.

"Once more, the interns bandaged me, and at ten o'clock in the morning I took the train to Friedrichshafen, where I recuperated before flying again."

In Friedrichshafen the next morning all the flags flew at half mast. Helmsman Marx was on his way to the boathouse to strip the launch *Württemberg* which had been decorated with flowers in the Graf's colors of blue and white. The flowers remained from the victory celebration prepared for the night before. On his way past the Deutsche Haus, Graf Zeppelin opened a balcony door on the upper story and smiling, called to Marx as if nothing had happened.

"God be praised, Marx! How are you? Why, Marx, you still seem to be hard hit by yesterday's occurrence. Come up here a moment."

Marx went up and the Graf opened the door, then led the perplexed helmsman to a table on which lay a great heap of money. "What do you think of that accident, Marx?

"That was sent to me by the German people, and there's more coming! So, Marx, now we'll really begin to build airships. Please go to Dürr's home and tell him to meet me at Manzell at 8:30. With God's help, we start again!"

The public contributions poured in. At the scene of the accident a man had swung himself on a table near the smoking ruins and began to speak. He appealed to the honor of the German people. He urged the crowd to voluntarily contribute to a new airship—so that Germany could continue to be first among the nations in the air. Newspapers had picked up the suggestion. The impulse was transformed into action throughout Germany. On the steamer *Konigin Charlotte*, ferrying between Friedrichshafen and Konstanz, the passengers and crew collected 600 marks; the Badisch Bowling Club sent 150 marks; the aldermen of Stuttgart 20,000; Friedrichshafen 5,000; the Mining Association of Essen 100,000 marks; Senator Possel of Lübeck, a like amount.

The newspapers continued to publish daily appeals, and printed lists of contributors. School children contributed, cities and villages, unions and the Hohenzollern associations. Altogether, in the end, the result of the spontaneous outburst of German national feeling totaled 6,096,555 marks.

The Luftschiffbau Zeppelin (Zeppelin Airship Works) was incorporated with a capital of one million marks. The Zeppelin Foundation was founded, with Dr. Hugo Eckener as its head. Its purpose was to use the contributions "for the advancement of airship travel." The Berlin Government reimbursed Graf Zeppelin for his previous expenditures, and he in turn repaid the investments of the stockholders in the liquidated Corporation for the Advancement of Airship Travel.

The "miracle of Echterdingen" relieved the Graf of his financial troubles. The subsequent airships, LZ 5, LZ 6, LZ 7 and LZ 8 had their mechanical troubles, but the tenth Zeppelin, the *Schwaben*, piloted by Dr. Eckener, inaugurated regular passenger service between German cities late in 1909. The world's first passenger airline, the Deutsche Luftschiffahrts Aktien Gesellschaft—DELAG, as it was soon called, built air harbors in Frankfurt, Berlin, Hamburg, Dresden. The airships *Schwaben*, *Viktoria-Luise*, *Hansa*, and *Sachsen* began to keep schedules as regularly as trains. Every German saw a Zeppelin in flight.

Altogether 37,250 passengers were carried on 1,600 flights. The ships spent 3,200 hours in the air, covering 100,000 miles—all without an accident. Tickets were available at all the branches of the Hamburg-America Line.

In the spring of 1913 a young Navy Lieutenant and naval architect learned airship pilotage from Dr. Hugo Eckener. In the fall, the Lieutenant was made Kapitän of the passenger ship *Sachsen*. At the same time he began training officers and crews in the newly organized Naval Airship Division. On the evening of July 31, 1914, Zeppelin

Captain Ernst A. Lehmann received a telegram from the War Ministry forbidding him to fly the *Sachsen* more than thirty miles from her home base.

The First War in the Air had begun.

In his *War in the Air*, H. G. Wells had been quite right. As it turned out, "that crazy old count," Graf Zeppelin, was nearly right.

The thing started, as everyone knows, when an archduke was shot in Sarajevo. Four years later, the casualty list was stunning:

| | |
|---|---|
| Known Dead: | 9,998,771 |
| Wounded: | 20,297,551 |
| Missing: | 5,983,600 |

The causes of such a slaughter were not entirely clear. Some great fault line ran beneath the foundations of Western society. Certainly there was an argument for the unification of Europe: there in the center where the machines were concentrated, they needed the raw materials which must come from the other great continents. But England knew her empire must be defended on Flanders field. Her experience with Napoleon had taught her so.

Republican France, the first nation to attempt to unify Europe, knew she must halt at any cost the advance of her ancient Teutonic enemy. The Rhine barrier, should it be flanked through Belgium, would lead to the fall of Paris—as it had in 1870.

Romanoff Russia, enigmatic for centuries, understood correctly but somewhat vaguely that her future, in an industrial age, was linked irrevocably with the outcome of events on the Rhine.

America and Japan finally saw that safe passage on the wide oceans depended very much on who controlled the continental ports and the strategic straits. And so millions of men stumbled into trenches and stayed there, slaughtering each other.

It was discovered, to everyone's horror, that no one knew how to stop the escalation of such a war. The old diplomacy was useless once populations were engaged. Universal guerrilla warfare was something different from the sport of kings. The very existence of Parliaments, Diets, and Congresses meant that peace terms must be without conditions—for every man, woman and child had done something for their country, and consequently all had some injury to redress. If the winner were to take all, then nothing but weeping and the gnashing of teeth could be the lot of the vanquished.

The old system (in which a small state or two was signed over to the victor and some ugly cousins were given over in marriage to cement the treaty) would not work. Unaware that kings no longer sat on thrones, the Germans found no one with whom they could treat.

The democracies, on the other hand, were infinitely stronger nations precisely because every man now shared in power, every man was a king. But the number of marriages that would have been necessary to give an enemy satisfaction were beyond their capabilities, in any case, and certainly would have horrified their sense of rectitude. So every home did its best for the war effort. While men died at the front, women and children worked in the factories—on the home front, it was called. The enthusiasm generated by incessant death was quite extraordinary.

The results were more obvious than the causes. England kept her empire, but lost the young men from the playing fields of Eton with which she had once governed it. The empire began to disintegrate under the governance of less subtle men. France emerged a victor shrouded in unrelieved grief, bitter and vengeful. America stumbled about in the conference halls of peace, aware now of her power, testing the chilly waters of European politics, then withdrew, baffled.

Everywhere the kings disappeared: they were obviously no longer useful. The Russians murdered theirs, then found they would need at least a generation to build a social structure to compare with the one they had overthrown. The German Kaiser took a train to Holland, leaving behind not only defeat but no social structure. Those few who had the courage to serve as conductors for his train were accused later of "stabbing the German people in the back."

The principal result of the war, however, was more subtle and more dangerous. The war revealed that the old Christian God, under whose aegis the marriages of treaty were once performed, whose Bishops had time and again "blessed this holy union" with at least one eye closed, this old authority to which even murderers must bow their heads, was now replaced.

Unaccustomed to playing the part of kings, every man chose his own heresy. Some chose materialism. Some chose idealism. And in the chaos, it soon came to pass that the great miracles might be performed by science. So everyone began to pray to the new God for deliverance.

Glory be to man in the highest. Heroes might once again walk the earth. They would only need some technical device, some magic sword or tarnhelm, like the one which could make Siegfried invisible, or take him in the twinkling of an eye wherever he might wish to be.

The Germans expected a great deal of their Zeppelins. During the war the first Zeppelin efforts ended in comedy, but by determined application they improved.

In the first days of August 1914, the Zeppelin ZV III took off from Treves to scout the French. When the ship arrived over enemy lines, the air was filled with bursting shrapnel. The Zeppelin was only a few hundred feet high. Thousands of soldiers competed in an attempt to hit a bull's eye in the 500-foot airship. The controls were shot off the craft, and thousands of bullets and shell splinters punctured the gas cells. The ZV III hovered defenselessly over No Man's Land, finally drifting down into trees in the forest of Badonvillers. The crew swung themselves overboard and the commander ordered his ship's papers destroyed. At that moment, a squadron of French cavalry dashed into the woods and attacked the wreck with drawn sabres. A Zeppelin destroyed by a cavalry charge! The old Graf was dismayed.

The German crew fled, marched east for eleven hours, and met the advance guard of the German Army. They filed the first report of the location of the withdrawing French forces. Soon the whole German Army began a forced march westward, and what had been No Man's Land was in German hands. The old Graf was pleased.

Despite the early misadventures, the German people hoped for and expected extraordinary accomplishments from their airships. Their animosity was directed principally against England, who had started a "hunger blockade," while she herself remained impregnable on an island fortress guarded by her Royal Navy.

The pressure of German public opinion for an air attack on London mounted. At first the Military High Command held off. The Kaiser was afraid it would be bad form to bomb the home of his dear cousins. Under the pressure of his admirals and generals he consented to bombardment of points of real military significance, but at first demanded the right to approve targets. Certain places, such as

Buckingham Palace, Westminster Abbey, St. Paul's Cathedral and the government buildings were under no circumstances to be affected. And there were to be no accidents!

There were many who considered such circumscribed aerial warfare an insufficient reprisal for England's insufferable blockade, and suggested the attacks should be extended to combined assaults of whole air fleets over Britain. Twenty great airships with three hundred incendiary bombs each could fly over London. Six thousand bombs, it was maintained, would start so many fires that it would be impossible to extinguish this gigantic conflagration.

The *Sachsen* had been converted into a war Zeppelin. Its Captain, Ernst Lehmann, had become the principal trainer of Zeppelin captains for both Army and Navy. He was asked his technical opinion. "The plan, as such, was feasible," he said. "But the thought of subjecting a defenseless civilian population, outside the actual war zone, to all the horrors of aerial warfare, and destroying priceless cultural treasures, was reason enough for all of us to reject the plan."

"As I was piloting one of the Army airships that were to fly over England, I was quick to realize what the Imperial command signified and what the consequences for me would be if I disobeyed it. So I spread out my map of London and drew around those buildings red circles resembling the danger circles which a sea-captain uses to mark dangerous reefs and sand banks."

Lehmann described one raid over London, on April 2, 1916. By then he had one of the new ships, the LZ 90, with much better performance capabilities than the old *Sachsen.* "Over the mouth of the Thames we were discovered, and a group of sea-vessels opened fire at us just as the searchlights began their restless playing in the sky.

"Without replying, we swung away at a right angle and climbed to 10,000 feet. There we resumed our course. The moon shone brightly through the windows of the control car, but it was due to set soon. A peculiar feeling overcame me as we hovered so high over the enemy's territory. Before going to sleep, every human being down there on the thickly populated island probably prayed to God that bad weather or moonlight might keep the German airships away, or that, if they came, they would be shot down.

"The moon went down and there was nothing but black space around us. From the window of the control car I could see nothing but a few clouds; down below the fog had become thicker, protecting us from detection by the searchlights as we crossed the outskirts of the city.

"The powerful beams of light were stopped at an altitude of 6,700 feet by a thin layer of clouds while, only 1,300 feet above that, we crossed the defense zone in a direct course for the Albert docks.

"There 'Archies' opened fire at us, awakened by the drone of our motors. The searchlights transformed the fog into an opalescent, milky fluid. The air was filled with bursting shells which were aimed at random and fell back down upon the sea of houses. The English anti-aircraft guns in this way anticipated us, for a great deal of the damage subsequently attributed to us was actually caused by them.

"The smoke and vapors of the metropolis were at once welcome and disadvantageous. They could not see us from below, but neither could we see anything from above. Then we approached a battery of searchlights and an anti-aircraft nest which was firing at us with unusual fury. I had saved my entire load of bombs, 5,000 pounds of them, and now judged it to be the right time to make use of them. First I dropped the smaller bombs to get my aim and extinguish the searchlights. And at that moment, my alert friend von Gemmingen noticed the first sample of a new kind of incendiary shell just as the rays of a gigantic searchlight broke through the clouds and fixed upon the grey hull of the LZ 90.

"This sort of phosphorus shell was quite different from the French type. They looked like blue sparks hissing toward us at extraordinary speed. More and more of them filled the air, and a few came so close that we felt we could have caught them through the window of the control car.

"Fortunately there was a cloud on our path, and when the ship came over it the searchlight lost us. Reappearing, we once more sighted the Thames, foggy and vague, but still visible enough to recognize by its course. Using a searchlight as a landmark, we navigated in the direction of the river flow and dropped our bombs one after another on a spot where, according to our map, the eastern docks and factories lay.

"We ourselves were unable to judge the result of our raid, but according to eye-witness accounts it must have been terrible. The crash of the hits mingled with the thunder of the defense batteries, the rattle of machine guns, the noise of the fire-engines racing to the fires, and the shrill piping of the ambulances speeding to the scene. Frightened out of their sleep, millions of people fled to the cellars, stumbling through the darkness and cowering together at every detonation. No one knew where the next bomb would strike, and this uncertainty was nerve-wracking. Women broke out in hysterical crying jags, children wept, and men, no longer able to endure it down below, rushed out into the streets with balled fists, as if wanting to strangle an enemy hovering invisible in the clouds above.

"This enemy was, God knows, only concerned with military objectives which made the capital of the British Empire the storehouse of the World War; but it was inevitable that many bombs missed their mark and demolished buildings around the docks. Those poor people saw their little goods and possessions go up in flames, and when they fled from their burning houses, they ran into a murderous rain of splinters, shrapnel and debris; it is immaterial whether the German attack or the English defense caused more victims.

"I was relieved when the lightened ship carried us up to 12,000 feet where we saw no more of the city. As we departed in the direction of the mouth of the Thames, I had the ship thoroughly checked. It had suffered not the slightest scratch. My returns from England were not always so uneventful."

At the beginning of World War I the airplane (as Wells had said, "on the Wright model") was a frail toy and the Zeppelin was the undisputed master of the skies. Frightened by their early losses, the English soon began to improve their defenses. They replaced their old anti-aircraft guns with more accurate French weapons. They reorganized their airplane squadrons, equipping them with faster, higher-flying planes. By 1916 British airplanes had become more than a match for the raiding Zeppelins.

Refusing to accept the reason for their growing Zeppelin casualties, the Germans increased the number of airship raids. At first the airplanes were able to reach a height of only about 13,000 feet, but they improved. In order to escape the planes, back in Friedrichshafen Engineer Dürr designed and built huge Zeppelins that could reach ceilings of more than 20,000 feet. But at such Himalayan heights the crews faced new problems. The airshipmen were forced to sniff oxygen to keep from passing out.

A combat plane pursued the LZ 55 to 25,300 feet, forcing its captain, Lieutenant Commander Hans Flemming, to involuntarily set an altitude record. Blood ran from the ears, mouths and noses of the airshipmen; vertigo attacked them one after another. The water ballast in the emergency ballast bags turned to ice in spite of the addition of alcohol. The gasoline supply was threatened. Frozen chips of oil were fed by hand into the coughing engines.

Worst of all, violent storms and strange new winds often raged at these high altitudes, quite independent of the more familiar weather on the ground. Because the "height climbers" flew so high above the clouds, where landmarks could not be seen, navigation became a matter of guesswork and sighting targets was often impossible. Time and again Zeppelins became hopelessly lost, and more than one disappeared at sea without a trace. Raids became somewhat difficult.

One evening towards the end of the war three Zeppelins heading for London were met by a new high-flying British biplane. At 16,400 feet the pilot banked into a head-on attack. In the second seat, his gunner let fly with the machine gun at the airship's bow. The gun was firing the new ZPT tracers—bullets explosively coated in phosphorus. The ZPTs blew a great hole in the outer fabric, then a fire started, followed in a moment by a tremendous explosion as the burning fabric ignited the hydrogen.

Down with the airship went Peter Strasser, the German Navy's Fuehrer of Airships, and his entire crew. The raids over London tapered off, then ended. At about the same time, the first War of the Worlds ended too. By then the Luftschiffbau in Friedrichshafen had built 88 Zeppelins. They were much improved machines over the comparably dinky little *Sachsen* which had first carried passengers for the airline DELAG.

Heinrich Kubis had been the first steward aboard an airship: he was the steward for DELAG aboard the *Sachsen*, under the prewar command of Captain Lehmann.

Chief Steward Kubis stood about 5 feet 9, his hair always brushed straight back, his bright blue eyes always twinkled. He enjoyed life immensely, but it pleased him most of all to meet famous passengers and to know the amazing little dramas of their lives. He read all the society columns avidly.

He was proud, and glad to tell anyone of it, that he had been born on June 16, 1888, the day Wilhelm II had been crowned Emperor of Germany. Before taking charge of the pleasures of passengers aboard the *Sachsen*, he had worked in the most fashionable hotels—in the Carlton in London, and then in the Ritz in Paris. He had met the Kaiser, even before the war, and the Empress, and Crown Prince Rupprecht; he had a discerning eye, Kubis said, for any person of quality.

As a matter of fact, Chief Kubis was charming. He knew instinctively not just the manners, but the small touch—a bouquet of flowers, a good sauce, or the right temperature for a champagne, which had made *la belle époque* a charming age. Kubis had learned in its school, understood the necessity of its lessons, and applied them vigorously. With a little effort, there was no reason why life should not be a pleasure to persons of quality.

When the war ended, Captain Lehmann and Dr. Eckener had set the Luftschiffbau to work at constructing ships. They would resume flights between German cities, just as they had before the war. In the fall of 1919 the *Bodensee* made 103 flights within 98 days. Captain Lehmann sailed her to Stockholm, and Chief Steward Kubis once again served the wines well, saw to it that the passengers were impressed, and promoted the notion that airship travel was not only practical, but luxuriously comfortable.

As a result, Captain Lehmann's conferences went well. The Swedish parliament seemed to be willing to approve a government loan for the establishment of an airship base in the capital. A Swedish company would be formed; it would order a ship of the *Bodensee* class which would be manufactured at the Luftschiffbau. Then the two craft would fly a two-day rotating schedule, covering the Stockholm–Berlin–Friedrichshafen route. Sweden, which had remained neutral during the war, meant to extend a helpful hand to a defeated Germany.

While Captain Lehmann was still negotiating in Sweden the Interallied Commission of the victorious powers ordered "all naval and military hangars and buildings for airplanes, amphibians and airships" destroyed or dismantled by February 15, 1921. The destruction was to be begun at once, except for those hangars whose maintenance was sanctioned for international air traffic—nine altogether; and those were awarded as reparations to the Allied Powers. Italy was awarded two, Japan one, and France six hangars at the Ahlhorn Naval Air Base. In addition, the Interallied Commission ordered the dismantling of all German airship hangars in municipal or private possession. The Luftschiffbau and every other German aircraft manufacturer were to be closed.

At the Luftschiffbau the unemployed workers had nowhere to go. Hunger was growing. The Luftschiffbau took up the manufacture of aluminum pots and pans.

The Allies made no secret of the fact that they meant to deprive Germany of the capability of building airships in the future. In a perverse way, German airshipmen began to take renewed pride in the bombing of London.

The sister ship of the *Bodensee*, commissioned as the *Nordstern*, was built to fulfill the contracts with Sweden. The Interallied Commission demanded it be surrendered as indemnification for the five naval airships sabotaged by their German crews in their hangars at Ahlhorn. The *Nordstern* was confiscated by the French, who renamed her *Mèditerranée*. The *Bodensee* was taken by the Italians and renamed the *Esperia*. The LZ 114, last ship to be built for the German Navy during the war but never actually delivered, was taken by the French and renamed *Dixmude*. It was the most advanced Zeppelin ever built, and could have flown to New York and back, non-stop.

The victorious powers meant to make use of Zeppelin's invention at Germany's expense. They expected to enlarge their own air fleets, and at the same time stop Germany from developing airship travel. But the lack of practical experience in airships—especially those of advanced design—resulted in disaster.

The English copied the design of the LZ 49, which had been shot down during a raid, and then captured almost intact. They planned to construct the copy to deliver it to the American Navy. They never finished it because another ship they had prepared for the Americans, designated ZR-2, crashed and exploded in the Humber River. The Americans grew wary of English design.

The Italians took the LZ 61, rechristened it *Italia*. On one of its first flights, as the Italians put it, "The *Italia* literally threw itself at the feet of the King with its motors wide open." The ship was completely wrecked. A number of the crew were killed. The Italians also had taken the LZ 120, Captain Lehmann's last war command. They were able to wreck it in its own hangar. They hung it up improperly.

The French at first did well with the *Dixmude*. They made the first air circuit of North Africa—flying 4,500 miles non-stop and staying in the air for 118 hours, 41 minutes. German airshipmen warned the French that the *Dixmude* had been designed for high altitude flying— above the storms, in clear weather. The French ignored the advice. Their government assured their press new records would be set by French airshipmen. The *Dixmude* took off on a low altitude trip, despite objections voiced to his government by her commander, du Plessis. Eleven days after take-off, two fishermen hauled in their nets off the coast of Sicily. The drowned Commander du Plessis was in the net. That's all that was ever found of the *Dixmude*. The French were discouraged from further airship adventures.

Of the confiscated German air-cruisers, the United States wanted none. But an American airship officer came again and again to the Luftschiffbau at Friedrichshafen. He inspected everything there with great patience and science. He finally revealed he was authorized to purchase a ship. Through the intervention of President Harding, the Allies in Paris reluctantly consented. In place of the two naval airships which had been allocated to the Americans by the Interallied Commission under the division of spoils, the Americans would contract for one to be built by the Germans in Friedrichshafen. The cost of the construction was to be borne by Germany, under the reparations clauses.

Under the circumstances it was not too bad an arrangement, for the German Government would otherwise have to pay three million gold marks in cash for the American claims. This way the money remained in Germany, creating employment, and kept the Zeppelin Company from closing down entirely. The ship was assigned dockyard number LZ 126. The American Navy would number her ZR–3, and commission her the *Los Angeles*. A German crew flew her to New York in October 1924. They were met as heroes.

\*    \*    \*

Although there was some work in the yards at Friedrichshafen, Chief Steward Kubis had no passengers to care for—thanks to the restrictions of the Allied governments. After the *Bodensee* was delivered to the Italians in 1920, he had to find something.

Married, and the father of a son, he cast about for some means of earning a living. Hunger was evident on every street corner. He finally began a small business: supplying pillows to be rented at railway stations, for the deluxe carriages, and placed behind the head as an added comfort to travel. The pillows were covered by good linen and Kubis saw to it that the linen was kept startling white. His connections had helped him get an exclusive contract. He knew how to hustle passengers into comfort. Nevertheless, the years from 1920 to 1928 were terrible years.

To expect each day that things might be worse than the day before came as a shock to a man devoted to the virtues of the 19th century. Kubis' attitude was epicurean, for what was culture if not an attempt to wheedle from the coarse material of life, by art and by love, its most delicate, its most subtle qualities: a good wine, a dry fresh beer, a classic cheese?

If one read what the Socialist newspapers had to say, the impression might be gleaned that before the war, life was poor, nasty, brutish and short—lived out in the squalor of industrial slums. But the painters had caught the spirit of things more truthfully: their impressions were of picnics in the shade of green trees by city streams, of cafes and dance halls and skating rinks in which costumes were exquisite and charm was diffused by the light through even the backbones of the models. When the painters saw sadness, it was bitter-sweet. They did not paint despair. Only after the war did Goya's sketches turn out to be realistic, and popular again.

Before the war, as Kubis so precisely understood, the pleasure of wealth was in having it, and not showing it. Even the richest men would play cards for only the smallest stakes, and those stakes were paid in gold coins whose value could be exactly determined.

With money stable, and manners fixed, "solid" men gave careful thought to their wills very early in life. They saved, of course. Every imaginable form of insurance could be bought: for houses, horses, carriages, for old age, in case of sickness, and even, in some cases, an insurance policy was set in the bassinet against the day a daughter

would marry. With a sufficient dowry, she need not marry below her
station.

Kubis could identify among the passengers on the prewar airships
the concentric rings of society. First there was the nobility. Then
"good society"—the lesser nobility, the higher officials. The army and
diplomacy were reserved for aristocrats of "the old families." Then
came the owners of major industries and the *haute bourgeoisie*—the
professionals. Many recognized artists, writers and musicians, and a
few sculptors moved through these circles, flattering them in the same
way that well-cut gems might adorn the neck of a good woman.
Nearly everyone lived comfortably and discreetly.

No one felt obliged to say "please," or "thank you" to anyone else.
It was a source of secret pride. It was true that men often abused each
other in the newspapers or in politics, but then they would sit down
together for a pastry and watch the potential variety in human character stroll past their cafe table. Although Jews might easily be proved
the "spoilers of modesty," "the wreckers of good art," and "the secret
influences behind the new industrial corporations," no one would go
about hating the occupants of the nearby table, some of whom were,
in fact, Jewish.

Many men were obviously portly—"worthy" it was called. "Sedate"
was a word of praise. Rhetoric had not yet been streamlined to con-
form with the rhythms of the new machines. Journalists dictated their
opinions to copyists. Neither the staccato rhythms of the typewriter,
nor the "hard news" story made much impression. The telephone was
uncommon and the declarative sentences of radio did not yet exist.
Consequently, speech, and the ideas it expressed, could be measured,
modified. What was tendentious would be qualified by complexities—
and the more graceful and balanced these modifiers were, the more
they were admired.

Flowers—not death's heads—were used as the emblems of political
parties: red designated the Socialist workers; white was the sign of the
Catholic centrists and the shopkeepers; the blue cornflower, favorite
of Bismarck, was the emblem of the German National Party. The appeals to make war were expressed in poetic images. No one knew yet
that tanks would grind the wounded beneath their implacable treads,
that bombs were indifferent to the age or sex of their victims.

One had to travel very little to know how much progress was being made: the houses of the little bourgeoisie in Vienna were solid testaments; and in Paris, by the Parc Monceau, the houses were glorious. Within just one generation there were street lights, autos, water without pumping it, electric motors, hygiene. People looked handsomer, healthier, happier. They went to resorts both in the summer and in the winter. They took up sports. Things were secure.

But these were the dream castles of security—the kind of dreams which it was supposed children had. Later it would be understood not even children actually had such dreams. If the confident materialism of the *belle époque* was a sweet dream, postwar Germany was a nightmare.

On June 28, 1919, the Weimar Republic signed the Treaty of Versailles. Not only did it give territories over to the Poles, which was in itself despicable, but the Allies demanded billions in reparations which could never be paid: 132 billion gold marks. In addition, it reduced the Army to 100,000 men; forbade planes and tanks; limited the Navy to ships of 10,000 tons. To ensure the payment of reparations, the Allied Commission took active control of many businesses. It was because of the treaty, and the Allied Commission, that Heinrich Kubis had lost his job as a steward to passengers. The government that signed such a treaty was doomed.

Power had been given to the people, in the form of its parliament: "A great experiment," it was said, "in Democracy." But what was the result? Anarchy. Chaos.

The communists, led by Rosa Luxemburg and Karl Liebknecht, marched down the Unter den Linden, proclaimed a Soviet Republic, and took control of the Kaiser's palace. Defense Minister Noske used regular troops to evict them. The Guard Cavalry Division dutifully slaughtered them all. No sooner were the communists chased out, when the Freikorps occupied Berlin. Then the workers all went on strike to chase Herr Kapp out. The parliamentary ministers all had to flee. Disgraceful!

To escape the provisions of the treaty, the General Staff organized in secret the Black Reichswehr who fought the Poles for a while, then decided they would sooner occupy Berlin. General von Seekt eliminated them, along with Communist governments in Saxony, Thuringia, the Ruhr and Hamburg.

To improve relations, the French, who must have their reparations come what will, occupied the Ruhr. Of course, no true German worker would touch his machine. The Army aided them with devices for sabotage and guerrilla warfare. The French stationed Moroccan black troops in the Ruhr who committed every atrocity; and as if that was not enough, the French arrested, deported, and executed, under the so-called rights of parliamentary law.

In April 1921, when the reparations were first demanded, the mark's value stood at 4 to each dollar. By summer it was 75 to one; by summer 1922 at about 400 to one; by January 1923 18,000 to one; by August 1923 it was calculated at 1,000,000 to one dollar. After that not even a trainload of marks would buy a cup of flour. A woman could be bought for a few ounces of sugar. In Berlin young men, even university students, painted themselves and went out at night to earn something with which to eat.

Under such conditions, every kind of riff-raff came to the fore. Men suddenly appeared with titles in their name. It the title might cost a fortune in the morning, it was only necessary to wait until the next afternoon to be a member of the nobility for a minor sum. The houses in which generations had made steady progress could be bought and sold in the hundreds—whole cities of them at one time—by men who had never saved anything, only borrowed. It was a time for wastrels, fools, and scoundrels.

And why not? For it was now the state which led the way. It was itself the biggest swindler and crook of all! A robber's state which stole from the honest and frugal man and gave to the adventurer.

By 1925 many thought the worst was over. Germany arranged to borrow $7 billion from the Americans, with which in turn the ministers pretended to pay the reparations. Minister Streseman got the French out of the Ruhr, and promised the Allies to leave the Rhineland unoccupied and unfortified. The Pacts of Locarno promised people peace for generations. The great industries, having liquidated all the debts they had earned in the war and even before that with valueless marks, began to retool. Workers could go back to jobs. The government increased social services, built theatres and sport stadiums, and swimming pools, and airfields. But no one would ever believe it again.

In order to display additional signs of a recovered Germany, the

Traffic Ministry contributed 1,100,000 new marks to the Luftschiffbau, and arranged guarantees of another 500,000 marks to insure passengers and crew. With the aid of the Weimar Republic, construction
of the *Graf Zeppelin* was possible—the first Zeppelin since the days
of DELAG to be built for peaceful transport. And so although the
airplane had defeated the Zeppelin at war, the Zeppelin survived.
Now its enormous lifting capacity and great range could prove its
advantage in luxury travel.

The old-style luxury that had added lustre to *la belle époque* had
been defeated by the war too. There was no use in order, sobriety, sav-
ings, stable families and good manners once it was demonstrated that
progress could be blown away by whirlwinds. Before the war luxury
meant a sense of style—wealth was to be spent to make life prettier.
What survived the war was the idea that the rich could buy pretty
things. What had been a secure style of dispensation had changed to
an insecure notion of acquisition. But if the old style was gone, there
remained a taste for the little niceties of luxury. Heinrich Kubis was
glad to give up the business by which he had survived—renting linen
pillows in railway stations—and once again begin to serve as the
epicurean Chief Steward aboard an airship. Although some very odd
people were now demanding the best tables in the better restaurants,
aboard a Zeppelin he still might serve, from time to time, some of the
Old Order.

# CHAPTER 2

# UNDER THE IRON LAW

"Nature (the Art whereby God hath made and governes the world) is by the *Art* of man . . . also imitated, that it can make an Artificiall Animal. For seeing life is but a motion of limbs . . . may we not say, that all Automata (Engines that move themselves by springs and wheels as doth a watch) have an artificiall life?"

—*Leviathan*, THOMAS HOBBES

THE Countess Brandenstein-Zeppelin, daughter of the Crazy Old Count, christened the LZ 127 the *Graf Zeppelin* on July 9, 1928 in Friedrichshafen. It was the 90th anniversary of the inventor's birth.

A number of trial flights were made over Germany: how proud the German people were to see one of their Zeppelins flying again! Then on the morning of October 11, 1928, the *Graf Zeppelin* was prepared to take off for the first passenger flight across the Atlantic to America. There was great excitement.

Chief Correspondent Carl von Wiegand of the Hearst Press was a passenger. He had secured the press rights for America. To fly the oceans as a passenger in great luxury only a year after Charles Lindbergh had been barely able to reach Paris alone—this was considered a great scoop. Two painters and two photographers came along. One of the painters was Honorary Professor Dr. Ludwig Dettmann. His artistic eye and skillful hand, he said, "reveled in the eternally changing play of color, light, air and water."

Two Americans, a Dr. Reiner, who owned a factory in Chemnitz, and a Mr. Gilfillan, a financier living in Switzerland, paid $3,000 each for cabins. Additional offers had to be rejected because of lack of space, although a rich Russian offered the same sum. The government sent a Senate representative along, and the Traffic Ministry, three men. Altogether there were twenty passengers and forty men in crew. Commanding were Captain Lehmann, with Captains von Schiller and Flemming as watch officers, and Dr. Hugo Eckener in overall charge.

When the Graf Zeppelin died in 1917, his nephew Baron von Gemmingen was made Director of the Zeppelin Corporation. Gemmingen had been Lehmann's bombardier. In 1923 he had died of cancer, and Dr. Eckener had succeeded the Baron. Dr. Eckener had always dreamed of establishing a transatlantic passenger service. He was a great expert at manipulating the opinion of the press in favor of Zeppelins, and it was to his credit that the Zeppelin Company was able to resume its business.

The only woman passenger, Lady Drummond Hay, a journalist for *The New York Times*, and a colleague of Carl von Wiegand, arrived so late at the hangar the airship almost sailed without her. The entrance stairs had already been removed. She was lifted aboard through the gondola door. But no sooner did she stand in the command gondola than she said: "Oh, for Heaven's sake, I've forgotten my coat!"

A fast auto was sent to her hotel to fetch the coat. Finally at 7:55, the *Graf Zeppelin* was cast off, and set sail for America. To find the best weather, the course was set to the south. By midday they passed over Lyons in the Valley of the Rhone, then out over the Mediterranean from the Côte d'Azur. They passed over Gibraltar just before dawn of the second day, then out into the Atlantic. On the morning of the third day, in mid-ocean, the ship was headed through a line squall marking the frontal edge of a low pressure area. The first gust of wind and rain shook the ship, knocking the coffee cups from the breakfast table. A good deal of crockery was broken in the pantry. Then the ship seemed to resume its smooth sailing.

Shortly afterward, Machinist Groezinger ran forward to report that the linen covering on the starboard stabilizer fin had ripped loose, and the shreds were flapping in the wind.

Dr. Eckener ordered the engines stopped and called for volunteers. His son, an airship engineer and helmsman, Knud Eckener, stepped forward. So did Engineer Helmsman Albert Sammt, Chief Helmsman Ludwig Marx, and three other brave men. Held by ropes, they climbed into the inside of the fin and made their way along the girders like seamen on yardarms in a storm—one hand for the ship, one hand for themselves. Below them, the sea raged. They relieved one another assisting Chief Rigger Ludwig Knorr.

He tore off the flapping shreds, tied the ends tight, spread blankets over the open section, sewed the blankets to the ship's envelope with rigger's thread and palm.

But the ship's skin was heavy with rain from the storm. With its engines still, it had lost some of its lift. The continuing rain kept adding weight. The ship was sinking slowly towards the white-capped seas. If he started the engines, Dr. Eckener knew the men, including his son, might be swept overboard. He waited until the *Graf Zeppelin*'s altimeter showed 300 feet. Then he gave the order: "Set the telegraphs for engines three and four at full speed ahead."

Fortunately, Chief Knorr's hands were quick. His volunteer repair crew had clambered back inside the ship's hull moments before the engines began once again to drive the ship towards New York.

To strain the damaged fin as little as possible, the *Graf Zeppelin* flew on at half-speed through storm after storm. At eleven o'clock in the morning on the 15th of October, they crossed the beach on the eastern shore of Maryland. At 12:28 P.M. they were over Washington, where they dropped a floral wreath for the President of the United States. Then over Baltimore, Philadelphia, and finally they circled the Statue of Liberty.

America's enthusiasm was incredible. There was so much tooting, howling, shouting and whistle blowing in New York Harbor, they could hardly hear their own engines. Navy fighters in escort did loops and barrel rolls. At 5:38 P.M. they landed at the U.S. Navy Zeppelin hangar at Lakehurst, New Jersey. The trip, with 20 passengers, had covered 6,200 miles and 111 hours in the air.

At two in the morning, the crew finally reached their accommodations in the Warwick Hotel in Manhattan. There were still diners in the restaurant and they instantly recognized the guests, stood and applauded. The official reception began the next morning. Autos decorated with German and American flags drove them up Broadway to City Hall. Confetti and paper streamers rained down from skyscrapers. Mayor Jimmy Walker met them and extended the welcome of the city.

For three days there were banquets, receptions, teas and dinners. The Presidents of Germany and the United States exchanged telegrams of good wishes. Dr. Eckener, Captains Flemming and von Schiller, and Captain Lehmann were received by Mr. and Mrs. Coolidge at the White House. The German Embassy gave a dinner that night, and every important military and political person attended.

The damaged stabilizer fin was repaired and on October 29, at 1:55 in the morning, the *Graf Zeppelin* started back for Germany. Twenty-five passengers paid the Thomas Cook Agency $3,000 each to make the trip. Helmsman Sammt brought along a dog—a Chow.

There were 48 bags of mail, 331 packages in the storerooms, and a bale of cotton to be auctioned off at the Bremen stock exchange for the benefit of the crew. While making an inspection tour when the ship was about over Nantucket, Captain von Schiller discovered a nineteen-year-old boy who had sneaked aboard at Lakehurst and hidden in one of the mail compartments. The stowaway was put to work for Steward Kubis, washing dishes and sweeping out the passenger cabins. The press made more of a sensation of the stowaway than the course of the trip. He was turned over to the American consul after the landing in Germany.

At seven in the morning on November 1, the landing lines were dropped in Friedrichshafen. A crowd of 30,000 had waited much of the night to greet the ship. Fireworks soared into the sky. Church bells rang. Spontaneously, the crowd began to sing: "*Deutschland, Deutschland, über alles. . . .*" After that, the band played "The Star-Spangled Banner." Five days later, they flew on to a triumphal reception in Berlin. The day of their reception was declared a holiday.

In the palace of the President, they were received by President von Hindenburg, hero of the Eastern Front. Each man in the crew was presented. The President shook hands with every one. He wore the black frock of civilian requirements, but he still had the bearing and clear eye of the old grey soldier. He addressed them:

"In this great airship, in its glorious flight through storm and fog, over continents and seas, the Fatherland saw a superb German achievement. You have in the best sense of the word completed a national exploit!"

In the succeeding years, the *Graf Zeppelin* was indeed to have astonishing success. It captured the imagination of people everywhere. It marked the beginning of air passenger service across oceans. At a time when the first mail planes were struggling to clear the mountains of Pennsylvania, the *Graf Zeppelin* could lift 20 passengers and 12 tons of freight, and cover 6,000 miles non-stop.

In 1929 it flew around the world in 21 days, starting at Lakehurst, stopping at Friedrichshafen, Tokyo, and Los Angeles. The press loved it. Lady Drummond Hay—on time this trip—reported again for *The New York Times*. From an altitude of 1,000 feet they flew over great barren wastes of Siberia never before seen by men. Over Western Russia a soldier with an excess of Soviet xenophobia emptied his tommygun at the great silver airship, but only succeeded in puncturing a few gas cells which Chief Knorr easily repaired.

The next year the *Graf Zeppelin* carried an international expedition of scientists to the Arctic to gather data on the weather and geography of that unexplored region. Then the ship began making scheduled runs between Germany and Brazil, making the round trip in 10 days, shuttling passengers back and forth to the large German colony that had settled in Rio de Janeiro.

By 1935 the trips had become almost routine. The service had greatly extended Germany's commercial interests in Latin America. In appreciation of the airship's effective public relations work, a German colonist in Rio, Hans Wagner, presented to Chief Steward Kubis what at first appeared to be a five-by-eight-inch painting of the *Graf* in the air over Rio's harbor.

The sky was a strange purple, the sea a brilliant blue, Sugar Loaf Mountain in the background dark and forbidding, but the ship a brilliant silver, set off with yellows. The picture was not painted with oils, but assembled from iridescent butterfly wings. The effect was eerie. Heinrich Kubis, probably the only crew member who could appreciate it, hung it in his dining room at home.

During her years of service, the *Graf Zeppelin* made 650 flights, 144 of them across the Atlantic, flew more than 1,000,000 miles and carried more than 18,000 passengers. The German Ambassador to

Brazil said that in the development of trade and the extension of German influence, the *Graf Zeppelin* was "worth more than 50 industrial captains."

Influence was something which concerned Berlin. Immediately after landing from a trip to Brazil in 1935, Heinz Wronsky, air traffic manager for the Zeppelin Corporation, handed Dr. Hugo Eckener a message to report to Berlin that night by train. Dr. Joseph Goebbels wanted to see him.

Dr. Eckener was not popular with the Nazis. He was by style an internationalist. They were nationalists. He had cultivated friends all over the world. They were untraveled. He saw technical achievements as a gain for mankind. They saw science as a tool for Germany. He thought transatlantic air travel would contribute to understanding between peoples. They thought it symbolized Germany's power.

He was essentially a man of good will. Before Hitler's election, the successor to Count Zeppelin had made radio broadcasts describing "the corporal from Austria and his bullies" as "adventurers with Germany's future." The men in Berlin resented being lectured by a representative of the Old Order.

When Dr. Eckener was seated in the office of the Minister of Propaganda, Dr. Goebbels came right to the point. Since the Zeppelins were the most prominent symbol of the new Germany on their foreign flights, the government wished to have the *hakenkreuz*, the swastika, painted on their tail surfaces. Drawings illustrating the prescribed form had been prepared. Dr. Goebbels presented them.

Dr. Eckener explained that the colors the Zeppelins flew were the traditional Black, White, Red; that the Zeppelins aimed to further international trade—of great benefit to Germany, and the peaceful understanding of peoples. The swastika was a symbol disliked by many. Its display would arouse animosity, and perhaps even demonstrations upon landing in foreign ports. Its display would do Germany no good, and besides would, in his opinion, do harm to the Zeppelin Company.

"The question is, Dr. Eckener," the Minister of Propaganda emphasized, "which Germany do you represent? The Germany of hunger, despair and defeat? The Germany of Hindenburg—a senile nincompoop whose grotesque insignificance raises in us the astonished question: How was it possible for this nincompoop to become Commander of the Imperial Army and President of the Republic? We have already made history in the streets. The old Germany is dead."

Joseph Goebbels sat behind a huge desk, clean of any papers, his chair pushed back, his legs nonchalantly crossed, his hands folded serenely in his lap. Dr. Eckener studied this fellow called by his fellow Nazis "our little Doctor." The Minister was small, and dark, of slight constitution. Dr. Eckener knew he had a crippled foot.

Dr. Goebbels' eyes shone as he spoke, but it was a cold brilliance, as if he were listening to himself and was amused by what he was saying. He looked like a satisfied cat playing with a mouse. It was not his appetite that made his eyes glow, but the delight he took from the game. The Minister continued.

"Come, Dr. Eckener. We have made our revolution. Germany has burned its bridges. We cannot go back, but neither do we want to go back. Together with our Fuehrer we are building a new Reich. Scratch your name in history with us. In any case, be kind enough to see to it that the *hakenkreuz* is displayed on your *Graf Zeppelin*. And on the new ship as well."

Dr. Eckener returned to Friedrichshafen the same day. He met with his captains and the key members of the Zeppelin works. The swastikas were painted on the tail surfaces of the *Graf Zeppelin* as prescribed.

Chief Rigger Knorr was a practical fellow, by 1935 Chief Inspector of Zeppelins as well as Chief Rigger, a scientist with his hands, an experienced man at construction—with or without the swastika on the tail surfaces.

As a matter of fact he had built Zeppelins under the Black, White, Red of Imperial Germany; for the Red, Black, Gold of the Weimar Republic; and if in turn he built them under the *hakenkreuz* of the Third Reich, it made little difference to him.

Like Steward Kubis, Chief Knorr was an old-timer. He was born October 8, 1891 in Berlin. In 1912, at 21, he had started as a cloth cutter at the Luftschiffbau in Friedrichshafen. During the Great War he had flown in raids over England and Russia. He had patched thousands of holes in gas cells and in ships' skins—the holes of machine gun bullets and shell splinters. Then he became one of the key men at the yards in the construction of Zeppelins. By the end of the war, they were building almost one ship a month.

In 1919 he would have been a member of the crew of the LZ 114 on its flight to New York. Captain Lehmann had planned to fly from Germany to New York and back non-stop—as a demonstration of the peacetime capabilities of Zeppelins. But the new national government had forbidden them to fly.

The LZ 114 had been designed to bomb New York and only finished just before the war ended. But the Weimar Republic decided that it would be bad diplomacy to appear over Wall Street, demonstrating how easily the feat could have been accomplished. Then the Allies had required the LZ 114 to be turned over to the French, and the manufacture of Zeppelins had been forbidden altogether. Well, one could hardly expect generosity from the victors.

Knorr was able to stay on at the Luftschiffbau while they manufactured pots and pans stamped with the company's LZ symbol. They had to watch, partly in admiration but partly in envy, as the R-34, an English dirigible copied from the captured German L 33, flew the first non-stop transatlantic air trip in July 1919.

Soon thereafter the Americans had built a hangar in Lakehurst 1,000 feet long and 263 feet wide to house the new ships they planned. It was ready in 1921. The English built a ship designated R-38 for the Americans. It was 700 feet long, 86 feet in diameter, contained 2,700,000 feet of hydrogen and powered by six 350 horsepower engines. It was badly built, however, and badly handled. On its last test flight it crashed into the Humber River and exploded.

The Americans had also bought a semi-rigid designed by the Italian Commander Nobile, called the *Roma*. It was a small ship, only 410 feet and 1,193,000 cubic feet of hydrogen. The Americans flew it into electrical wires at the edge of Langley Field and it too exploded. Eleven crewmen were saved, but 33 died.

After that the Americans decided their airships must contain helium, instead of hydrogen. Helium not only was not explosive, it could be used to put out fires. In Amarillo, Texas, and Dexter, Kansas, the Americans had all the helium in the world—no other country had any, except perhaps the Russians. The only trouble with helium was that it had only 90 per cent of the lifting capacity of hydrogen. It was also 10 times more expensive, even for the rich Americans.

As far as Chief Knorr could see, hydrogen worked much better. Its use meant the ships could carry greater loads; it was relatively inexpensive, and available in every part of the world. If proper precautions were taken, nothing need go wrong with it.

After all, during the war German ships had been filled with machine gun holes, hit repeatedly by anti-aircraft shells, hit by lightning in storms, and even once or twice completely covered with the dancing static electricity discharge known to seamen as "St. Elmo's Fire" —a sight which at first frightened the men. Chief Knorr had been aboard to see it.

The whole ship had glowed an eerie blue. At their posts in the stern the machine gunners had sparks dancing at the tips of their fingers in a weird magic. When they asked Captain Lehmann about it, he laughed and explained. As the ship moved through the clouds it accumulated an electrical charge, much in the same way a child would when he dragged his feet across a thick carpet. There would be no discharge of the static electricity unless the child then touched someone else, or a doorknob. Since they were at an altitude of 8,000 feet, they would find it difficult to become a conductor to the ground: "Only do not drag one foot on the ground as we sail along."

Static electricity would certainly never bring a Zeppelin down. In any case, as Chief Knorr would explain to the younger men, the only way Zeppelins were brought down was after the English had introduced the phosphorus bullets. Phosphorus started either the outer fabric afire or lit the materials of the gas cells. Then once the material was burning, oxygen could make the combination with hydrogen, and the burning fabric provided the ignition. In peacetime, German Zeppelins had flown more than a million miles of passenger service without even one injury of any kind, and with certainly none of the "accidents" to which the Allies seemed so prone.

Chief Knorr could recall that in 1923 the Americans finally built for themselves a ship they called the *Shenandoah*. It was, in fact, a copy of the Zeppelin LZ 49 which had crashed in France during the war. The Americans had to add extra frames on the inside of the ship —make it longer—to provide for more gas bags, because their helium did not lift as well as hydrogen. Captain Anton Heinen went to Lakehurst to teach them how to fly. Once when they moored the

*Shenandoah* improperly, it broke away in a bad storm. Captain Heinen had to fly the ship back and save it.

By then the Americans had come to their senses and commissioned the Luftschiffbau to build the LZ 126 for the U.S. Navy. The yard had work again: a ship of German construction, under expert German command, would show what Zeppelin men could do. It was built at 670 feet, a maximum diameter of 92 feet, and a capacity of 2,470,000 cubic feet of helium. With Dr. Eckener commanding, and Captain Lehmann as his alternate, it took off on October 12, 1924. Eighty-one hours later—and 5,030 miles—the LZ 126 landed at Lakehurst. The U.S. Navy landing crew was expert at handling the landing lines. They had had plenty of practice from handling the *Shenandoah*.

The Navy rechristened the LZ 126 the *Los Angeles*. According to the contract of delivery, nine members of the German crew remained at Lakehurst to train the Americans in the ship and in its operation. The remaining Germans included Captain Flemming, Navigation Officer Walter Scherz, Helmsmen Ludwig Marx and Albert Sammt, Mechanics Groezinger, Pfaff, and Martil, and Chief Rigger Ludwig Knorr.

In addition, by a contract entered into between the Luftschiffbau and the Goodyear Tire and Rubber Company, the Goodyear Zeppelin Company was created. It would make use of the Zeppelin Company's patents. Mr. Vissering, of Goodyear, Dr. Eckener and Captain Lehmann were elected its directors.

Chief Designer Ludwig Dürr, Chief Engineer Eric Heligardt, and others moved to Akron, Ohio, to help the Americans get started on design and construction of their Navy airships *Akron* and *Macon*. Although the French and English still had the power to ban the construction of Zeppelins in Germany in 1924, they could not stop a private American company from making use of German talent.

In 1925 after a national tour, the officers of the American-built *Shenandoah* flew into a violent thunderstorm over Ohio. The ship had already had structural failures which should have served as a warning. The extra frames installed to provide for the extra cells of helium instead of hydrogen were a risk. When the storm dashed the ship up and down in the air, it broke up under the strain into three parts at 5,000 feet. The command car was not built into the frame, as were the command cars of German ships, and it pulled away from the rest of the airship and fell to the ground.

In one of the three remaining sections, the helium continued to lift the frame, and Commander Charles E. Rosendahl—who happened to be in that section when the ship broke up—took command and sailed the section as a free balloon. He stayed in the air making lazy circles of about ten miles diameter for an hour after the rest of the Shenandoah had gone down before he came to earth. Nevertheless, 14 men died (all those in the command gondola) while 29 survived.

Two years later, in May 1927, Charles A. Lindbergh flew his Spirit of St. Louis from Roosevelt Field in Long Island to Paris, non-stop. He had great improvements in his plane over those of the World War I models: a Sperry gyrocompass; cambered wings; a 225 horsepower Wright Whirlwind air-cooled engine; improved gasolines. While one swallow does not a summer make, some visionaries began to think that improved airplanes might someday compete with Zeppelins in long distance flights if not in payload.

About the same time the political climate had eased a great deal, and Chief Knorr was back in Friedrichshafen to supervise the rigging of the LZ 127, the Graf Zeppelin. He was proud not only that he had been part of its construction, but that thereafter he had not missed a single one of its flights. He had ridden in the ticker tape parade in New York in 1928. He had shaken the hand of President Hindenburg. He had flown around the world in 1929, went along on the trips to Cairo and the Arctic, and on every trip to Rio.

While the Graf Zeppelin was setting records, the other nations tried to keep up. The English flew the R-100 to Canada and returned in the summer of 1930. They wanted to send the R-101 on a triumphal tour of India the same year. It was another badly designed and handled ship. With their Air Minister aboard, they crashed in France on the way to India and the ship exploded. The English gave up dirigibles.

In 1933 the Americans crashed the Akron in a storm off the New Jersey coast. The causes were not clear. Only three men survived, while 73 drowned, including Rear Admiral Moffett, Chief of the U.S. Navy's Bureau of Aeronautics. It had been his idea to make the Zeppelins into something like flying aircraft carriers.

The Americans perfected a method in which their Zeppelins acted as long-range scouts for their fleet. Airplanes could be launched from a bay in the belly of the airship, fly off and zoom over the enemy, return to the airship for refueling. The plane would fly up under the airship, attach itself to a hook, then turn off its engines. The hook ran to a derrick which pulled the plane into the belly of the ship where there was a hangar for the planes.

Since the airships by then had a range of nearly 10,000 miles, and air speeds about three times as fast as either cruisers or aircraft carriers, the combination of airship and airplane appeared to be devastating in the American war games.

In the spirit of her husband's vision, the widow of Admiral Moffett christened the *Akron*'s sister ship, the *Macon*, in March 1934. During war games in the Pacific in 1935, the *Macon* broke up off Point Sur, California. Again the cause was structural failure in the stern, just forward of the rudder fins and horizontal stabilizers, and probably as a result of the lengthening of the ship to contain the less buoyant helium. Only two men died, and 79 were saved, but the Americans gave up Zeppelins too. Instead they would concentrate on airplanes.

The unfortunate accidents to the *Shenandoah*, *Akron*, and *Macon* had strengthened the arguments of the airplane men. It was useless to argue, as the Zeppelin men did, that airplanes had at that time just as many accidents. The airplane technicians countered that the Zeppelins were too vulnerable to attack in war; Zeppelins were dinosaurs, there was no sense in continuing their development.

It was all very well to talk of "passenger services," but the cost of developing large, modern, technical devices must be paid by the State. The main function of the State was to protect its people in war. Therefore, the course of technology ran between the channels demanded by war. The Iron Law of technology was: if there were no use at war in the device, then in a practical sense, the technology had no utility. From the earliest times it had always been so.

Things designed for pleasure, for the beauty of their form, for the delights of peace—such as Zeppelins—were no more than art objects, things like millionaires' yachts, or Santos-Dumont's enchanting balloon. They might very well promote peace, but the War Department was not in the business of supporting pleasure.

Among the technical men it was well known that Germany had on the drawing boards airplanes such as the Messerschmidt fighter plane. The British had planes of similar characteristics, the "Hurricane" and the "Spitfire," as they were called. In the United States, the engineers were refining the designs for the Bell "Aircobra." Any of these fighters could knock down a Zeppelin in seconds with phosphorus coated bullets.

By 1935 aircraft design had made considerable progress. The directional gyroscope had been added, the artificial horizon, then radio beam landings. Better metals allowed for unitized construction, laminar flow wings. The variable pitch propeller, the 425-horsepower Wasp engine, and then the 925-horsepower Cyclone had brought speeds up to 180 miles per hour. In 1933 Boeing's 247 was introduced as the first commercial U.S. transport. It only carried 10 passengers and its range was insignificant compared to Zeppelins, but the airplane men were learning. Besides, the War Department would pay the development costs.

In March 1936, when the *Hindenburg*, the LZ 129, was making its trial flights, Douglas Aircraft Company began the trial flights of the DC-3, a 21 passenger plane with 220 miles an hour speed, powered by two 700 horsepower air-cooled engines. It had a heated cabin that gave it the ability to fly at 20,000 feet—above most bad weather. But its range was still only 1,200 miles, and Chief Designer Dürr and his engineers at the Luftschiffbau did not see any practical competition in transatlantic service yet.

Dr. Hugo Eckener could have scoffed at the attempts of other nations to inaugurate transocean passenger services, if he were that sort of fellow. Plans were being made to fly seaplanes in a series of short hops across the Pacific. By building innumerable fueling stations, the amphibians would land and take off at island after island until they reached China. With the *Graf Zeppelin* Eckener had easily sailed across non-stop. Britain's Imperial Airways announced plans to fly by seaplane from New York to Bermuda. Non-stop, they said. Dr. Eckener could afford to be charitable. He said he thought Zeppelins and airplanes would eventually complement each other.

Thanks to the success of the *Graf Zeppelin* he could easily show Berlin that transatlantic service between America and Germany added to Germany's prestige. The commercial and financial extensions of Zeppelins were important too: they earned foreign exchange for Germany—which Finance Minister Hjalmar Schacht wanted keenly. And Dr. Eckener had other reasons as well: he was convinced that Zeppelins served the cause of peace, a cause which won him no credit in Berlin nor any arguments with the technicians of war, but which was his own central motivation. He used his considerable skills as propagandist and salesman to advance his life's work.

As a result, early in 1935 a special corporation was formed, the Zeppelin Airship Corporation. The Zeppelin Luftschiffbau—the construction company, bought up 58% of the new corporation's stock; the National Government of the Third Reich and Lufthansa, the government's airline, paid for the other 42%. Captain Lehmann and Herr Karl Christiansen, the Police President of Magdeburg, were named as directors. Construction was started on the LZ 129.

To get the money the great ship required, Dr. Eckener had to accept the State's director, a man with no experience whatever in Zeppelins, but it was done for a good cause. In any case, in operating matters the Police Chief would have to bow to their experience.

As Chief Ludwig Knorr tirelessly pointed out, experience was one of the main ingredients in correct technical construction. At the yards in Friedrichshafen Ludwig Dürr, chief architect, had been conducting experiments and designing rigid airships since joining Graf Zeppelin in 1899. Chief Helmsman Marx had trained recruits since 1900. Dürr's brother-in-law, Lösch, was superintendent of the foundry. Schwarz, who had escaped the burning LZ 4 in the miracle at Echterdingen, was a foreman in the manufacturing department. Futscher was a machinist on the DELAG's *Deutschland* and the *Viktoria Luise*. Karl Friederich Beuerle had been with DELAG too before he circled the world on the *Graf Zeppelin* as Chief Engineer. On the LZ 129 Beuerle would be replaced as Chief Engineer by Rudolf Sauter, who had served a long apprenticeship with the Daimler Motors Company.

Besides Chiefs Kubis, Knorr, Sauter and Chief Electrician Philip Lenz, there were many experienced men to see to the millions of details of accurate construction.

To construct the LZ 129 a new hangar was built—one large enough to accommodate the construction of the big ships planned. Then the foundry began the work of fabricating more than 10 miles of girders made from Duraluminum, a light alloy of copper and aluminum. Not all the experience in making pots and pans was lost.

The Duraluminum girders were of a triangular design to add strength, but save weight. The first step was to assemble giant rings laid out flat on the hangar floor. When riveting of each ring was complete, it was hung up from the main brace in the hangar's ceiling. Eventually 16 giant rings, each 14 stories high, hung in their apportioned places.

Then longitudinal girders of the same triangular design were assembled. They ran lengthwise connecting the bow rings with the stern rings. There were 36 of these long girders. The base of the triangle of the girders faced inboard. It was riveted to the base of the triangle of the rings, which faced outboard. So the horizontal rings and longitudinal girders were fixed face to face.

At that stage in the construction the naked frame could be compared to the skeleton of some fantastic whale. The rings formed its rib cage—blunt in the nose, thick in the middle of its body, tapering again in streamline to its tail. The lengthwise girders formed a circle of backbones, but the whole impression, though huge, was airy, lacy and light—adapted to its intended medium, the sky, instead of the deep pressures of the sea.

At the tail of this odd monster a vertical fin was built into the frame, from its bottom to its top about 150 feet. Similarly a horizontal fin, or wing, stretched laterally the same distance. The marine biologist would have to note that its vertical fin gave it the aspect of a shark, the horizontal the aspect of the porpoise, or whale family. At the aft end of the vertical pin was the rudder, such as those in ships, to steer to left and right. The horizontal fin had an "elevator" to steer up and down.

From the very bow to the very stern in the center of its ribs there ran a central backbone—an axial girder. It served two purposes. First, guy wires of steel ran from each ring's diameter to this center backbone. By increasing their tension with turnbuckles each ring's shape could be maintained, and strengthened, by strain. Struts fanned out from the axial girder to stress the interior sectioning.

Second, once the ship was completed, this interior backbone also served as a gangway—the so-called "middle" gangway for access to the interior of the ship from bow to stern. At the center of the ship's diameter, the middle gangway was (at the ship's midpoint from bow to stern) about 75 feet below the top and 75 feet above another gangway —the lower gangway—which also ran the length of the ship, again from bow to the tail, along the belly of the ship.

Because of the ship's whale-like shape the bottom gangway curved up in the blunt bow to meet the middle gangway. In the tail, the bottom gangway ran to the point at which the vertical fin intersected with the tapering hull. There a set of stairs descended in two flights so that crewmen could clamber down into the fin itself and manage the retractable rear landing wheel and stern docking lines at the appropriate moment.

Hung up in the hangar when the rings and girders had been assembled and when the struts were affixed, the guy wires tensioned, and the frame of the tail and fin assembled, the next step was to stretch a strong cotton fabric over the whole, like a skin. It gave the airship its smooth form, and saved the interior from the winds and the elements.

It was cut and sewn at machines, then stretched and laced section by section onto the outer frame. The outside of the cotton was doped with five coats of cellon, mixed with silver to reflect the heat of the sun. On the inside, on the top of the ship, it was also painted red as insulation against the sun's ultra violet rays. As men worked on its interior the electric lights, marking their tiny efforts, shone through the cotton skin giving it a ghostly cast.

The 16 rings also served to compartmentalize the ship in the same way an ocean ship is sectioned off. Each compartment contained a gas cell. In the *Graf Zeppelin*, LZ 127, these gas bags were stitched together from cotton fabric, then backed—lined—with the outside membrane of the large intestine of the ox. It had taken about 50,000 membranes to line each cell. The membranes were cemented to the cotton. They were chosen because the intestine of the ox was considered the most impervious substance, consequently the hydrogen would not be able to leak through what was called "Goldbeater's Skin."

For the LZ 129, however, an improvement was made even on "Goldbeater's Skin." A gas-tight film, chemically produced and similar to photographer's film, was cemented between two layers of fabric. Then sections of this new surface were stitched into bags, and the bags hung in the interior of the ship—one bag for each compartment.

Each bag was surrounded by a netting of line, just as were the balloons flown over the siege of Paris in 1870. Once the bag was inflated, it lifted against its lines. In turn, the lines lifted the ship. Each bag was sheltered in its own compartment by cotton partitions from the next, and in addition, by lines from the girders and frames so that the surface of the bag would not chafe. When fully inflated, the bags would completely fill their compartments. When gas was lost, the top of the bags would still strain against their net, but the bottom would fold in on itself. In walking along the axial backbone —the middle walkway—an experienced rigger like Chief Knorr could estimate the pressure in each cell by putting his hand against the cell's surface and feeling the skin of the bag. A loose bag equaled low pressure, a tight bag meant high pressure. Over the years a man like Knorr learned to guess within a percentage point the gradients between.

There were, of course, valves for each cell—valves to let off pressure should the ship need to descend, valves to regulate the flow of inflation. Each valve for each cell could be operated from the command gondola. Each cell was metered too, so that in the command gondola a reading could be made as accurately as Chief Knorr's more informal method.

When all 16 of the LZ 129's gas cells were fully inflated with lifting gas they contained 7,200,000 cubic feet of hydrogen—enough to lift a gross weight of 236 tons. Even after lifting its own weight, and that of its engines (which had only to work to drive the ship ahead), and their fuel, the remaining payload was more than 20 *tons*—which was precisely the advantage of Zeppelins.

At a cruising speed of about 80 miles per hour, with a full payload, the LZ 129 had a fuel range of about 10,000 miles—or about 5 or 6 days continuously in the air. At lower air speeds, it could theoretically stay up longer.

In November 1935 on a trip to Rio a revolution started on the ground while the *Graf Zeppelin* was en route in the air. The ship throttled down, floated over the South Atlantic, waited five days until the revolution was over, then landed. The LZ 129 had almost half again as much lifting capacity as the *Graf Zeppelin.*

The new LZ 129 also had much grander passenger accommodations. Instead of being contained in a gondola slung below the ship, the new accommodations were built on two decks up inside the hull. Access from the ground was by a two-stage hinged stairway, which was let down by lines, but which, when folded up, was flush with the ship's hull. This main gangway was about 120 feet aft of the command gondola.

Climbing the stairs a passenger would first arrive inside the ship on "B" deck. An aisle running forward on the starboard side passed by windows on the right hand, and the hot and cold shower rooms on the left—divided for ladies and for gentlemen. At the end of the aisle was the entrance to the bar. Through the bar, where a steward would be in attendance day and night, there was a double lock door, sort of half a revolving door, which led in turn to the smoking room. Entrance and exit to the smoking room would be controlled by the bar steward.

On the port side of "B" deck, there were additional baths and showers for the crew, then working forward again along the windows lining the aisles to the left, there was the crew's mess, next the kitchen, and finally the officers' mess.

Upstairs on "A" deck a wide aisle ran laterally across the ship. On the starboard side was a large lounge with groupings of comfortable chairs and tables. They were made of aluminum and so light they could be lifted with two fingers.

Forward of the lounge, and divided from it by a wall, there was a library and writing room. Along the windows of the starboard side, which ran the length of "A" deck, there was a promenade of about 130 feet. Benches were built in beneath the windows, so that passengers might gaze out and be amused by the passage of the ship over continents and seas.

A similar promenade stretched the length of the port side, again with comfortable benches. Above the benches a low counter hardly waist high formed the sill of the windows, which slanted up and out, following the form of the ship. Inboard of the port promenade, behind a railing low enough to keep the view unobstructed, was the dining saloon. It was served by a small pantry on "A" deck, which was in turn fed by a dumbwaiter from the kitchen on "B" deck directly below.

Spanning the center of the ship on "A" deck and served by two center corridors, 25 staterooms were arranged side by side and running fore and aft. Each stateroom contained an upper and lower berth, its own toilet, hot and cold running water in a washstand. During the day, the upper berth could be folded up into the wall, and the lower made into a settee—much like Pullman compartments on a train. During the day, each cabin was its own comfortable sitting room. The walls were decorated in pearl grey linen. The ship was electrically lit throughout. There was a bell to summon the steward for wine, or for playing cards.

Chief Steward Kubis would supervise a crew of six stewards, plus a stewardess for the care of children and helping lady passengers with their hair. Chef Maier supervised a crew of four cooks and a mess boy. There would be 17 mechanics, and three engineering officers under the supervision of Chief Engineer Sauter. In addition, there were Chief Knorr and his two riggers, Chief Lenz and two electricians, plus radio operators, helmsmen, elevatormen, navigators, and ship's officers. There would also be a ship's doctor.

Depending upon the number of passengers (anywhere from 30 to 70 could be comfortably accommodated) and the number of crew (if there were fewer passengers, additional crew could be carried for training purposes), the ship could travel comfortably with 100 souls and all their needs in food, wine, water, and comfort for a week in the air.

Each of the main rings which formed the ribs of the ship was, by custom, numbered according to its distance in meters from the very stern. Hence, the stairway which led down into the tail from the main, or lower, walkway along the bottom of the ship, began "aft of Ring 62." Similarly, it would be said that the small freight room, the one designed for the transport of animals and such, was just forward of Ring 62. The same Ring 62 separated Gas Cells IV and V, but Zeppelin men by tradition referred to the position of things in the ship by reference to their ring numbers. The very stern being Ring "o"; and the very tip of the bow on the LZ 129, "at 246.7," which was also the length of the ship in meters.

Hence forward of Ring 62 were the small freight compartments and the crew's quarters for the riggers. Crew's quarters were similar to passenger quarters—with double bunks, but they did not fold away. Between Rings 77 and 92, there was a large freight room.

At Ring 92, lateral walkways extended all the way across the ship up at the middle gangway level. The walkways went through hatches on the side of the ship, then out to the aft engine gondolas, mounted on struts outside the ship.

Each engine pod was itself streamlined much like an egg and inside the egg the engine was mounted on a special pad to reduce vibration. Two men could work inside the pods, which had their own windows outboard. In each pod was a 16-cylinder V-type Mercedes Benz diesel engine driving a four-bladed propeller mounted aft. The propellers were wood and 20 feet in diameter. The lateral walkway at Ring 92 connected engine gondolas #1 (starboard) and #2 (port).

Fuel tanks were spaced through the ship forward from Ring 92 to Ring 140. At Ring 140 another lateral walkway vertically amidships extended across the ship to engine gondolas #3 (starboard) and #4 (port). Altogether the four engines could deliver 5,000 horsepower.

In addition to the fuel tanks, there was a large freight room between Ring 123.4 and Ring 140; and another between Ring 140 and Ring 156.5. Altogether, the LZ 129 had a capacity for more than 13 tons of freight, mail and baggage.

In the same section was the electrical power plant of the ship—the domain of Chief Electrician Philip Lenz. Arranged in two rooms with a metal door lock between them were two 30-kilowatt diesel-powered generators in two electrical net systems—so that if one were faulty the other could provide.

Besides the regular lighting on a 220-volt system, there was a backup lighting system on a 24-volt net, three pump engines, two ventilator engines, two motors for the steering apparatus (which could also be manually operated), two motors for antenna winches (one for the refrigerator, one for the dumbwaiter), one transformer for the gyrocompass, four transformers for the radio room, four ovens and three boilers and food warmers in the kitchen, and finally, six preheaters for the cooling water of the engines.

Crew's quarters took up most of the keel space between Ring 156.5 and Ring 173 and the two-deck passenger area between Ring 173 and Ring 188. Just aft of Ring 203 a post office was situated to port and the radio room to starboard, on either side of the walkway. Immediately ahead of them a gangway ran downstairs to the command gondola, which was suspended below the skin of the ship, providing visibility in every direction except up.

The gondola was about 28 feet long and 9 feet across at its widest. It was, of course, streamlined too. A retractable landing wheel fit into its bottom. Facing forward was a stand for the rudder wheel and on the port side a stand for the elevator wheel. The helmsman stood sideways. While the steersman read his compass, the helmsman read his altitude gauge and his inclination.

Behind the steering compartment were a pair of navigating, or chart rooms. The whole of this little ship hanging beneath the big ship was surrounded by glass windows. The gauges for reading the pressure in the gas cells and the valves for each cell were on the rear wall of the steering compartment and at the elevatorman's left hand. The gauges and controls for the ballast were above his right hand at the port side windows.

Distributed throughout the ship were containers of water ballast. Once the ship had been inflated by hydrogen, and balanced, ballast would have to be released to gain buoyancy. The containers were of fabric. From the very bow, or the very stern, 500 kilograms of water could be released to change inclination as well as buoyancy. Amidships, the tanks on either side of the walkway were of 2,000 and 2,500 kilogram capacity. They could be emptied partially, or totally, by the elevatorman through wires running to his stand in the control car.

Telephone lines ran from the control car to various command posts in the ship. In addition there were speaker tubes, in case of a loss of power. Engine commands were signaled to the individual engine gondolas by a mechanical telegraph—like a ship's. By placing the signal lever at the required position in the command car, each mechanic would receive the necessary order: "Reverse, Slow Ahead, Stop, Fast Ahead!"

Above the command car and inside the ship, the main walkway arched up in a slow curve to meet the bow "at 246.7." For the last 75 feet the ascent was steep, and so the walkway gave way to steps. At the top of the steps there was a kind of shelf inside the bow of the ship, from which the riggers could manage the mooring apparatus and its lines.

Along the steps, looking down, and on either side of the mooring cone, there were windows. As a result, from head on the ship looked as if it had four closely spaced eyes in its nose, then a trail of eyes down the throat of its belly to the command car.

The *Graf Zeppelin* (LZ 127) had been an experimental ship whose exploits quickly became routine. Its success, however, had been so spectacular that the Luftschiffbau skipped over the plans drawn up for the LZ 128 and went on to build the LZ 129. By March 1936 it was ready to be commissioned.

# CHAPTER 3

# LATEST IN THE LINE

"All visible objects, man, are but as pasteboard masks. But in each event—in the living act, the undoubted deed—there, some unknown but still reasoning thing puts forth the mouldings of its features from behind the unreasoning mask."

—*Moby Dick*, HERMAN MELVILLE

On Wednesday, March 4, 1936 Dr. Hugo Eckener took the new LZ 129 for a three-hour trial flight over the Bodensee. The airship had not yet been named. Captain Ernst A. Lehmann was in command. The new diesel motors were pronounced much quieter than the gasoline motors of the *Graf Zeppelin*. There was practically no vibration, and the ship was easy to handle. They landed at 6:25 P.M.

The next morning the ship was up again at 8:53 A.M., this time with 90 people on board, among them Lieutenant Colonel Breithaupt, a former Zeppelin captain in the war and the representative of the Air Ministry. After a few turns over the lake, making various calculations on the ship's handling ability, and after testing the kitchens—Kubis selected Hungarian goulash with a good red wine for lunch—Dr. Eckener decided to pay a call.

A radio-telegram notified Mayor Fiehler, and at 12:30 the LZ 129 arrived over Munich. Crowds came out to welcome the new ship. By radio the Mayor asked what the ship's name was. Dr. Eckener answered "*Hindenburg*." Upon landing that night, he was again summoned to Berlin.

"Dr. Eckener," Minister of Propaganda Dr. Goebbels began: "You seem to think you know how to manage the affairs of the press better than I do. I see that your test flights were thoroughly covered by the foreign press, and in addition, you thought it would be gallant to name this creation of the new Reich for the old grey man of the old regime."

Dr. Eckener was 68, a proud and independent man, most always direct, and he felt himself quite as much a German patriot as these ruffians who now spoke for Germany. Patiently, and in the face of Goebbels' own choice for the airship's name, he explained that naming the ship "Adolf Hitler" would gain the Zeppelin Company no good will in trips to America—or anywhere for that matter; that "Hindenburg" was certainly an honorable German name; and that in any case, he was himself no more than a mere technician—not a politician with votes to be won by pandering to the current hysteria.

"Dr. Eckener, let me explain." The Propaganda Minister almost seemed patient. "We are the State now. We have put up the money for your ship. More important, we are the essence of the German people brought up to this date. We are not only its laws, we are its achievements. We are Beethoven, we are Mozart, we are Schiller, and Kant and Wagner. And we are your airship.

"We are the mothers and fathers, the grandmothers and grandfathers; and we are the sons and daughters. We are the tillers and workers, yes your mathematicians and technicians too, the engineers and architects. Who are you? From whom do you get your orders, your mandate, your power?"

The disciple of Zeppelin was silent.

"What you want to be is your own little God. But you lack the magisterial authority. We represent the Volk—the German Volk. You want things to stay the way they were; but we are making progress. You cannot hide behind your technical apparatus as if it were kitchen skirts from which you can peek when frightened! I have given orders today that in Germany, at least, your 'Hindenburg' ship will be referred to only by its number, LZ 129. What the foreign press calls it is not my concern.

"Moreover, I warn you that I would regret giving orders that in the future the German press should not mention your name at all, nor mention the name of your son Knud, who played the hero on the *Graf Zeppelin*'s wing. The only heroes in the Third Reich are those who belong to the party—which I understand you are disinclined to join. Well then, so be it."

Once again Dr. Eckener returned by train to Friedrichshafen, and once again consulted with his collaborators of the years at the Luftschiffbau. There was, of course, nothing they could do.

On Friday, March 6, the LZ 129 as it was called in Germany, and the *Hindenburg* elsewhere, made a three-hour trial flight. On board were Dr. Eckener, eight Zeppelin captains, functionaries from the Air Ministry, ninety members of the crew and the Zeppelin Corporation's staff, and Dr. Eckener's personal guests. Among Dr. Eckener's guests was Lt. Commander Scott Peck, official observer for the U. S. Navy.

Commander Peck declared the engines far more powerful and much faster than in American dirigibles. He praised the performance of the new Zeppelin, especially its efficient streamlining. He added: "I consider all possibilities of danger in the new Zeppelin eliminated."

The world press was fascinated. The Commissioners of the Air Ministry pronounced the new ship airworthy. The German press reported it all—except they referred to it as the LZ 129, and they did not mention the *Hindenburg* name.

The next morning, Saturday, March 7, Chancellor Hitler ordered three battalions of German troops to occupy the Rhineland. They paraded across the Rhine bridges at dawn. Two hours later the Fuehrer was on the rostrum at the Reichstag before a delirious audience. After a long harangue about the evils of Versailles and the threat of Bolshevism, he announced that France's pact with Russia had invalidated the Locarno Treaty, which had guaranteed a demilitarized Rhineland.

Rudolf Sauter, Chief Engineer of the *Hindenburg*, was a Nazi: Party Card #890755.

Born in Tettnang, near the Bodensee, trained as an engineer in the Daimler works, he said he had always favored the party right from the beginning. He just didn't get around to joining it formally until February 1, 1932. By then he was already 30 years old.

Some of his shipmates would characterize him as basically an opportunist, but that was not true. He was bluff, thought he was suave, admired in himself the air of charming rogue which in part he displayed, and yet he would not inform on his shipmates in the same way that, say, Helmsman Helmut Lau might—Lau was both "party" and "SS."

Good old Sauter really loved Zeppelins. He loved engines too. And he loved Germany. He saw the National Socialist German Workers Party as a natural expression of the will of the German people, even a necessity, in the face of the treachery of Versailles, the greed of Jewish bankers, and the ineptitude and anarchy of the Catholic and Communist "Democrats."

Since he was born in 1901 he had been the perfect age to win the worst possible of all educations from the war, the Soviet governments after the war, the inflation, and then the Depression. He had seen with his own eyes that the strong in life survive and the weak do not—which was, after all, nature's rule, was it not?

He had seen anarchy and chaos in Munich and Berlin—not to mention a half dozen other cities of which he knew. Were not the Spartacists led by Jews? Had not the so-called "people's state of Bavaria" been the work of Kurt Eisner, a Jewish writer?

In fact, the Soviet Revolution in Russia was led by Trotsky and Zinoviev—Jews, both of them. And during the period of the "experiment in Democracy" was not the press mostly Jewish, the theatre Jewish, and the big department stores Jewish? What then was the result of these social experiments? The Credit Anstalt in Austria failed in 1927 and the world banking system subsequently collapsed. Was not the Credit Anstalt the Rothschild bank—the principal Jewish bank?

And when the socialist states failed, and the banks failed, what did the journalists have to say then to help the working man? The landlords still rode around in their big cars and went to pretty theatre parties in Berlin. The working man could just as well starve.

Well, as far as the party was concerned, it was time for law and order; and some discipline. "Germany for the Germans," and then they would work themselves out of their poverty. And had it not been done? Was there not work for all? And couldn't Germany take its place in pride with the other nations again? Wasn't the *Hindenburg* itself an example of what might be done? Rudolf Sauter was proud to pass out the party's literature and make its arguments.

Aboard the *Hindenburg* in 1936 Rudolf Sauter was a happy man. The great interior of the ship—in the areas off the walkways and be-

yond the freight rooms and working areas—had such a fantastic com-
plex of struts and arches and wires and space. It reminded him of the
Cathedral in Ulm, except in the *Hindenburg* there was nothing super-
stitious about it—Designer Ludwig Dürr and his staff had calculated
to the millimeter every one of those braces and in a way even the
mathematics of the open space too.

It was the open space which gave the effect that charmed Sauter.
The sun shone through the linen exterior in much the same way that
it would stream through the vaulted arches of a cathedral—the criss-
crossing rings, girders and struts outlined against the light like gigantic mullioned windows. Then at night the electric lights would seem
like votive candles, each one lit beneath some area of work. Especially
when the airship floated in the hangar, when the tiny lights could still
be seen through the translucent linen skin, it seemed to Sauter as if
each light was a reminder how much he loved the quiet machine it
guarded, each light sought intercession for each working part, and the
whole effect combined to reassure him of the miracle of power.

Chief Sauter was in charge of the engines which drove this cathedral through the sky. His engines weighed 4,320 pounds each and
could develop 1,200 horsepower each at 1,400 r.p.m. That meant he
was getting better than 4 pounds per horsepower from diesels—which
compared to gasoline were much cheaper. Diesel eliminated the fire
hazard of carrying gasoline aboard; eliminated the need for an electrical ignition system; or carburetors; simplified the radio and navigation
problems; and could give great performance at high altitudes—if
they ever needed it the way the wartime Zeppelins had.

Bent over his engines Sauter could read their chant as well as any
choirmaster could read the tones of twenty boys in a church. In a curious way his engines, in their slow start, and then the steady drum of
explosions in each of the 16 cylinders, moved in Sauter a faith somewhat similar to the faith in transubstantiation.

Well, not exactly, of course. But the oil which was their fuel had
come up from the bowels of the earth, constituted from leaves and
ferns and mosses, once living carbon rings compressed down there for
eons, a sticky wine sucked up from its underground vats, and then
refined.

When it arrived in each cylinder, it was exploded under compres-
sion without spark, successive controlled fires in each tabernacle,

pushing the cylinders down one after another in their disciplined order. Each one was exactly the same as its neighbor; each must wait its turn to do its work—the timing exact; each push combining perfectly with the pulls of its compatriots in the engine's ordained cycle. Was that not how things should be ordered? Could anything be accomplished without order? What if each cylinder decided for itself its own moment to do its work, why the machine would accomplish nothing, it would fly apart!

Power—effective power, depended upon each part consenting to the engineer's plan, and then following it exactly. If only everyone could see that with proper planning they could arrange not just 16 cylinders, but 32, or 64, or 128, or thousands, even millions to work together.

In any case, when the ship was under way Chief Sauter would scramble over the catwalk to the egg-shaped gondolas standing out from the hull. In the gondola 16 cylinders made a terrific racket, which he immensely enjoyed. It was difficult to hear anything at all in there, indeed it was difficult to even think. Orders had to be given by sign. Once back across the catwalk in the ship's hull, he could say: that's power, all right, the noise of pure power—running in an orderly way.

After the first test flights in which everything went perfectly, the *Hindenburg* and *Graf Zeppelin* were scheduled to take part in the Rhineland election. For after occupying that historic German region with troops on March 7, the Fuehrer had generously called for new elections to be held Sunday, March 29.

On the starboard and port sides of the bow of the LZ 129 the name *Hindenburg* had been painted in large block letters. Amidships were the five interlocking rings of the Olympic circles—the games were to be held in Berlin that summer. As the ship was being led out of the hangar, a 35-degree crosswind was blowing. The inexperienced ground crew pulling the great ship out of its refuge were carried off their feet by a capricious gust of wind. The stern fin was pushed to the earth and bent. The *Graf Zeppelin* began its propaganda attack on German cities alone.

The *Hindenburg* was returned to its hangar. The bent pieces were sawed off, and Chief Knorr patched fabric on the stump of the rudder. Captain Lehmann was prepared to take off again immediately, but Dr. Eckener was furious. In full view of the crew, and within earshot of the representatives from the Propaganda Ministry, Dr. Eckener berated Captain Lehmann for risking a great ship for nothing more than a cheap political trick.

Nevertheless, Captain Lehmann brought the *Hindenburg* out of the hangar again and took off. The ship steered perfectly, he said. They joined the *Graf Zeppelin* over Nuremberg. In the belly of the ship was a large radio and a loudspeaker for broadcasting election speeches. From a release mechanism in the stern, little parachutes carrying leaflets fluttered down to the millions of voters below.

The leaflets said: "The Reich is free and happy;" and, "Thirty-seven parties destroyed the Reich in 15 years; one man—Hitler—built it up again in three."

Silesia and Dresden were covered by clouds, but for four days the *Graf Zeppelin* and the *Hindenburg*, huge swastikas on their tails, loudspeakers blaring military marches and slogans, cruised—over the Gulf of Danzig, Tilsit, Königsberg in Prussia, over the national monument in Tannenberg.

At Tannenberg the crowd below sang *Deutschland* and the ship's crew joined in over the loudspeaker. The motors had been stopped, and the ship floated.

When the motors were started again they continued over Nedeck where Marshal Hindenburg had lived and died, then Marienburg. Then to Lübeck, Kiel and Hamburg. They cruised for an hour over Hamburg at night—a sea of lights below, the whistles, fog-horns and sirens of the merchant ships hooting greetings. Again the motors were cut, and in the light of torches below the crew could make out the faces turned upward—a sea of red faces bathed in the glow of reflected fire. The ship was so low the crew could hear from below the repeated "Heils!"

On the second day they flew over the Olympic village being constructed in Berlin. There they received a telegram from the Fuehrer: "I thank the crew and passengers of the *Hindenburg* for the greetings sent me from the Tannenberg Memorial. I reciprocate them heartily and wish you further good flights. Adolf Hitler."

Apparently the Fuehrer was not subject to Dr. Goebbels' restrictions and could call the LZ 129 by its given name. He had just begun a radio appeal to Germany when the ships, after visiting Magdeburg, Dessau and Leipzig, returned to Berlin again. By then it was night. Giant searchlights from the ground caught the two ships in crossed beams. Searchlights from the two ships played down on the crowd below.

After the Fuehrer's speech a description of the appearance of the city below mixed with campaign propaganda was broadcast from the *Hindenburg*, picked up, then relayed by ground stations to the national radio network. In addition, the ground radio kept up a running description of the two ships' maneuvers. To the delight of tens of thousands of school children jamming the Lustgarten, the Zeppelins released thousands of tiny Nazi flags which floated down on tiny parachutes.

Then the ships went on to see the swastika flaming on the tower of the Schwanenburg Lohengrins at Cleve. By the next morning they were over the Ruhr; over Essen, Dortmund and Witten, where the foundries and smelteries were permitted to smoke again. Finally over Cologne on Sunday morning, where Germans were voting in that city on the west bank of the Rhine, now once again under the protection of German statesmen.

Aboard the *Hindenburg* a voting booth had been set up too. There were 104 people aboard and the official tally showed 104 votes "ja." Later, Dr. Eckener was reported to have said to an American journalist, Mr. Louis P. Lochner of Associated Press, that there were two more "ja" votes than there were persons on the ship.

This was not at all true, according to party members Rudolf Sauter and Helmut Lau. They had followed instructions exactly. There were 104 persons aboard the ship. Their orders were to count blank votes as "ja" votes. This had not been necessary because all ballots were marked. What had happened was that two ballots were marked "nein," but for the good of the Zeppelin family the two "neins" were changed to "jas." Nevertheless, this led to some difficulties at district headquarters.

Party officials pointed out that before the vote was taken the ballots should have been marked with either skimmed milk, or by using blank typewriter ribbon. By doing so it would have been possible to identify which two people had cast the "nein" votes. But those supervising the votes aboard the *Hindenburg* had failed to take the proper precautions. Consequently the matter had to be dropped without being able to identify the two votes against the interests of the German people, 99% of whom had voted to support their Fuehrer.

The election ended Sunday. The following Tuesday the *Hindenburg* took off for her maiden flight to Rio de Janeiro. In the off-watch hours Chief Sauter was enthusiastic. Germany had successfully extricated herself from the League of Nations in 1933. Then by 1935 General Goering announced that Germany would have an air force again, and then the Fuehrer announced the reconstitution of the German Army with military service compulsory. Britain had agreed to let Germany build ships. With rearmament begun, the factories ran day and night again, and for all there was bread again. The Lord obviously helped them who helped themselves.

The *Hindenburg*'s course to Rio had to be lengthened by making a detour around France—for political reasons it was said. Two days out from Rio an American Associated Press story from Berlin came over the ship's radio. The story reported that Dr. Eckener had placed the *Hindenburg* "into election propaganda during the four days preceding the balloting only under pressure and with great misgiving." *The London Daily Express* radioed for confirmation of the Associated Press story.

After consulting with the eight licensed Zeppelin captains he had with him aboard the ship, Dr. Eckener radioed his reply to London:

"I am without news from Germany and your inquiry surprises me as a bad joke. My attitude during the elections was only that of a voter and I refused to participate in any kind of propaganda when I was invited to do so.

"I never protested against the use of the airship at the elections, for it is known that it was so used and that I am the Chairman of the Board of the Zeppelin Corporation.

"I expect to return to Germany with the *Hindenburg*, and to retain my post as long as I can thereby be of service to mankind in the development of air travel."

Upon landing in Rio, the men of the Luftschiffbau learned from the Associated Press Service that in conformity with orders issued by the Propaganda Ministry, the Reich League of Periodical Publishers, which was part of the Reich Press Chamber, had issued the following instructions to its members, who included the publishers of all newspapers and periodicals:

> We request our members to bring to the notice of their editorial and writing departments the following instructions and insure its unconditional observance:
> The name of Dr. Hugo Eckener will no longer be mentioned in newspapers and periodicals.
> No pictures nor articles about him shall be printed.
> We learn that the reason for this is the very strange stand assumed by Dr. Eckener.

In the crew's mess, Rudolf Sauter had some trouble standing off the objections. Chief Knorr thought it very strange that the associate of Count Zeppelin since the days of the "miracle" at Echterdingen, the man who had started the DELAG and saved the company after the war, the man who had really given every one of them their employment—it was strange that this man should be disgraced by the Nazis.

Chief Kubis allowed that if Prince Rupprecht had been named regent, none of this would have ever happened.

Party member Sauter could only lamely explain that it was not possible to make an omelette without breaking some eggs, and that it must be admitted that Dr. Eckener had put the party into some embarrassment by his outspoken speeches. Perhaps, in any case, it might be worked out.

On the way back from Rio the *Hindenburg's* #3 diesel stopped. Perhaps it had got wet in a rain squall. Nothing Sauter could do would start it again. The airship had to fight its way back from Africa to Friedrichshafen against fifty-knot winds with only three motors. Joseph Leibrecht laughed at Sauter: "God is punishing you with water, Mr. Chief Engineer."

On April 16 Dr. Eckener went to the Propaganda Ministry in the company of General Goering, head of the Air Ministry. No one would disclose the events of the meeting. Upon emerging Dr. Eckener, in the company of General Goering, would only say:

"It is naturally not delicate for me to say anything. That is obviously up to my Chief."

But neither would General Goering say anything. It was believed that Dr. Eckener would command the first flight to New York despite the row. Meanwhile the diesel motors were sent, along with Chief Sauter, to the Daimler Benz factory in Stuttgart for overhaul. There were those who said the engines were due for overhaul before the four days in the air of the Rhineland Propaganda attack. The ship should not have been used in such a wasteful way.

On April 23 the local Nazi officials in the Zehlendorf Borough, on the western outskirts of Berlin, were informed by the Burgomaster's office that Eckener Avenue was to be renamed Adolf Hitler Strasse.

This was followed by fantastic rumors in Germany: that Dr. Eckener was dead; that Dr. Eckener and his son Knud had been arrested for high treason—allegedly for selling German Zeppelin plans to the United States; that Dr. Eckener had committed suicide.

Nevertheless when the *Hindenburg* took off from Friedrichshafen at 10:27 P.M. on May 6, 1936, Dr. Eckener was there in the command gondola. The flight was the inauguration of the first North Atlantic air passenger service. When the great airship arrived over Times Square on May 9 New York was in an uproar. The maiden voyage took only 60 hours.

During 1936 the *Hindenburg* made 10 round trips to the United States. They were a great success. By the end of the year the first regular transatlantic passenger service by air began to be accepted as a somewhat ordinary occurrence.

But in the beginning America was almost as crazy to see the new Zeppelin, and cheer it, as the Germans in the Fatherland. Sure, the *Los Angeles* had been flown over in the Twenties, and the *Graf Zeppelin* had won a ticker tape parade in 1928, but in 1936 the Depression was not wholly over yet and the *Hindenburg* was something to cheer, to admire for its technical virtuosity, to believe in as an example of what the future might bring. Things were moving again. The mass of people really enjoyed the sight of it. They followed its adventures on the front pages, and they listened on the radio. Relatively few were put off by the swastikas so prominent on its 150-foot tail.

Throughout the year, Chief Engineer Sauter's motors performed faultlessly. Chief Rigger Knorr climbed through the ship's interior day after day, his young charges following him and learning, but there was hardly anything to patch or mend. He told them stories of the old days. After each crossing as hydrogen was valved off, it was refilled. As ballast was dumped on each trip, they topped the tanks again. Young Eric Spehl developed a taste for American movies. He saw A *Night at the Opera* with the Marx Brothers, *Riffraff* with Spencer Tracy and Jean Harlow, and *Mutiny on the Bounty* with Clark Gable. Spehl retold the stories of the films endlessly to his crewmates.

Chief Steward Kubis was pleased again about the kind of passengers he could serve. It was almost like old times—in some ways better. On the maiden voyage journalists predominated, naturally.

Among them, however, were Count von Schwerin, the correspondent for General Goering's newspaper, *Essener Zeitung*; Countess von Waldeck who wrote under the initials "R.G." in Berlin and whose husband, the Prince von Waldeck was a very high state official; Madame Tatiana from Paris; Lady Grace Drummond Hay, the ever-present correspondent for *The New York Times*; the explorer Sir George Hubert Wilkins and Lady Wilkins; Carl von Wiegand of the Hearst Press and Louis P. Lochner of the Associated Press; and Mr. and Mrs. Walter Leeds from Palm Beach, Florida. They were very rich and prominent Americans, according to Chief Kubis, who still read the society columns without fail.

Some of the passengers expressed amazement (and a few, righteous annoyance) that Dr. Eckener's name was printed on the crew list without an indication of rank—an apparent slight to the veteran Zeppelin hero.

Dr. Eckener, however, smiled good naturedly and said: "This list was probably printed during my trip to Berlin. You see, however, my name is at the top."

On the maiden voyage Professor Franz Wagner of Dresden played the ship's piano in the lounge while Lady Wilkins, who was once a distinguished actress, sang. The concert was broadcast by radio to New York from the ocean by Dr. Max Jordan, "the flying announcer," then relayed from station WJZ over the NBC Blue Network across America.

In addition, on the first trip the Reverend Paul Schulte, "the flying priest," said Mass in the air for the first time. He arrived with a papal document "authorizing" him. It said Pope Pius XI considered the passenger lounge of the *Hindenburg* a place of dignity and of history;

further, the great airship was so steady that sacrificial wine would not be spilled. The two conditions on which the church needed assurance before permitting Mass to be said and sung were satisfied. For some reason, the official passenger list did not contain Father Schulte's name.

The *Hindenburg* arrived over New York for the first time at 4:55 o'clock in the morning. Throughout the night thousands of New Yorkers had waited patiently on roof tops, or nestled in window sills, scanning the sky to catch a glimpse of the new ship. The *Hindenburg* came in over the Bronx, swung south over Queens and Brooklyn, then circled north again to pass directly over the Times Building at 5:07 A.M. The sky was beginning to turn from black to blue when the ship beamed its searchlight into the throng waiting in Times Square below. Cheers went up, again and again. Then, the soft drone of its motors faded as it headed towards its landing at the Lakehurst Naval Air Station.

The ship first made a pass over the air station. Its commanders could read the wind directions at 200 feet, and at the ground, from anemometer readings electrically displayed atop Lakehurst's meteorological station. Then the ship swung, its engines idling, and settled toward the mooring mast. When one engine was needed, only that one functioned. When lift was necessary, water ballast poured from the ship. When it rose too fast, hydrogen was valved off until the ship's nose hovered a few feet from the connecting cone atop the 75-foot mast.

Landing lines were dropped. The Navy crew quickly attached them to lines prepared on the ground. A great steel cable was wound down from the ship's nose. It was attached to a winch powered by diesel on the railroad car on which the landing mast rode. The winch engaged and the airship was reeled in like a fish until its nose cone locked into a cup atop the mast. Within three minutes mail bags were being thrown down to waiting crew members.

While a hundred Navy crewmen steadied the ship with lines let down from both sides, the rear landing wheel was fixed into another railway car at the ship's stern. This second car rode on a circular track. Once tied down astern, the Navy crewmen could let go their lines.

The ship was cradled between two railway cars on tracks. If the wind direction changed, the rear car was free to run on its circular track. Since the nose was at the center of the circle's radius, the ship could swing to the wind.

Later the airship was towed by the diesel-powered landing rig at the bow along double tracks set 200 feet apart. They led from the landing circle's center into the immense hangar. The stern car followed docilely behind with the ship's tail, until the whole of the ship had disappeared into the hangar. The rolling mast and stern car on rails were, in effect, land tugs. In the hangar the ship would be safe from any gust of wind. The passengers disembarked.

On the *Hindenburg*'s first trip more than 100,000 people drove the simple New Jersey roads to have a look at the new wonder. Miserable traffic jams were created in little Lakehurst. Parking about a mile from the hangar, sightseers made the trip by a 5¢ bus ride. A tour was arranged in the hangar, but tourists could not go inside the ship.

Special planes flew Captain Lehmann and Dr. Eckener to New York where the German-American Chamber of Commerce had arranged a dinner in the Waldorf Astoria. The big ballroom had been decorated in flags, bunting and banners. The two national flags, the Stars and Stripes and the Swastika, hung side by side. Before the speeches began, the lights were turned down, and a spotlight illuminated a huge heap of ice cream shaped like a Zeppelin, presented by the Association of German Bakers. It would not have been complete without its swastikas.

The next day Captain Lehmann and Dr. Eckener flew to Washington and were presented to President Franklin D. Roosevelt at the White House. With German Ambassador Dr. Hans Luther present, Dr. Eckener explained that the *Hindenburg*'s ten trips of 1936 were to be a demonstration of the practicality of transatlantic passenger service. Germany was building another still larger Zeppelin—the LZ 130. He hoped that if the Germans could show success by example, America would join Germany by also building two ships. Then regular and frequent sailings could be scheduled, the considerable overhead shared, and understanding built between the two peoples. Dr. Eckener also hoped that America would make helium available to Germany soon. Both the *Hindenburg* and the new ship had been designed to accommodate helium, but would fly on hydrogen until America lifted the embargo on the rare helium.

President Roosevelt was "very interested and very hopeful" at the prospect of a regular two-and-a-half-day airship schedule to Europe.

Captain Lehmann and Dr. Eckener later appeared at a press conference. Standing side by side on a little platform set up in the hangar at Lakehurst, Captain Lehmann stood erect and stocky in a trim uniform of midnight blue. Dr. Eckener, in civilian clothes beside him, was described as "the grizzled successor to Count Zeppelin." They answered question after question.

"Are you in command?" a blunt questioner asked Captain Lehmann. He answered quickly with a ready smile:

"Yes."

"Then is Dr. Eckener's position advisory to you?" the questioner persisted.

"Oh yes," answered Captain Lehmann. "We consulted together on every decision," and he turned and smiled affectionately at the elderly veteran under whom he had received his training. He added emphatically, however, in answer to another question, that Dr. Eckener's position was not "supervisory" as well as "advisory."

Dr. Eckener denied emphatically that he planned to take up residence in America.

"I, a man 68 years old? Such a thing would be feasible for a man twenty years younger, but in any case it would be out of the question for me, for my place and my work are in Germany and I hope to have many more years for it."

Dr. Eckener explained that published stories had made a great deal more of the incident in which he decided against the use of the Zeppelins for Nazi electioneering. He denied the report that his name had purposely been left off the news stories of the *Hindenburg*'s exploits.

"I was on a South American trip when these things were reported," he said, "and when I returned I went directly to Berlin and saw General Goering and we straightened out the misunderstanding."

Perhaps it was just a misunderstanding. On its return flight to Germany, the *Hindenburg* landed at the new airport at Frankfurt-am-Main. A huge new hangar had been built to serve as the terminal for transatlantic crossings. The Gauleiter of Frankfurt, Jacob Sprengler, presented to Dr. Eckener a silver cup bearing the inscription: "To the leader of the dirigible *Hindenburg* in commemoration of its landing at the new Frankfurt airport."

Dr. Eckener's name began to creep back into the newspaper accounts of the *Hindenburg*'s adventures. There were indications that the rousing reception given to the *Hindenburg* and its crew in the United States had helped Dr. Eckener regain favor in parts of Germany.

But orders were issued again by the Propaganda Ministry that Dr. Eckener's name was not to be mentioned. Interviews about New York's reaction to Germany's great airship achievements were reported from Captain Lehmann. General Goering was considered Dr. Eckener's hope. The General was chief of Germany's Air Ministry, licensors of the ship. He was *de facto* director of Lufthansa Airlines, who in turn shared the stock of the Zeppelin Corporation with the National Government. General Goering sent the company a telegram of congratulations. Unfortunately, it did not mention Dr. Eckener's name in either the address or the text.

After the Rhineland elections and the New York maiden voyage, the rest of the season seemed almost anticlimactic. On the *Hindenburg*'s second crossing Dr. Eckener excused himself "because of work as Chairman of the Zeppelin Corporation." He spent some time at Kressbronn, his lifelong home on the shores of the Bodensee. Captain Lehmann had a home overlooking the lake too, right near by. But Captain Lehmann was busy commanding the airship on its transatlantic journeys.

Meanwhile, Chief Kubis kept a log of the passengers. There were Mr. and Mrs. Gardner Cowles—he was the executive editor of the *Des Moines Register*; Dr. Matthew Taylor Mellon of Pittsburgh; Mr. Ben Smith—famous as "sell 'em Ben Smith," the most famous of the "shortsellers" in Wall Street; Roger D. Lapham, President of American-Hawaiian Steamship Lines, and his friend Captain Reiber, Chairman of the Board of the Texas Oil Corporation; Norman Holden, the British financier; Captain Frederick E. Guest, M.P., former British Secretary of State for Air, and who had married one of the American-millionaire Phipps girls; Mrs. Conrad Berens, whose husband, an ophthalmologist, had invented the contact lens. Everyone who came and went was recorded by the press. Everything the ship did made news.

A Mrs. Harriet Hague, 85 years old, went back to the United States by ocean liner. She told the papers she was through with Zep-

pelins because they were too safe to be much fun: "It was too boring," she said. "You can't even feel seasick."

A thirteen-year-old American boy scout flew across and upon landing was met by a delegation from the Hitler Youth. He was reported
as being surprised they spoke English. And a six-month-old baby
made the trip. His mother and the boy had their picture taken at the
gangway as they landed. Prize fighter Max Schmeling crossed after
defeating Joe Louis. He was met by ecstatic crowds at the Frankfurt
Airport.

In July the *Hindenburg*, on its return trip to Frankfurt, flew over
the docks at Southampton, England. That annoyed the English.
They pointed out that aboard the airship were Luftwaffe officers.
The airship, the English said, had flown as low as 100 feet, had fol-
lowed the course of the Manchester Ship Canal, and flown over the
Calshot Airstation and the Portsmouth Navy Yard.

The matter was brought up in Parliament. The Ambassador from
Great Britain requested the Government of Germany to see to it that
the *Hindenburg* did not fly over England ". . . except when forced
to do so by urgent necessity of navigation."

On a later flight Mr. Elliot White Springs, a famous pursuit pilot
in the Canadian Air Force in the Great War, author of the best
selling *War Birds*, and owner of the Springmaid Mills in South Carolina, met Captain Otto Forster, Luftwaffe, a one time member of
Baron Richthofen's Flying Circus Squadron. The two men admitted
they had probably shot at each other many times during the war, but
now "a cup of wine had passed between them."

In August, Heinz Wronsky, traffic director of Lufthansa Airlines,
announced that the *Hindenburg* already had proved to be too small
for the traffic demands—it was "booked to 101 percent of capacity."

Wronsky was interviewed in New York after having made the trip
himself. He said new cabins were being added to the *Hindenburg*—
accommodations for 25 more passengers. He added: "On several voyages passengers have spent the night in the lounge without sleeping
rather than postpone their voyage."

The new fare of only $400 (compared to the old fare of $3,000 for
the Latin American trip of the *Graf Zeppelin*) was cited as one of
the factors in the ship's popularity.

Wronsky had served as a traffic manager for Pan American, held membership as a "Quiet Birdman" for his own flying achievements, and his father, Martin Wronsky, was one of the directors of Lufthansa.

Off the record, Wronsky was asked his opinion of the German regime—especially of the Nuremberg Laws passed the year before which excluded Jews from public life.

He admitted that Jewish artists were hard hit—actors, singers, authors were jobless in Germany. No medical licenses could be issued to Jews.

He had joined the party on September 1, 1932 for "economic reasons." But the Third District Court in Berlin had turned both his father, Martin Wronsky, and himself out of the party because his grandfather, Meyer Wronsky, was Jewish. Both of Meyer Wronsky's parents were of Jewish descent, the court found, hence neither the son, Martin, nor the grandson, Heinz, could remain in the party.

Heinz Wronsky said he "had to be very careful because he had a little of the blood back there."

Wronsky made his transatlantic trip at the same time as Douglas Fairbanks and his wife, the former Lady Ashley. Wronsky said her perfume carried through the linen walls of the passenger cabins. Her presence had made the trip a dream. He noted that Douglas Fairbanks had worn bedroom slippers throughout the trip. The slippers had the initials "DF" on them in diamonds and precious stones.

Late in August, the *Hindenburg* was used again as a propaganda symbol when it flew over the opening day ceremonies of the Olympic Games in Berlin. The 100,000 people present in the new stadium were enchanted. The gossip was that with the ship overhead, no one would pay attention to the Fuehrer, and he had ordered: "*Hindenburg Auf!*"

On August 22, more than one hundred "anarchists" wearing evening clothes and masquerading as peaceful visitors boarded the liner *Bremen* in twos and threes. She was docked at Pier 86, Hudson River, at the foot of West 46th Street in New York. The liner was preparing to sail at midnight. The troupe boarded about 11 P.M. Once on board they whipped off their outer wraps. Underneath they all were wearing white sweaters which said: "Hands off Spain."

At a fireworks signal, they ran through the ship passing out anti-Nazi handbills. Then paraded yelling: "Hitler must be kept out of Spain."

A riot call brought large squads of New York police to the scene—70 patrolmen, 8 emergency squad detectives, 4 radio cars. Young men picked up deck chairs and swung at police. Cries of "Communists" went up by spectators. Eight women and four men were arrested and taken to the West 47th Street station. New York Police said it was the second incident of the year aboard a German liner—the first occurring on the Hamburg-American Line *Hamburg*, but not generally reported. Security was increased both in Germany and in the United States at the Zeppelin hangars.

In September the *Hindenburg* carried its 1,000th passenger, Mrs. Frances Springs of Mort Mill, South Carolina. She received a gift of a Duraluminum tray at a ceremony before the airship sailed.

While Mrs. Springs was aboard on the trip to New York, fifty-four lives were lost as a hurricane swept up the Atlantic Seaboard. The storm veered out to sea south of New York, but many New Jersey towns were isolated. Shipping was seen as imperiled by the hurricane's 100-mile-an-hour winds. Dr. James H. Kimball, chief of the New York Weather Bureau, refused to forecast the weather for the German airship as it neared the North American coast.

Commander Lehmann skirted the storm and even took advantage of its anti-cyclonic winds to boost his speed. He sent a radiogram to *The New York Times*: ENTERING HURRICANE AREA WITH HIGH VELOCITY WINDS ENABLING ARRIVAL OVER NEW YORK BEFORE DAYBREAK SUNDAY STOP HURRICANE IN BAR AT FULL FORCE.

Upon the *Hindenburg*'s arrival it was revealed that the Dutch were thinking of constructing two airships to enter transatlantic travel. Paul W. Litchfield, President of Goodyear-Zeppelin Corporation, indicated negotiations had already begun between Germany and the United States for the building of "at least one" Zeppelin.

Philadelphia, Washington and Miami put in bids to be the terminals for the new service, but Baltimore was said to be especially favored because its winds were one half those of Lakehurst, on the average, and fog was infrequent.

Before ending the season in October, the *Hindenburg* took 84 American passengers for a ride over six states. The group included leading figures from American finance, industry and aviation. It was said that progress was being made towards the financing of two rigid airships. Chief Steward Kubis laid on a lovely lunch with sweet German white wines, ice cold beer, brandy and champagnes.

Dr. Eckener was back in the news again—at least in the American news. He offered the plans of the *Hindenburg* and its sister ship, the LZ 130 under construction in Germany, to the builders of the proposed American airships.

"I never had the intention of making flights from Germany in German ships only. Eventually we could have three or four ships—two German and two American. German ships need your facilities and your American ships will need our facilities."

During the stormy North Atlantic winter, the *Hindenburg* made trips to Rio de Janeiro. Eighteen trips were announced for the 1937 season to New York, the first sailing to be at 8:00 P.M., Monday, May 3, 1937.

Shortly after sunset on Sunday, May 2, 1937, the crewmen of the Zeppelin *Hindenburg* gathered in the Heldenkeller, a weinstube and rathskeller, in Frankfurt, Germany.

Their meeting was not any official affair; nothing more than a gathering of the men of the Zeppelin family. The occasion, the sailing on the morrow of the first trip of the year to New York, was the sort of occasion for which it was thought appropriate to have the wives and girl friends come along. The officers, of course, would not be in the Heldenkeller. Nor, in fact, would every last man of the airship. Some would have other business to attend to, or other pleasures, and would perhaps come along later.

But the Heldenkeller was a warming place for a family—such as the Zeppelin family—to gather. On the walls of its main dining room were portraits of Germany's great airmen. There, Baron Richthofen, commander of the famous squadron; there Goering, winner of the *Pour le Mérite,* and the squadron's last commander; there a scene in which the biplanes of the Great War dueled in arcs among the clouds; and there the Graf Zeppelin himself was shown standing with the Kaiser beside the *Sachsen;* there Captain Heinrich Mathy, who had set the heart of London afire; there Captain Peter Strasser, Fuehrer of the Navy Zeppelins who saved the German fleet at the bat-

*Count Ferdinand von Zeppelin* (1838–1917)　　　The Zeppelin Museum

*The LZ2 crashed near Weilburg in January 1906 after its rudder controls jammed at 1,300 feet.*

*The LZ4 cruised the 24 hours required by German Army purchasing agents, but then exploded at Echterdingen.*

*The German people voluntarily contributed enough money to found DELAG, the world's first airline. Before World War I, ships like the Sachsen carried 37,250 passengers without accident.*

*Left: Alberto Santos-Dumont,
aéronaute, dandy from Brazil,
and darling of Paris.*

*A holiday crowd came to watch "le petit Santos" take off from his
hangar in St. Cloud, circle the Eiffel Tower, and return in less than
30 minutes.*

Bettmann Archive

The Zeppelin Museum

*In 1929 Dr. Eckener piloted the Graf Zeppelin around the world. Twenty passengers cruised in luxury for 21 days. At this stop in Los Angeles an early Goodyear blimp was tethered alongside.*

*Dr. Hugo Eckener, director of the Zeppelin Company and successor of Count Zeppelin.*

*The Hindenburg in production at the yards in Friedrichshafen. From inside the frame, looking up along the keel towards the bow, the first panels of linen have been sewn into place above the man at right.*

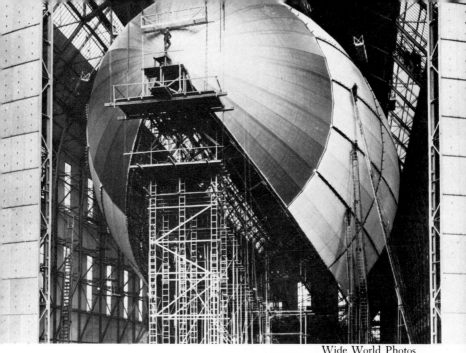

Wide World Photos

*Chief Knorr's riggers pose atop their ladders at the bow. One can see through the rings and girders to the hangar windows a quarter of a mile away.*

*With the outer skin sewn on, but before the partitions between each cell have been built, gas bags were hung inside as a test.*

The Zeppelin Museum

*Captain Ernst A. Lehmann, Dr. Eckener's successor as director of the Zeppelin Company, won the Iron Cross twice flying Zeppelins over England during World War I.*

The Zeppelin Museum

*In May 1936 the* Hindenburg *inaugurated scheduled transatlantic passenger flights, docking at Lakehurst, New Jersey. Aft of the command gondola in the ship's flank, are the windows of promenade deck.*

The National Archives

*Over the Wilhelmstrasse in Berlin, the* Hindenburg, *on the left, and the* Graf Zeppelin *took part in Nazi propaganda during the Rhineland plebescite in 1936.*

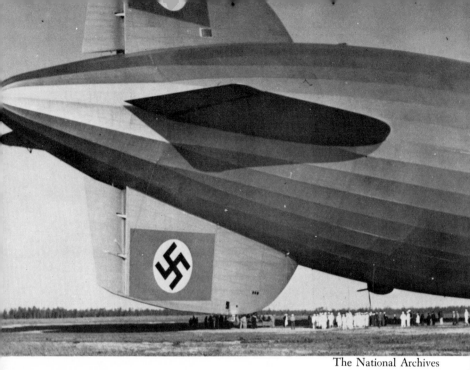

The National Archives

*The ground crew from the Naval Air Station at Lakehurst secured the giant tail to a railway car. Dr. Eckener argued that the swastikas would win Zeppelins no friends, but Dr. Goebbels insisted.*

*The nose of the Hindenburg being fitted into the mooring mast at Lakehurst by rigger Eric Spehl.*

*American Airlines arranged connecting flights from Lakehurst to the west. There were some who saw in the tiny DC-3 the possibility that airplanes might even replace Zeppelins.*

*In the dining saloon, fresh fruits and the best wine.*

*In the promenade lounge, no pitching or rolling or vibration as there would be on the great ocean liners.*

The Zeppelin Museum

*Through open windows, cruising along at 80 knots, passengers could hear dogs barking at them just 500 feet below.*

*Passenger cabins were like Pullman compartments. From outside cabins, travelers could lie in bed and watch the sea through a window.*

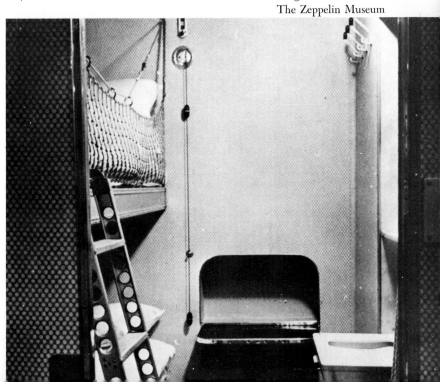

In the tradition of the best European hotels, stewards shined the shoes left outside a passenger's cabin overnight.

The smoking room was guarded by a double-locked door. A steward kept the only matches passengers were allowed.

*By valving off hydrogen or dumping ballast from the controls in the gondola, the airship could maintain its trim.*

*Inside the gondola, the wheel at right set the course; the elevator wheel at left allowed the ship to climb or dive.*

*The narrow lower walkway led from bow to stern along the ship's belly.*

tle of Jutland; there Captain Hans von Schiller, survivor of incredible adventures in the war, winner of the American Harmon Trophy, new commander of the *Graf Zeppelin*, and at this moment probably arriving in Rio; there a portrait of Dr. Hugo Eckener; and next to him a portrait of Captain Ernst Lehmann, with both his Iron Crosses.

The crewmen of the *Hindenburg* were surrounded by the history of the men and the dream of which they were the inheritors—a long line of hopes and failures, of invention and art, of tragedies and comedies, of fools and heroes. There were men there at the tables who could cite not only the glories of the round-the-world trip of the *Graf Zeppelin*, not only the excitement and fear when lightning had flashed into a warship's hull, but also the time remembered when a neighbor whom they still loved had poured water by mistake into the gasoline tanks.

At the tables, Joseph Leibrecht sat chattering with Mechanic Johnny Doerflein and Rigger Hans Freund. Frau Leibrecht was in Lindau still. Chief Sauter and his Frau sat across from Chief Radio Officer Willy Speck and his Frau. Their discussion was serious, measured.

Chief Kubis filled in details in the story of the family von Waldeck for the benefit of Stewards Eugen Nunnenmacher, Wilhelm Balla, Fritz Deeg, Max Henneberg and Severin Klein.

A whole table was taken by mechanics who, without their women present, put down the beer steadily and whose voices grew in volume and proportion. There were Rudy Biallas, Albert Holderried, Richard Kollmer, Alois Reisacher, Raphael Schaedler, Willy Sheef, Joseph Schreibmueller, Alfred Stoeckle, German Zettel. If a head-count were taken they would discover that Bahnholzer, Bentele, Deutschle, Fischer, Moser, Ritter and Steeb were absent. Perhaps they would come along later. It did not really matter.

Sitting with Chief Knorr were Ernst Huchel and his Frau (whose father had died in a Zeppelin shot down in the war); Ludwig Felber (once a rigger and soon to be helmsman); and near Knorr as usual, Rigger Eric Spehl. With the handsome 25-year-old Spehl was his girl friend, Beatrice Friederich.

The other women did not like her. She was, they said among themselves, not right for that young man—why, she was at least 31, six years his senior. She had already had two husbands, and at least one notorious lover in addition. Too many men for one woman. And she was too much for Chief Knorr's young pupil.

Chief Sauter also felt it inappropriate that Rigger Spehl should be seen in the company of Frau Friederich. He knew that she was on the list of potentially dangerous citizens at the Gauleiter's office. But Chief Sauter was an advocate of the party and its benefits for Germany, not a stool pigeon. He would not report Spehl's association.

At another table, sitting with Helmsman Kurt Schoenherr, and Radio Officers Herbert Dowe, Franz Eichelmann and Egon Schwiekart, Helmsman Helmut Lau noted the association of Eric Spehl and Frau Friederich. Unlike Sauter, Lau would report it. It was his duty to do so.

Helmut Lau was, like Spehl, in his twenties. Lau was fair-haired too. Lau was short—5'7″ or so, in contrast to Spehl's six feet. Lau had blue eyes too, but they were set close and were quick in comparison to those in Spehl's open farm boy's face.

Lau had placed his fortunes with the party (party card #1,731,232) and with the Schutzstaffel (S.S., or Blackshirts—S.S. #143,449). He held the rank of Unterscharfuehrer, or Sergeant. He was no man to trifle with.

As his fuehrer, Heinrich Himmler, had put it there were probably many people in Germany who felt sick when they saw the black tunic. He could understand that. But he believed that now was Germany's time. If they were to lose, they would lose everything. If they won, nothing would be measured on scales.

Of course, Helmut Lau did not wear his black tunic regularly. He wore the uniform of the Zeppelin men, just like the others. His reports went directly to Sturmbannfuehrer Karl Hufschmidt. He understood that from Hufschmidt they were even considered by SS-Obergruppenfuehrer, Prince von Waldeck, next to Himmler himself. In any case, Germany had many enemies, and reports were necessary.

Spehl's girl friend, Frau Friederich, was listed as a potential enemy. Lau knew her, at least by reputation, as many men did in Frankfurt. She certainly had some crazy ideas.

While she was aware that she had earned an odd reputation among the virtuous wives and mothers with whom she often had to associate, by the necessities of her sex, Frau Friederich had not yet been much more than annoyed by their gossip and certainly not chastened.

As she saw it, without a man there was no way for a woman to get outside a very limited sphere of action. She really liked men. She wasn't so sure other women liked much more than house and home. They had their men as talismen of achievement, and somewhat boring symbols of security. Instead, she saw in men an opportunity for adventure. In most cases, the gossip of the other women was salted with envy.

Well so be it. She had just been unlucky with the men she had chosen. First, there had been the artist—a great beautiful man, with a huge head and great round shoulders. She had been only 19, and he was, in fact, a bit older; perhaps 40, maybe 45. If he was not a very good artist, it hardly mattered for he was a work of art in himself.

She knew that someday when she was old and bent, she would still be able to recall how her soul flew up from her spine, night after night, with him. She would never fear death when she was old, because with him she had already died a thousand times and she could remember many of those times with a sweet glow.

They stayed married for about six years. Then one day he simply disappeared from Frankfurt—as she had to admit he probably had done with others before. Still, let the good burghers' wives gossip about that if they liked. She had him for a while, while the best they had ever had were men who would insist on their breakfasts on time.

It was just unlucky that once, when he did come back, he had entered their apartment before she got home that night. When she turned on the lights in their sitting room, he was sitting there. And he saw the two jockeys with whom she had been laughing outside the door just a moment before. He beat one of them terribly and the other one barely got away. Then he left again for good. She didn't blame him. It was the right thing for a man to do. The divorce was executed by mail—of course he had no money to send her. He had never had any money.

Her next marriage came quickly and lasted only six months. He owned a part of a bar in Frankfurt. It was just a mistake for both of them. Then there had been a succession of good friends, but not one seemed to have the capability of doing anything that would matter.

They were all ordinary good fellows—careful and prudent and some of them even wise in their way. Fortunately, she then met a man with something to him: she called him "the patriot." She fell deeply in love again.

They spent a great deal of time together in the bars and cafes popular with the Left. The talk was heady. In the cafes all could agree they had a grand enemy—the State itself. Endless schemes were propounded to survive—survive until, as the doctrine went, the last stage of capitalism, the fascist regime, made conditions so intolerable that the workers would revolt. Then there would be the future—endlessly discussed too, from an agenda of the day's outrages. For each outrage, from surly railway clerks to the banality of the capitalist press, there was some corresponding utopian program—not too exact in its details—which required considerable discussion. The dialectics could be savored, turned, tasted. Her man, particularly, was increasingly full of anger and energy. His eyes would flash across a cafe table when some point was made. She could close her hand on his, which he often would not even notice, and she could feel his energy flow.

They had lived together, in her place, for almost a year. The war in Spain began to preoccupy him. In November 1936 he had gone. In January 1937, he was reported killed. In an odd way she felt no loss, but somehow a gain, although she grieved for his empty place in her bed, and it took some while before his scent was gone from her linens. But then she had met Eric Spehl.

Eric was so Catholic. That attracted her. She had once dreamed of being a nun—before she met the artist. Her mother had wanted her to take orders. She had asked her father what to do.

He had not given her any answer, but he had never had any answers to anything anyway. At about the same time she had discovered the communion of seduction and took it up instead of the cloth. Although she had bungled a good many, she sensed that seductions were *actes gratuits*, what her artist had explained to her were *beaux gestes*. If the other women judged her to be a provoking woman: rebellious, flirtatious, and a fantastic flattery to the man she might be with, well, the hell with them. The men at least knew she was as complicated a structure, with as many struts and ribs, stresses and strains as their damn Zeppelin. And among all their blue uniforms, the intense Catholic farm boy from Göschweiler, her Eric Spehl, was the only one worth looking at.

She could bring to Eric what she had learned from her artist, and what she had learned from her hero in Spain, and from some others too. Together they talked about their childhoods and about what it would have been like if Eric Spehl had become a priest and Beatrice Friederich had become a nun.

She was, at 31, a long way from being a nun. And with her help, at 25 he was gaining some distance from being a priest. She had encouraged him in his hobby—the beginnings of a skill as a photographer. He had told her the stories of the American movies he had seen. They began to talk about going to America. If they went to America perhaps he could earn a living as a photographer. He began to encourage her that they might someday go to the land of golden dreams.

Eric Spehl and Beatrice Friederich sat together at Chief Knorr's table in the Heldenkeller as lovers, and they were obviously quite happy with each other. Indeed, this night they seemed particularly happy.

At the table there was some laughter about how the Sicherheitsdienst, the S.D., the security service of the S.S., had conducted their investigation of the *Hindenburg* in its hangar that day. Chief Knorr held forth.

He described how, as they rounded the corner of the hangar, they first saw the line of S.D. men stretched across the hangar entrance; how the dogs had barked and how Eric Spehl—a farm boy like that—had jumped. Everyone at the table joined in the laughter and Eric Spehl joined in with them.

Then Chief Sauter took up the story. The S.D. men had been assigned in twos to each of the chiefs. They were to look for "bombs." Joseph Leibrecht, in the generator room, had told the S.D. men about the time on the *Graf Zeppelin* someone on the crew had smuggled aboard four monkeys. The monkeys had escaped their hiding place and were discovered clambering through the interior arches of the ship. The S.D. men did not believe Leibrecht, but it was all quite true, Chief Sauter had assured the S.D. He did not, however, tell

them that it was Leibrecht himself who had attempted to smuggle
the monkeys from Brazil to Germany.

Which reminded Chief Knorr of the time someone had hidden
pineapples in the rigging next to the gas cells. The pineapples had
cracked somehow and Watch Officer Sammt had discovered them. As
he walked along the middle gangway they had dripped on his hat.

If a young boy could stowaway, as had the young man discovered
on the *Graf Zeppelin* after leaving New York, if monkeys and pineapples could be hidden, certainly the S.D. men were not going to find
any bombs. Chief Knorr could assure them all of that. If there were
bombs to be found, the Zeppelin men who knew their ship inside and
out would do the necessary work. They all had a good laugh at the
S.D. men, who had been exceedingly cautious and tenderfoot on the
high middle gangway.

The S.D. men had not been satisfied until they had "inspected" the
galleys and storage bins of Chief Steward Kubis. The S.D. "inspectors" opened four jars of caviar, 6 bottles of Riesling, and did in two
packages of hothouse strawberries in the thoroughness of their duties.

Since the ship was already provisioned for the flight tomorrow,
Chief Kubis had protested. They had replied, "Let the Jews you fly
do without." Kubis would have to spend valuable time in the morning replacing the stores from local shops. Who had ever heard of a
bomb hidden in strawberries? There was such foolishness these days.

In the background to the accounts of the S.D. search, the table of
mechanics had long since finished their spargel with chicken and rice.
The smoke and the noise were rising—for most Zeppelin men were
Southern Germans from the shores of the Bodensee. In South German tradition it was only natural to bang the table with steins, to sing
a snatch of song now and then, and to laugh with the gusto of men in
a group at a table.

Eric Spehl and Frau Friederich slipped away first. At the bachelor
tables there was talk that he was returning to his last; and whether he
would last; and whether he was her last; and such. The married couples soon followed. The bachelors probably stayed on quite late.

Their ship waited for them in its immense hangar. The area was lit
inside by arc lights, which cast an eerie green glow on the white linen
belly. One hundred feet up, as its flanks curved inward towards the

top of its back, the lights of the hangar gave way to shadow. But from within little electric lights, powered by a connection direct from the ship's main fuse board to the ground, dotted its interior axial spine. Two S.D. men stood guard up in there, waiting for relief, counting the minutes until they could have a smoke.

Outside, in the hangar's strange recesses, shadowed by grotesque shapes from the machinery outlined by the arc lights, pairs of S.D. men walked with rifles slung at their shoulders. At first, they had talked together as they walked, but then the hangar had oppressed their chatter. The Alsatian guard dogs walked with their tongues out too. Though there was no reason in the world why their tails should be down, they were.

At night near the Bodensee, at Kressbronn, in the house of Marie and Ernst Lehmann, the Alps across the lake were invisible, though the dots of light that marked the shore towns of Switzerland could still be seen. From the east, around the shoulders and over the heads of the Arlberg, the wind swept down, gave the lake its hiss and swish, rustled the new buds on the apple trees in the garden. It was no winter wind, not shrill and harsh, but heavy and soft with the promises of spring.

They had not been arguing really, and his final decision was, by her insistence, postponed until morning. They loved each other in the quiet gentle way which often occurs when the lovers are not so young anymore.

She had been married before, to a man in the business of supplying film for photographers. They had two sons and a daughter. Then she had met Captain Ernst Lehmann in Munich. She could not help it, she was in love with him.

The divorce had been quiet. The Zeppelin captain, a hero in Germany, was the most gentle of men, gentle from the immense strength that lay deep within him, and from which she drew laughter and joy and peace.

In 1934 she bore him a son. They named him Luv, and they never knew whether to laugh or cry at the gift God had given them. During Lent Luv had caught a cold, which turned into an infection of the middle ear. They had driven him to the doctors at the University in

Munich. They were the best. The boy died on Easter Sunday. It was unexplainable.

She had cried a great deal then, but Ernst did not. He held her every night, and in his arms the pain had begun to seep away, gradually.

Marie Lehmann was worried about "my Zeppelin captain," as she had called him when she still used to tease him. She knew that the politics of the regime had been pressing in on him; that the affair with Berlin and Dr. Eckener had saddened him—they had worked as comrades for twenty-seven years; that there were troubles in the *Hindenburg* because political men were pushing, or being pushed, to the fore.

She knew too that a woman may grieve for the loss of a son, but the loss was something so secret, so huge to her man that her pain was nothing to his complaint with God himself. She did not want to have to depend upon him, but she could not help it. She wished she could cheer him, take his mind away from his troubles, get him to laugh again and play the piano again.

Their argument that evening, such as it was, revolved around whether he actually needed to go to America on the first trip of the season. She thought he should rest away from the Zeppelin Corporation's affairs for a while. Captain Max Pruss was scheduled to command anyway. He didn't really need to go. She sent her reasons out in sorties.

It was May on the Bodensee, the time he loved best. They were going to have to move to Frankfurt before Christmas anyway. He had the plans of the house they would build in Zeppelinheim to work over. The workmen would need their orders. It would help her if he stayed. She needed him.

In the papers in the past fortnight there had been the news of the aerial bombing of a little Spanish town named Guernica. For some reason, Ernst had insisted on saving all the issues, something he never did before even on the most important political matters. The English had accused the Luftwaffe of destroying the town "for practice."

Ernst had said the English were right, that's what had been done. He talked on at dinner of his own bombing raids over London, but his description was not the one she had expected from the winner of the Iron Cross. He kept talking about how terrible it must have been for the people waiting in their houses. He seemed doubly sad.

She had blurted out that she had been to a clairvoyant when they had visited Vienna two weeks ago. The gypsy woman was incredibly dirty. She had said "Your husband is an airship Captain, but not always. Warn him not to ride on the *Hindenburg*. I see it in flames beyond the ocean."

Marie Lehmann said she was afraid. Then Ernst had been both stern with her, and almost his old wry self. Gypsy ladies could not be said to set the schedules of Zeppelin captains.

They had laughed a bit with each other, and she teased him about whether gypsy ladies might not provide better weather forecasting services than some he had been forced to use. And he said gypsy ladies were known to provide all kinds of services. They had a glass of port and went to bed in each other's arms.

# CHAPTER 4

# UP SHIP!

"But tell me, Circe, who is to guide me on the way?
No one has ever sailed a black ship to Hell."
                    —*The Odyssey* x: 501-503, HOMER

MONDAY, May 3, 1937. In Frankfurt, Germany, the sun rose at 4:34 Greenwich Mean Time—or 3:02 Central European Time, which was about one minute and 50 seconds earlier than it had the day before, a calculation the sun itself never made.

At the airport the sun was obscured by a high overcast. A very light drizzle was falling. Joseph Leibrecht, the Electrician, Chiefs Knorr, Kubis, Sauter, Riggers Spehl and Freund, Helmsmen Lau and Schoenherr, radio officers, stewards and cooks, mechanics and elevatormen, navigators and ship's officers were at work early in the hangar and in the ship, finishing the endless preparations for voyage. There was much coming and going. Kubis had to replace the strawberries "inspected" the day before. Chief Knorr sent Spehl for some extra needles. Chief Radio Officer Speck replaced a tube. Navigators and officers began to etch in their weather maps.

There was light rain in Berlin too. On the way from the airport to the Wilhelmstrasse three Luftwaffe officers sat in the back seat of an official government Mercedes. Along with its driver, it had been provided by the Schutzstaffel. Their appointment with S.S. Sturmbannfuehrer Hufschmidt was at 10 o'clock sharp. After lunch the three men would fly back to Frankfurt and board the *Hindenburg*.

\*      \*      \*

Colonel Fritz Erdmann, the senior Luftwaffe officer present, was until recently Chief of the Luftwaffe Intelligence School at Halle. At the intelligence school they taught Radio Navigation, the Techniques of Direction Finding, Advanced Cartography, the Techniques of Reading Photo Maps, the Assessment of Bomb Damage, Estimation of Enemy Ground Tactical Capabilities, Calculation of Enemy Geopolitical Strengths, Strategic and Industrial Bombing.

After the expansion of the German Air Force began under General Goering two years before, they were able to give up practicing in gliders and flying sport planes in "Aero Clubs" and the school had expanded considerably. Colonel Erdmann was satisfied. At Halle they provided a rigorous and disciplined course in modern warfare.

Now, however, he had a new post. Although he had hardly begun, he liked his new assignment a good deal less. He was Chief of the new "Special Intelligence" division of the Luftwaffe. He had responsibilities in internal security and in the estimation of Enemy Strategic Operations Capabilities. The new counter-intelligence division was hardly three weeks old, and no better organized than the Halle School had been when it started. Colonel Erdmann already saw that its implications were political. He would be involved with spies and the reports of spies, which made him uneasy. He would be involved in Berlin politics. But the General Staff had decided he was exactly suited to organize the new division precisely because he had done such an excellent job at the Intelligence School.

With him in the back seat of the official Mercedes were Major Franz Hugo Witt and First Lieutenant Klaus Hinkelbein.

Major Witt had taught Geopolitics at the Intelligence School. His studies on the meaning of the Ukrainian grain belt were brilliant. At war, Germany must have clear access to grain or be defeated by "saltwater" navy blockades. He was also an excellent flyer.

Lieutenant Hinkelbein had an odd, quick, acquisitive mind. He was a daring flyer, but perhaps had not yet had the proper opportunity to apply himself to any serious study. At the Intelligence School he was popular with the young pilots, if somewhat irreverent in his manners to the older men.

Both men would fly with Colonel Erdmann to New York and back on the *Hindenburg*, partly as a reward for their excellent service at the school, partly because the Air Ministry had ordered the three of them to make the trip (but the orders also required them to report to the S.S. in Berlin first—as they were about to do), and partly because the Luftwaffe had sent along "observers" on almost every Zeppelin voyage.

The "observers" from the Intelligence School were airplane men, and learned virtually nothing of any use about flying on a Zeppelin voyage. What they did learn had to do with long-range navigation, weather forecasting, and a good deal about the topography and landmarks of France and Britain.

It was one thing to locate the Portsmouth Navy Yard on a map, or with aerial photographs at hand to study. It was quite another to fly over it (or near it, now that the British had objected) and see with a trained eye the course of rivers, the outlines of hills and valleys and towns.

Naturally, the Luftwaffe "observers" never made these trips in uniform, lest they offend the diplomatic sensibilities of England and France, and indeed, America. They always traveled in mufti, and on the ship's manifest as "passengers." The world, after all, was at peace and appearances must be maintained.

The training of competent intelligence officers, in the barracks at Halle, or by observation in the field, was a practice with which Colonel Erdmann was familiar. Dealing with the political men in Berlin was something else. As they approached the Wilhelmstrasse he speculated on what possibilities were inherent in the special orders for this trip. It would come down to spies of some kind or another.

Well, dealing with the S.S. was preferable to dealing with the local Gestapo types. On one or two occasions, involving minor matters for his men, he had found it necessary to enter local Staatspolizei Headquarters. They were always noisy, dirty, badly organized places. In general, the responsible officers were ambitious louts. Schoolmasters in uniforms. From his experience the S.S. officers were men of much higher calibre, frequently from good families, with university educations, generally excellent manners, and their operations handled in an orderly, serene, and discreet manner.

Just as he expected, they were met at the door of S.S. Headquarters and greeted with proper respect, then escorted by a neatly uniformed adjutant to the offices of Major Hufschmidt.

The Major rose from his desk immediately, apologized "for the necessity of requiring this meeting on the day of a long voyage," and asked if the Colonel would object to his finishing the cigar he had thoughtlessly just lit.

Colonel Erdmann did not object at all, and under the circumstances accepted one of the Major's cigars. The Major lit it for him. It was exactly ten o'clock on the clock on Major Hufschmidt's wall.

On either side of the clock there were photographs of Adolf Hitler and Heinrich Himmler. Himmler's moon-shaped vapid face looked like another schoolteacher's, thought Lieutenant Hinkelbein, who proceeded to count the objects in the office. There were the three chairs the Luftwaffe men occupied, the one which Major Hufschmidt swiveled restlessly behind his desk from time to time, the black desk on which there were three black telephones, the humidor for cigars, two black ashtrays (one for the guests), a stand for two gold pens—it appeared to be made of cheap black onyx, and a steel ruler of the kind architectural students often carried. It was about three feet long.

If the pens and penstand counted as one, the office contained 16 objects, including the photos and clock. Except for the three phones, the desk was empty. Apparently a very efficient fellow.

"I am in charge of special state security problems," Major Hufschmidt began. "I report directly to Herr Himmler. We have today a special case to deal with and, Colonel, we very much need the cooperation of the Luftwaffe, especially of your new unit. In fact, Colonel, it is essentially a Luftwaffe matter."

Colonel Erdmann nodded. A "Berlin" problem, obviously. Major Hufschmidt continued.

"You are aware I'm sure, Colonel Erdmann, how important a symbol of Germany's growing strength the Zeppelin *Hindenburg* has become. Last year the airship made 10 very successful trips—from the propaganda point-of-view—to New York. Neither the English nor the French were capable of building or flying Zeppelins. But Germans are without question masters of this art."

Major Hufschmidt went on to describe one of the results of the Zeppelin flights to Rio. The German colony there had even erected a small replica of the Brandenburg Gate near the airfield. Above the gate German eagles guarded the interests of the Greater Germanic Reich in that remote part of the world.

"The great airships promote our commerce, extend our influence, earn exchange for the Reichs Bank. The *hakenkreuz* of the new Germany has been displayed not only to millions of workers in German cities, but in the major cities of the world as well. It is a sign that we are to be reckoned with. Those who have seen the *Hindenburg* float serenely above their heads, know well of the revolution we have made here."

Colonel Erdmann examined the Major's cigar. It was not a bad cigar. The trouble with these men in Berlin was they believed their own arguments. Rio was a long way away, he thought, much further than they realized. The revolution in Germany made very little difference to those millions of people so far away.

Major Hufschmidt was warming to his subject: "Unfortunately this German achievement encourages envy in certain circles, and especially within the conspiracy between the Jewish capitalists and the Bolshevists. We have received information that an attempt to sabotage the airship upon its arrival in New York might be made. Sabotage might cause an international incident of the sort which would be in the interest of Germany to avoid. First of all, we do not wish to have passengers, particularly American passengers, sent to their death in a German ship on American soil. More important, no matter who might perpetuate such an ugly deed, we do not wish to leave the impression that Germans are so undisciplined in the New Reich as to engage in these sorts of criminal activities."

Major Hufschmidt paused. His cigar had gone out. He put it down. He took up the ruler and played idly with it. He fit its ends into his palms so that he appeared to be balancing it along a horizontal line across his chest. At the same time he could compress it slightly and then it bent. Lt. Hinkelbein considered its gentle arc.

Colonel Erdmann asked: "What is the source of your information?"

"I cannot specify that exactly to you, Colonel, but as you know we have a good many sources. I will, however, review the major elements of the case with you, as a courtesy and since it is your responsibility."

"This is a civil matter. I do not see how this is my responsibility!"

"My dear Colonel. The airship *Hindenburg* is financed by the national Government and by Lufthansa Airlines, as well as by the Zeppelin Corporation. All German air matters are under the direction of your Air Ministry, headed by your commander, General Goering.

This naturally includes the flights—and the safety—of the airship *Hindenburg*. As you undoubtedly already know, Colonel, there was a small disagreement last year over the proper employment of the ships between Dr. Eckener and Minister of Propaganda Herr Goebbels. As the result of the meetings which then took place, all responsibility for the airships would rest in General Goering's Departments. I have the papers if you like. The Air Ministry in turn has designated you as its expert in such security problems. Is this not so?"

Colonel Erdmann thought through his alternatives. He obviously would be faced with "the papers" in a moment. The best thing to do would be to begin work on the problem.

"All right then." The Colonel thought to himself: so this is how the fat gets into the fire.

Major Hufschmidt put down the ruler, picked up his cigar and relit it. After the concentration the first few puffs required, he continued.

"You have as you know, Colonel, the complete cooperation of the S.S. To begin with, may I call your attention to the disturbances last year aboard the Steamships *Bremen* and *Hamburg* in New York. Communists, masquerading as legitimate passengers, boarded the ships in twos and threes. Once on board. . . ."

Colonel Erdmann interrupted: "I am already familiar with the political situation, Major. Be kind enough to tell us about airship problems."

"Well, then. In March 1935, a bomb was discovered in the main dining saloon, beneath a table, of the *Graf Zeppelin*. Our assumption was that some passenger had left it there. Fortunately it was found before it was detonated by a timing device.

"Last year, a passenger traveling under a forged Swedish passport, and an assumed name, disappeared before he could be arrested. He landed from the *Hindenburg* in Frankfurt, took rooms in the Frankfurter Hof. Since he was on the list of suspicious persons, when he absented himself from his room, it was searched. Complete plans and technical drawings of both the *Hindenburg* and the *Graf Zeppelin* in great detail were found in his room. Somehow he must have been warned, because he never returned. The Gestapo handled the affair and has been unable subsequently to find the culprit."

Colonel Erdmann could easily believe such Gestapo stupidity. They were always too late, or arrested the wrong man, or concerned themselves with the case of a pickpocket as if it were a matter of state, while more important matters got away.

Lieutenant Hinkelbein was studying the portrait of Hitler. Moustaches should always either be full, or at least extended to the corners of the lip. The Fuehrer's little brush was bad style. Now there were tens of thousands of them, just like it.

Major Witt also understood the incapabilities of the Gestapo. He nodded sympathetically to Major Hufschmidt, who continued.

"We have information that last month in a bank controlled by Jews in Paris, a plot to sabotage the *Hindenburg* was discussed as a means of embarrassing the Government of the Reich. Fortunately, we also have friends in the board room of that bank. They reported the matter to us. It appears that the discussions were just so much talk, but we took certain measures anyway—as a precaution, and we feel that the discussions will not be repeated for the time being."

Lieutenant Hinkelbein figured somebody got murdered.

"Recently, however, we have been hearing from some new sources. These reports indicate that an attempt at sabotage is possible on the next trip to New York. That is, of course, today's flight. The attempt is to be made after the *Hindenburg* has arrived in American territory."

Colonel Erdmann asked: "Why over American territory?"

"We don't know the answer to that exactly," said Major Hufschmidt. "We only know that is what our sources indicate."

Major Witt asked: "What kind of sources, German or American?"

"These sources are remarkably varied. Some from the weinstubes and gutters of Germany. Others from America. The reports are curiously consistent on one point, which I reemphasize: the sabotage is to happen in America, not in Germany. In order to impress upon you the seriousness of the matter I shall depart from our usual procedure somewhat and identify for you some of the raw reports."

Major Hufschmidt leaned back in his chair for a moment as if extending his concentration. He had picked up the ruler again and was flexing it between his palms. He could not help but give the impression of the very competent and well-informed intelligence officer.

"You may not be aware that our German Ambassador in Washington, Dr. Hans Luther, has customarily received hundreds of letters and a good many phone calls in the past year. These communications either threaten the airship, complain of it in American skies, or warn of its destruction. Most of these, of course, are cranks.

"Nevertheless we investigate many of the warnings to discover if there is any connection between the good Germans kind enough to warn us of difficulties and plotters against the prestige of the Reich.

"Recently we have heard from a Mrs. Annaliese Kraatz, who, if I remember correctly, lives on Pine Street in the city of White Plains north of New York City. Then we also examined the connections of Willy W. J. Weber, who I believe lives on a Stanhyse, or Stanhyte Street, in Brooklyn. We have received information from Williamstown, Massachusetts and from Bridgeport, Connecticut."

Lt. Hinkelbein was wondering what sort of fellow takes a job like Hufschmidt's. Did he just decide one day he would like to sit behind a desk in a uniform? Where would he come from? Lt. Hinkelbein decided the Major probably collected stamps when he was a kid, and pasted them into books, and liked it very much, and now he collected stamps of a new order.

"On April 8 a letter was written to our German Ambassador from a Mrs. Rauch, owner of the Six Point Tavern at Hopkins and 26th Street on the north side of Milwaukee, a city which is in Wisconsin.

"This last letter is quite specific about specifying a time bomb. Our lady correspondent urges us to stop the flights of the airship in order to save people's lives, and so forth.

"We have learned she is involved with a man called Georg Pfister, who is an illegal alien in the United States, and on occasion most helpful to us in small ways. He is a cook at that city's Schroeder Hotel. The city has many good and loyal Germans, but it has a great number of very active communists as well.

"We have encouraged a Bund there, and the Bund requires that members must swear they have no Jewish blood in their Aryan veins —which is amusing if you think about it for a minute, because America is so completely a mongrelized nation."

The world is mongrelized, thought Colonel Erdmann. Only here in Berlin is everyone so pure. And yet he had smiled in acknowledgment to this Major's little pretension. Perhaps politics was an infection that was caught like colds. The Major was rushing on about this cook's woman.

"Despite Mrs. Rauch's odd credentials we have reason to believe we ought to take her correspondence in this case seriously. A copy of her letter has been forwarded to Captain Lehmann at his home in Kressbronn, along with the appropriate explanations. It should have reached him this morning.

"We have also taken the precaution to have the ship thoroughly searched in its hangar and guards have been posted to guard it. We have arranged for the passengers to be searched this afternoon before they board."

Major Hufschmidt picked up one of the telephones, calling his orderly. In a moment he had placed before him a thick manila dossier. The orderly said: "Heil Hitler!", clicked his heels, then nodded to the three Luftwaffe officers and closed the door again as he left.

"I have here the information on your fellow passengers." The Major opened the manila covers, and began to turn over the papers one by one. Lt. Hinkelbein prepared to take the notes.

"Adelt, Mr. Leonhard B. and his wife Gertrud. Both journalists until 1933. He from Berlin *Tageblatt*; she as a cultural critic in Dresden. Since 1933 they have been supporting themselves by writing pamphlets and brochures. He is collaborating with Captain Lehmann on Lehmann's autobiography. They are close friends. The Adelts are also close friends of Stefan Zweig, the Austrian Jew writer, now in London.

"I will insist you consider a certain element of risk with these two. First of all, they are both Catholics. As you know we have just arrested another 1,000 monks and nuns and charged them with sexual crimes, which is not of course the main question, but rather who is to control the education of our German children, these perverts or the doctrines of the new order. Well, understandably a number of the Catholic intellectuals are somewhat upset. We have had to send them to Dachau for some reeducation.

"I do not know whether this will be necessary with the Adelts. But she has already had her press card lifted, and he is not only a friend but a pupil of the Jew Zweig, and they both have a number of Jewish and leftist international connections. They bear watching.

"Anders, Ernst Rudolf, owner of Selig & Hill Tea Merchants, also Dresden. No risk there."

"Belin, Peter. . . ."

"Just a moment, Major," Colonel Erdmann interrupted. "Exactly what do you propose we are to do if we decide one of these passengers is a potential saboteur?"

"Why, Colonel, I believe you have all the necessary powers or would have in conjunction with the officers of the *Hindenburg*, to arrest the suspect and forestall the disaster. That would seem self-evident."

Colonel Erdmann did not see what was so self-evident. Exactly how did one begin to avert this kind of disaster? What were his flyers to do aboard a Zeppelin? Major Witt's mind was also racing ahead: damn communists! They were capable of anything. Lieutenant Hinkelbein was finally interested.

"You say the passengers will be thoroughly searched?" Colonel Erdmann had no experience in searching passengers.

"They will be searched at the Frankfurter Hof, then transported to the airfield by secure busses. Their luggage will be searched completely. All matches, all cigarette lighters, all photographic equipment, even flashlight batteries will be taken from them. We have arranged to have small bags prepared with each passenger's name. When the trip is over, we shall return their belongings to them in the bags. They may keep the bags as a memento of their trip, courtesy of Lufthansa Airlines. I think it will aid you, however, if I proceed through the background of those on the list."

"Proceed," was all the Colonel said.

"Yes, we were at Belin, Peter, an American student at the Sorbonne, age 25, graduate of Yale University, from a rich and well connected Wilmington family. No risk.

"Then we have Dr. Birger Brinck, journalist from Stockholm, the *Tidningen*. No risk.

"Clemens, Karl Otto, from Bonn. A photographer. We might have a problem here. Mr. Clemens makes the trip to visit his cousin, a Mrs. Leif Neandress, 549 Studio Road, Ridgefield, New Jersey. He is going at half-price fare. In return for the special fare he is photographing the trip for the Zeppelin Corporation. Unfortunately this is an arrangement worked out by the Company's traffic manager, Mr. Heinz Wronsky, formerly a member of the party, but expelled because of Jewish blood. In addition, these press arrangements favored by Dr. Eckener might eventually cause us trouble. We have strong suspicions of Dr. Eckener. Photographic equipment is often used, as you know, as part of the detonating device for small bombs. It would only take a very small bomb to ignite the hydrogen in an airship, then. . . ."

Major Witt, excited by Major Hufschmidt's expressive shrug, interrupted: "They are foolish machines, airships, they have no future. . . ."

Colonel Erdmann demanded the briefing continue.

"The Doehner family: Father, Herman Doehner, General Manager of Beick, Felix & Co., Chemicals, Mexico City; Mother, Mrs. Matilda Doehner; daughter, Irene, age 16; two boys Walter, age 8 and Werner, age 6. No risk.

"Dolan, J. Burtis. 47 years old. American. President of Lelong Importing Company, a perfume business, Chicago. Home address 734 Kenesaw Terrace, Chicago. Married, 4 children. Despite strong French connections, no risk.

"Douglas, Edward H., 39 years old, an American whose home is Belleville, New Jersey, but who has remained in Europe since supposedly being discharged as a Petty Officer in the United States Navy in 1920. He is divorced from his wife Martha, who with their daughter Dorothy lives in Switzerland.

"This man is employed by H. K. McCann & Company, the advertising agents of the American General Motors Corporation. Mr. Advertising-Man Douglas is a spy."

The S.S. Major went on to explain how General Motors had bought Adam Opel, A.G., which made the most popular car in Germany; how the company also manufactured, or sold, spark plugs, batteries, motors for refrigerators, diesel engines, generators, brakes and brake linings, Allison aircraft engines, roller bearings, and many other related engineering products in Germany.

In addition, the company owned and managed the Vauxhall Motor Company in England. Their General Manager in England was Mr. Nicholas Vansittart. His brother, Sir Robert Vansittart, was chief of British Intelligence.

Major Hufschmidt explained how Douglas got his information on German steel production, ball-bearing plants, aircraft assembly figures —indeed anything manufactured in Germany—from his superiors at General Motors. Under the guise of "marketing information"

Douglas sent it to America. The material went "directly to the Department of Intelligence of the U.S. Navy."

Yes, the S.S. had been aware of this activity for some time, but the question was somewhat sensitive. General Motors was the largest employer in Germany. The men who hired Douglas and paid him—his superiors at the highest level—were the actual thieves of the material, sending it not only to the U.S. Navy, but then in turn to British Intelligence. In fact, the responsible Director of the parent Corporation was now on active duty with the American Navy Intelligence (but secretly) for precisely the purpose. His spying was official spying with the connivance of his government. But Hufschmidt implied that higher authorities than even Himmler himself had blocked the arrest of either Douglas or his superiors . . . "the men who fed him the data."

"Nevertheless Douglas is going home. He will probably not return because we have indicated by the arrest of some of his coworkers at the Opel works that we know of his activities. We released them after interrogation, and he has booked passage. But he is a most dangerous spy."

The three Luftwaffe officers considered all they were learning: so, the Americans prepared for war too! Major Hufschmidt turned the typewritten pages of the dossier files.

"The next names are no risk. Ernst, Otto, a seed trader from Hamburg and his wife Elsa. He is 72; she is 62.

"Moritz Feibusch, age 57, a Jew from 2601 Lincoln Way, San Francisco, California. This man is a tuna fish broker and broker of canned and fancy goods, but you can never be too careful of the artful Jew.

"Grant, George, age 63, is Assistant Manager of the London Office of the Hamburg-American Line. He does some silly little spying for his England too, but he's no risk.

"Hirschfeld, George W., age 36, Cotton Broker from Bremen. A businessman. No risk.

"Mrs. Maria Kleeman, age 61, Bad Homburg. No risk.

"Knoescher, Eric, age 38, Importer, Zeulenroda. Another businessman. No risk.

"Leuchtenburg, William G., age 64, now an American citizen, home at 49 Maplewood Street, Larchmont, New York. He is president of the Alpha Lux Corporation, 194 Front Street in Manhattan. No risk, another businessman.

"Margaret G. Mather, a spinster, 48 Via Antonia, Rome. This is one of those rich American ladies who have traveled the world. If she weren't in her sixties, she would be a risk only to bachelors.

"Philip Mangone, in his fifties, home 25 East End Avenue, New York. A dress designer. No risk.

"Colonel Nelson Morris, 46, Chicago, Illinois. His military title has no significance whatever. His family are rich meatpackers. During the war he ran a meat plant in France.

"O'Laughlin, Herbert James, age 28, 914 Bonnie Brae Road, River Forest, Chicago. He is an employee of the Consumer Company in Elgin, Illinois. He is flying home from three weeks vacation. No risk at all.

"Osbun, Clifford L., age 37. Export Sales Manager, Oliver Farm Equipment Company, home 904 Vine Avenue, Park Ridge, Illinois. A young businessman, no risk.

"John Pannes and his wife Emma, home Manhasset, Long Island. He is the passenger agent of Hamburg-American North German Lloyd Lines in New York. I have met them. They are a very charming couple.

"Reichold, Otto, about 35 years old, of the Reichold Chemical family in Vienna. We don't think there is any risk here. We would be grateful for any information you can assemble about Vienna, as a courtesy, naturally.

"Spah, Joseph, about 35, an acrobat and comedian. His home is in Douglaston, Long Island. His professional name is 'Ben Dova.'

"Under the guise of his artist freedom, this man has been traveling frequently through Germany. We have a great number of significant reports. And we advise you that this comedian, this acrobat of the stage, is in fact a very dangerous man.

"He travels as an American, but with a French passport. He was born in Strasbourg, which at the time he was born would make him German today. This aroused our suspicions.

"In Munich he spends his time in the company of anti-party people. In Berlin, he has made a habit of dining regularly at the Restaurant Hurcher, which as you know is the habitual dining place of General Goering and his group and which, it seems to us, is certainly far too expensive for such a simple comedian.

"Finally, he has been keeping company regularly with a striptease artist by the name of Mathia Merrifield. She is an American woman who in turn is being supported by a man so high on our list of dangerous persons he may not last the month. What is most curious is that she speaks no German and her lover no English.

"It is no more than a suggestion, of course, Colonel, but I would have this Spah watched day and night."

The S.S. Major paused. Lieutenant Hinkelbein looked up from his notes. The Major was bending the steel ruler almost double. Colonel Erdmann tried to estimate how frank Major Hufschmidt was really being. These people in Berlin were not beyond causing an incident themselves, then blaming others. They had done it before.

Or perhaps, letting an incident they expected to happen actually occur, then blaming the lack of prevention on the Luftwaffe. It was well known that General Goering and Herr Himmler had certain disagreements.

"Let me assure you," the Major picked up again, "you have the essentials of all we know about this Joseph Spah. We shall assign, in cooperation with the Zeppelin Corporation, a man whose name is Emil Stoeckle, who will also travel as a passenger, but whose duty is to search the mail on board, using the special equipment we have developed. Let me list two more passengers for you. . . .

"Vinholt, Hans. Copenhagen, age 65, retired banker.

"Rolf von Heidenstamm, a former submarine officer in the Swedish Navy, President of the Lighthouse Company of Sweden, and representative of the American Gas Accumulating Company of Elizabeth, New Jersey. Despite our previous 'Swedish' problems, no risk. That's the list."

He closed the dossier, picked up the phone, the adjutant appeared again and whisked it away. The Major put down his ruler, got his cigar going again. He seemed pleased with his performance.

"We really have very good sources, Colonel. For example, we expect the Paris-Marseilles express to be bombed by the leftists on Wednesday night. . . ."

"You'll stop it of course. Why that's an express!"

"Not at all, Colonel, that's a French matter. Just mark my words."

Colonel Erdmann considered it.

Lieutenant Hinkelbein wondered aloud why, if they were so sure about sabotage, they didn't just cancel the trip, or mix it up somehow. Colonel Erdmann silenced him with a glance, asked about the reliability of the crew.

"We have a number of sources of information among the crew and from certain officers. There are no indications of unreliability—just the usual barracks gossip.

"I cannot in fact promise you, Colonel, that there is any danger. I only think that in the circumstances every precaution should be taken. The Jew Feibusch bears watching. It is not out of the question that he might be recruited to perform some symbolic act at the behest of his miserable people. The Adelts are the sort of people we shall arrest sooner or later for some political crime, we lack only the instance at the moment—and who knows that they have not gone about providing us the reasons. We know Douglas is a spy, and perhaps on his way home he will follow one more order. He has the technical knowledge, and our sources, you will not forget, indicate that should some event take place, it will occur on United States territory—to embarrass our government even further.

"Finally, Mr. Joseph Spah, masquerading as an artist of the stage, we can assure you is a dangerous man. He enjoys money. As far as we can tell, these artists have no compunctions. Making fools of our government would be a lark for him. But I sincerely hope that we are wrong and that you will have a most pleasant voyage to America and a safe return."

Colonel Erdmann flushed slightly. He was not pleased. On the one hand he thought Major Hufschmidt had too many suspects—a tuna fish salesman suspected of sabotage because he was a Jew! That was laying it on too thick. He calculated the S.S. knew better than that themselves. They were just covering every possibility. On the other hand, how could he be sure they were not correct?

"Major," he said, "it must have occurred to your headquarters that we are not detectives. We are flyers. We have no experience with your sort of work. We are military intelligence officers. Surely it should be recognized that this is a Gestapo matter, not something for the Luftwaffe."

Major Hufschmidt seemed vaguely amused by something, but there was no diffidence in his reply: "Colonel, I sympathize completely with your position. But the Luftwaffe has already accepted responsibility, and I have been only doing my best to make your task easier. Perhaps you should record your misgivings by letter to your command."

The clock behind Major Hufschmidt's head stood at exactly one minute before noon. "In the meantime," he said, "I am sure you will not want to miss your connection to the ship."

The Luftwaffe men stood up. Major Hufschmidt escorted them to the door, then the adjutant to the car, which was waiting. The adjutant held the door for Colonel Erdmann. They left for Staaken airfield, and Frankfurt.

In the car they were mostly silent. Lt. Hinkelbein noted that most of the women wore only light topcoats. It would soon be time for summer dresses. Major Witt interrupted their sightseeing by remarking: "Information derived from lovers of cooks, barmaids, whores, striptease dancers and acrobats is not what the Luftwaffe would rely on for accuracy!"

That cheered them all up considerably, especially Colonel Erdmann. They passed the Brandenburg Gate, through Adolf Hitler Platz to the outskirts. Colonel Erdmann was beginning to concoct a plan. If the passengers were really thoroughly searched . . . he'd have to observe that. Then suppose the S.S. were right. If an attempt was to be made at the American end, then whoever was guilty would have to do something—make some sign. He would make some move different from the other passengers in order to get at whatever it was that would constitute the sabotage. He could then be arrested; a preventive arrest hopefully. On the other hand, perhaps the whole thing was the invention of the S.S., or the Gestapo who had bucked it to the S.S. and they were all just covering themselves, in case. Well, he was now their "in case."

They were at the airfield where a new Heinkel was already warming up. They would be at the Frankfurter Hof in Frankfurt when the passengers were searched at four o'clock.

\*          \*          \*

At the same time the Luftwaffe officers were in the air between Berlin and Frankfurt, an indifferent sun was rising on Eastern Daylight Saving Time at the United States Naval Air Station, Lakehurst, New Jersey.

Immediately after his breakfast the station's commanding officer, Lieutenant Commander Charles E. Rosendahl, U.S.N., began preparing for the *Hindenburg*'s arrival on Thursday.

Commander "Rosie" was first stationed at Lakehurst in 1923. He had been navigating officer on the ill-fated *Shenandoah*. When that Zeppelin broke up in a thunderstorm at 6,000 feet, he sailed his third of the broken ship to the ground safely. He was a hero to both American and German Zeppelin men.

In 1926 he was made Commander of the *Los Angeles*. He had been the first commander of the *Akron*, but had been on fleet sea duty when she crashed. In October 1928 he sailed on the *Graf Zeppelin*'s maiden voyage, and in August 1929 as a guest on her round-the-world trip. Although the *Los Angeles* was officially decommissioned, thanks to "Rosie," she was berthed at Lakehurst. Navy men could practice ground handling procedures and maintenance against the day when American Zeppelins might fly again.

It was said that sometimes the "ground practice" required Commander Rosendahl to take the *Los Angeles* a short distance into the air, but this had never been officially confirmed since after the *Akron* and *Macon* disasters, U.S. Navy dirigibles were not supposed to fly.

At Lakehurst, besides officers-in-training in meteorology, navigation and radio, there were 92 Navy men trained in ground handling: men like Chief Boatswain's Mate Frederick J. "Bull" Tobin, another survivor of the crash of the *Shenandoah*; Lieutenant Raymond F. Tyler, in command of the mooring mast—the land tug apparatus, with 20 years' experience in Zeppelins; Lieutenant R. W. Antrim, who would stand atop the mooring mast—75 feet up—and guide the airship's nose cone into the mast's cup, and lock it.

In addition to the Navy men, 139 civilians—local men hired at $1 per hour—would assist the Navy men at the spider lines and landing lines let down from the airship before it was winched into the nose cone and locked down at the rear railway car. After the *Hindenburg*'s ten dockings and launchings of 1936, the civilian crew could be considered reasonably experienced.

The contract with the German Zeppelin Corporation stipulated that the use of Lakehurst as the western terminal would be at no cost to the United States Navy. The American advantage in the contract was that Navy men could be kept in training against the day when American Zeppelins might fly again. The Germans needed the mooring facilities, the use of the great hangar, and the American manpower.

At the end of 1936, the Zeppelin Corporation and the Navy had agreed that landings would take place at either 6 o'clock in the morning, or 6 o'clock in the evening, regardless of the time the *Hindenburg* arrived over the field. In order to save money, ground crews need only be called an hour before these times. If, for example, head winds delayed the *Hindenburg*'s arrival past the 6 A.M. landing, ground crews would not stand by at $1 per hour per man. The airship could cruise around until 6 P.M.

The arrangement also made sense for the considerable crowd of people involved in docking a Zeppelin. There were the Customs and Immigration men from Philadelphia; the mail and freight services from New York; the connecting aircraft flights which had been arranged with American Airlines. DC-3 passenger planes stood ready to meet the airship and fly passengers on to Newark and then Chicago, non-stop. Moreover, there was always the press to be accommodated. And to the queries of anxious relatives and friends, it would be better to give an exact landing time.

It was Commander Rosendahl's responsibility to orchestrate these crowds of people and their varied interests. In addition, "Rosie" was the ambassador of good will for Zeppelins. After the *Hindenburg* landed this Thursday, his wife Jean had planned a dinner for the ship's commanding officers, for Nelson Macy of the American Navy League, for the German Consular Officer, William von Meister, who was also the Vice President and General Manager of the American Zeppelin Corporation, and for Herr von Meister's mother.

Then there were the problems of the base's security; the handling of the inevitable crowds of tourists and sightseers; and the sometimes delicate relations with the local townspeople.

Last year Mayor Harold J. Fuccile and the town council had prepared a code of ethics, which included a pledge not to charge more than 25¢ for parking. The town tradesmen had invested some $5,000 in sandwiches, ice cream, and "perishable" souvenirs. It didn't work out too well.

The sandwiches and ice cream spoiled. The "souvenirs" largely went unsold. Mayor Fuccile, who owned the barbershop, operated the bar in the Pine Tree Inn and sold insurance, said the town folk "did pretty fair on meals, but got stuck on the incidentals." It was the pennants marked "Hindenburg" and the toy balloons in the shape of Zeppelins that went unsold.

Asked his opinion for the excess inventory, Mayor Fuccile pointed to the swastikas on the toys, replicas of the real thing on the ship, and said: "Hitler," but he would not elaborate.

Commander Rosendahl thought it was probably more likely that since the *Hindenburg* arrived and sailed right on time, visitors had no reason to hang around.


The public relations department of American Airlines had been asked to think of ways to promote the company's new plane, the DC-3, and the new service inaugurated in 1936 from New York to Chicago. Its speed and convenience was to be emphasized. They would also emphasize the safety of flying. Too many people still remembered mail planes disappearing in the hills of Pennsylvania.

But mail pilots, old stunt flyers like Dick Merrill, were contracting to fly the Atlantic, and they were always "just making it," leaving an unfortunate impression about the safety of aircraft travel; or worse, they were reported skidding their single engine planes to a crash landing in some bog in Newfoundland.

American Airlines thought the DC-3 was different. It could fly with its pressurized cabin at 20,000 feet, above the worst weather. It had a range of 2,000 miles. The plane's enthusiasts were already talking about flying the ocean, and replacing the Zeppelins. Of course it was too early to tell. They would need field facilities at some place like Gander, and then in Ireland.

The huge Zeppelins could lift 240 tons and carry 100 passengers; the DC-3 could only carry 21 passengers and two tons. But the DC-3 had the advantage of speed. With extra tanks a plane might fly to London at 200 knots and get back again before the Zeppelin could make one crossing. And designers were talking about the next genera-tion of planes with four 1,000-horsepower engines, bigger payloads and even higher speeds. The thing to do in the meantime was to promote the national use of the DC-3—especially New York to Chicago.

On the recommendation of the public relations department, American Airlines started a service connecting passengers from the transatlantic Zeppelins from Lakehurst through Newark airport to Chicago. If Zeppelins were stealing all the headlines, the DC-3 could tag along for a while.

For the *Hindenburg*'s first trip of 1937, the public relations department had arranged to fly Herbert Morrison, an announcer for Chicago's WLS, the "Prairie Farmer Station," to Lakehurst—along with Morrison's sound man, Charles Nehlsen. They could use a small shack on the edge of the field to record. Morrison would describe the landing, interview passengers—especially those flying on to Chicago, then edit the show and play it back on Saturday night's "Dinner Bell" program.

On Monday, Morrison's calendar showed "Wednesday—fly to Lakehurst."

Although Lakehurst, New Jersey, was hardly within New York City's jurisdiction, the Department of State had requested the assistance of the New York City Police Department.

It seems that State was worried about the "potentially awkward" incidents which had occurred aboard the *Bremen* and *Hamburg*. Then a bomb had recently been discovered aboard the liner *Europa*. Mr. von Meister of the Zeppelin Corporation had complained to State that on previous trips, "nuts" had taken pot shots at the *Hindenburg* from the ground with rifles—although it was presumed the shots had been air rifles because they had either not reached the Zeppelin, or bounced harmlessly off its linen skin.

Detective Arthur C. Johnson, Alien Squad, New York Police Department, was assigned the case. Johnson was a specialist with 27 years on the force. He had been on the Dutch Schultz murder, and the Lindbergh baby kidnapping. His chief facility was a nearly photographic memory for faces. He could stand beside the gangway of a ship and, as if by magic, spot Nazis or Communists attempting illegal entry.

Naval Intelligence alerted State that three fairly important Luftwaffe officers were traveling in mufti as passengers, due to arrive

on the *Hindenburg* Thursday at 6 A.M. In turn, State had contacted
New York Police. His captain had assigned Johnson with the instruc-
tions: "Don't let any of those goddam Nazis slip into the country."
Johnson entered "Thursday—Lakehurst" into his appointment book.

He enjoyed his work. In fact, Johnson enjoyed life. He was about
six feet. His weight was a secret, but was estimated by more disin-
terested observers as better than 280 pounds. Along Broadway they
said he could eat four dozen oysters for an appetizer. It gave a man a
certain reputation. He was also marvelously well-informed. He listened to the news constantly: "Hello America, this is Berlin speaking. . . ."

He kept up with H. V. Kaltenborn, with Lowell Thomas; read
Walter Lippmann, Westbrook Pegler, Drew Pearson; had read John
Gunther's *Inside Europe*, and Sinclair Lewis' *It Can't Happen Here*.
He followed every detail of the sit-down strikes, the war in Ethiopia,
the war in Spain. But his favorite source of information was Charlie
McCarthy. On Monday mornings he would review the entire Chase
and Sanborn Hour, virtually line-for-line, with his working partner,
George Ballenstadt.

Ballenstadt got to hear the program twice that way, but he didn't
mind because big Arthur C. Johnson was a formidable man. "He
wasn't too quick on his feet, but he was sure."

At 4 P.M. Central European Time, officials of the S.D. in the company of Zeppelin Corporation representatives began the search of passenger baggage. Tickets and passports were shown. The baggage was
assembled in the main dining room of the Frankfurter Hof. It was
photographed with X-ray machines and weighed.

Miss Margaret Mather, born in the United States, direct descend-
ant of Cotton Mather, citizen of the world, resident of Rome, age 59,
spinster, was a formidable woman, but she weighed only 98 pounds.
Though her passport said she stood five feet zero inches tall, that
probably included her practical heels.

When her baggage was weighed she was found to be 15 kilos in excess, for which she had to pay. Only 20 kilos—about 44 pounds—were
allowed. She argued that she weighed 20 kilos less than the average
man, but she was told "it was the rule."

She was a character out of Henry James. Her father had been born in New York in 1835—three years before Count Zeppelin. He was Frank Jewett Mather, a successful New York lawyer, and the father of eight children. They spent their summers at Quisset, near Wood's Hole, on Cape Cod. From a New York house to the Cape and back each year—it was an orderly world. Summers could be devoted to literature, some tennis and swimming, and sailing.

The story went that when she was about 17, there had been a sailing accident out in the bay. Miss Margaret and her brother made it to shore safely, but the young man who had been engaged as a tutor for the summer was drowned. Miss Margaret was grief stricken for some time.

When she was 28, her brother Frank Jewett Mather, Jr. contracted typhoid in Florence. Her father had retired, and together with her mother and father, Miss Margaret nursed the young man to health. The whole family lived for a year in a villa in Capri. Young Mather recovered and in 1910 was appointed Marquand Professor of Art and Archeology at Princeton University.

Miss Margaret's father and mother stayed on in Italy. Her father had a bit of heart trouble, but Florence and Rome were pleasant. Her mother died in 1920. Miss Margaret cared for her father until he died in 1929, at the grand age of 94. Then she took an apartment at the top of the Spanish Steps. From the second floor you could see St. Peter's.

Her own life seemed charmed. She told a story on herself: she had been driving a car fast, and alone, on the back roads in the hills of Italy. She must have let her attention wander because she went off the road, down a steep embankment, and the car had rolled over a number of times before it finally came to a stop. Steam and smoke were pouring out of the overturned car, but somehow she was uninjured and wriggled free. When she had stepped clear and smoothed her skirt, she looked up and there were two Italian shepherds, standing below her, leaning on their staffs. They crossed themselves, to ward off the dangers emanating from her spirit—there are two kinds of angels!

In the early twenties Miss Margaret developed a taste for flying. Indeed, she loved it. She was quoted as complaining about the new planes that were all shut in. She liked the open cockpit, two-seater kind, where you wore goggles and a helmet against the wind, and could really see out. She did not fly herself, but hired pilots. She had flown over the Mediterranean, over what she called the "Grecian Islands," through the Gulf of Corinth, over Italy and the Dolomites, over "the high secrets," she said, of the Albanian mountains, over the African deserts, over France and Germany.

She wrote some poetry, knew the museums of Europe by heart, and traveled every year in the spring to New York to shop. She had to do her buying in the teenage department to get things to fit. Then she would visit her brother at Princeton, and then go up to Quisset for the summer.

The grey, angry Atlantic made her very seasick. She had seen the *Hindenburg* over New York the summer before. "The lavish comfort and entertainment of the steamers meant nothing to someone who was a sea-sick wretch," she said, and so she was delighted to book passage for her annual trip by Zeppelin. She payed half her fare in registered marks, which made the trip even cheaper.

She had been visiting in England, flew from London to Cologne Sunday night, then down to Frankfurt in the morning in a gentle rain. She saw the great Zeppelin hangar at the field, and asked if she could leave her luggage at the airport, but it was not allowed. She must transport it to the city, to the official starting place, the Frankfurter Hof.

She had to kill time then. She visited Goethe's House, and the Opera House. Then she hired a taxi and drove out of the city across the river through the beech woods. She thought them "most enchanting with their young green leaves." She could not explain the thought that came to her: "What a beautiful farewell to earth."

When she had taken some tea and returned to the Frankfurter Hof, the main dining room was full of uniforms—black and grey on the officials; midnight blue for the representatives of the Zeppelin Company.

She was surprised to see how few women there were. During the folderol of inspection—they searched every box, the linings of suitcases were slit, the bon voyage candy boxes opened, and the men had to give up the matches and lighters—Miss Margaret Mather struck up an easy conversation with some of her fellow travelers.

She learned from Mr. and Mrs. Otto Ernst that they too loved flying. They were going to fly to New York, spend a week, then fly back. It was the perfect vacation.

She judged Mrs. Adelt to be about 35; a very pretty woman with short blond hair, well turned out, and with the most enormous big blue eyes. Mrs. Adelt had flown on Zeppelins many times before. Both she and her husband were journalists. Never had there been such an inspection of baggage. Gertrud Adelt said: "This is more like a conscription for a galley than a luxury trip."

A young man, whose name turned out to be Karl Otto Clemens, had cameras of all kinds about his neck. The inspectors confiscated from him the flashbulbs he said he needed for indoor shots, but they were relentless. Flashbulbs were not allowed.

It was not until seven o'clock that the passengers were escorted to three big busses, driven across the Main Bridge and through the woods to the airfield. On the way in the bus, an old man who had apparently overindulged during the lengthy inspection, began to sing. He was actually quite drunk.

By the hangar, tethered by its mast to the ground, was the great silver ship, and at the sight a great wave of joy swept over Miss Margaret. Gone were all her "doubts and reluctance."

There were more inspections in the hangar again. One of the passengers, a Mr. Joseph Spah, had slipped away and not been aboard the bus. He arrived by car at the hangar entrance with a box wrapped in brown paper under his arm. A long discussion ensued which she could not hear. He kept laughing at them, and making sweeping gestures, turning on his heel as if to walk away, then spinning around to face them again. He seemed to be an amusing fellow. The inspectors, however, were stony-faced.

She edged over closer and saw that they were making him unwrap the package. He did it elaborately, taking off first the outer wrapping, and then what was obviously gift wrapping. She could see that inside was a doll—of the sort little girls loved and which were well made in Dresden. Mr. Spah was furious.

They took the doll over to a large machine which must have been an X-ray machine and photographed it before they would return it to him. The official even lifted the skirt of the doll. Mr. Spah laughed at them again and said: "It's a girl, dummkopf."

It was still drizzling as the passengers crossed the brief space from the hangar to the Zeppelin. Stewards with umbrellas escorted the ladies. Miss Margaret was escorted up the main gangway, and then to her cabin. She thought it tiny, but was thrilled by it. A complete little house decorated with pearl-grey linen walls, a washstand and cupboards, and cut jonquils in a vase standing by her bedside. She was in one of the new cabins on "B" deck. She had her own window, slanting up in the shape of the hull, but after a hasty look, she went up to "A" deck to watch the casting off from the promenade lounge windows.

There she found Mrs. Gertrud Adelt again and together they watched, despite the rain, a great many spectators waving. It was the first time, according to Mrs. Adelt, that friends and relatives were not allowed to go on board before the sailing—to say their goodbyes and present their gifts themselves.

There was a detachment of Nazi youth parading quite close to the ship and there was a fine German brass band. The musicians were dressed in blue and yellow uniforms, and some of the instruments were decorated with streamers in the same colors. In the rear center, beside the tubas, was an instrument shaped like a huge lute, but filled with bells, instead of strings. It had yellow and blue horse tails hanging from it.

The band played the traditional German folk song *Muss I denn?* which Gertrud Adelt said began:

> *I now must leave this little town*
> *While you my sweetheart must stay behind. . . .*

Then the band played the *Horst Wessel* song, which was supposed to have been freshly composed by a Nazi killed in a brawl in 1930, but was actually an old Viennese air. It ended:

> *For the last time the call to arms is sounded!*
> *For battle, now we stand prepared.*
> *Soon Hitler's flags will wave in every street,*
> *Our servitude will last but little longer. . . .*

Then they played *Deutschland Über Alles,* and everyone expected the ship to cast off. Instead, the loudspeaker in the ship blared out to the ground: "Will the wife of Colonel Erdmann please come forward. . . ."

Mrs. Adelt said: "Ah, the privileges of these military men."

A handsome brunette woman stepped from the crowd. While the ship waited, she walked out of sight beneath the promenade windows, under the belly of the ship to the gangway. She soon appeared on "A" deck. She and her husband embraced. His knuckles were white on her arms. They said nothing at all to each other. She was crying. Then she turned and retraced her steps. She reappeared again beneath the windows of Promenade Deck, but did not walk all the way back to the crowd of spectators, standing alone directly beneath her husband at the windows. She waved the handkerchief with which she had been mopping at her tears. The band struck up again: a reprise of *Deutschland Über Alles, Über Alles in Der Welt.* . . .

The mooring lines were cast off, the nose cone at the bow disconnected by Chief Knorr and Eric Spehl. From the lift of its hydrogen, the great ship began to rise.

Captain Pruss had given the command: "Up Ship!" Except that the bandmaster seemed to be getting smaller, there was no sign that they were airborne, no sense of motion—not a quiver.

Searchlights from the field played across the flanks of the silently gaining airship. At about 300 feet, the telegraphs from the command gondola signaled, and Chief Sauter's men started their diesels. From Promenade Deck, they seemed distant. Muffled. At 8:15 the *Hindenburg* set course 281 degrees (about northwest) to join the Rhine at Koblenz.

The twilight was shrouded by the overcast. As the ship pulled away from the spectators, the Nazi youth ran after it full tilt, their caps flying, until the fence at the end of the field interrupted their pell-mell chase. The last searchlight held a circle on the swastika on the lower tail fin, then was switched off. There was nothing for the spectators to do but go home.

The bomb which was hidden on board was an extremely simple, but practical device. In a cotton bag it contained four dry cell batteries of the "C" type. They provided the energy for a flashbulb detonator which in turn would ignite a quantity of phosphorus. The timer, of the type used in cheap photographic kits, had not yet been started.

In the command gondola Captain Lehmann watched without comment the performance of his Zeppelin captains. In his breast pocket he had a copy of the letter from Mrs. Rauch of Milwaukee, forwarded from the German Ambassador in Washington, then from S.S. in Berlin to his home in Kressbronn.

Lehmann had taken the train to Basel, then to Frankfurt, arriving at the *Hindenburg* while the passengers were having their baggage inspected. He had surprised Kubis at the head of the gangway. Kubis had saluted and blurted out in surprise: "Captain, where is your luggage?"

Captain Lehmann had with him only his toilet kit. He had stopped at his apartment in Frankfurt and picked up the architectural plans for the new house in Zeppelinheim—he would work on them during the trip. It was Dr. Eckener's dream to provide good housing and a pretty community for the men of the Zeppelin family. To that notion Captain Lehmann could agree. He had Kubis send one of the stewards to the car to fetch his accordion. Kubis read concern on his chief's face. As the two men walked toward what would be Lehmann's cabin, the little Captain said:

"Kubis, I thought my being on board would give my boys more assurance—you know."

Now with the noise and excitement of the take-off behind them, the quiet efficiency, the orderliness, of his men in the command gondola soothed Captain Lehmann.

With Dr. Eckener confined to his home in Kressbronn, Lehmann had taken over almost all the corporate duties. Captain von Schiller now commanded the *Graf Zeppelin* to Rio. And with this crossing Max Pruss now would take over the North Atlantic runs of the *Hindenburg*. Lehmann had trained Max Pruss twenty years before as an elevatorman. Pruss was as sure of himself and as moderate in command as was Lehmann himself. Pruss had also been a Navy man and studied at Kiel. He had commanded the *Graf Zeppelin* 16 times across the Atlantic.

With Pruss in the gondola were Albert Sammt, Heinrich Bauer,

Walter Ziegler—all qualified and ranked as captains, and serving as watch officers. The Corporation had more captains than ships. Captain Anton Wittemann traveled on this trip as an observer.

Kurt Schoenherr stood at the helm. On the left side of the car Eduard Boetius handled the elevator wheel. In the compartment behind them Christian Nielsen and Max Zabel bent over the navigating maps and the weather charts. Up the stairs into the ship in the radio room, Chief Radio Operator Willy Speck and his crew worked their dials.

One radio officer would sit on the 900-meter band until they had cleared Ireland, then on the 600-meter band at sea. A second would keep in communication with Hamburg on short wave, reporting position, altitude, course every fifteen minutes.

By radio they picked up reports from ships at sea. By marking in the ship's position, wind direction, barometer, and cloud cover, the navigators could keep redrawing the maps.

The *Hindenburg* also had an official radio channel and provided a commercial radio service. News broadcasts were picked up twice a day in English and German. Private calls and messages could be worked through Nordreich radio in Hamburg, Mackay Radio on the North American coast, and WCC—the RCA service. As usual when a trip began, passengers were jamming Willy Speck's facilities with messages to the ground. They almost all said the same thing: "SAILED AT 8:18 FROM FRANKFURT ABOARD HINDENBURG ARRIVING NEW YORK THURSDAY 6:00 A.M. LOVE. . . ."

Chief Kubis had the trip's first crisis to manage. It seemed that Mr. Joseph Spah had arranged to ship his dog, an Alsatian bitch of nine months, with him on the ship. Now Spah demanded to see the dog, which was in the animal freight room all the way aft at Ring 62. Spah claimed: "No one can feed my dog but me."

Kubis had the sense to say he would check with the Captain first. He sent a message forward to Captain Lehmann, who asked Kubis to bring Mr. Spah to Kubis' small office behind the stairs on "B" deck. They could meet privately there.

After their "Grüss Gotts," Spah explained to Captain Lehmann that he had expected to ship his dog to New York by steamship. In the Zeppelin Corporation offices, when he had bought his ticket, they had urged him to ship the young dog on the *Hindenburg*. They said many other animals—dogs, birds, fish and even pet deer—had made the trip and there would be no problem. He had understood he would be able to feed and handle his dog himself. The dog was young and skittish anyway and would certainly be frightened now that she was in the air in a Zeppelin. He had, he said, begun the training of the dog to help him in his comedy act—the dog would pretend to leap at him from behind and he would fall down. Now Spah thought he would give the dog to his children. It was such a sweet dog.

"Besides," said Spah, "I must take great care of this dog because she is royalty. Her name is Ulla von Hooptel. She has proper papers. A pedigree!"

Kubis winced at the *von*. Now even dogs were giving themselves titles. Captain Lehmann, however, couldn't help but smile with the compact, quick-witted Spah. He found it pleasant to look into eyes that sparkled and danced.

"Mr. Spah," he said, "can you explain to me why it was that you did not join the others in the bus on the way to the airport—why you found it necessary to make your own arrangements?"

"Ah, that! Well there is this very pretty lady—she is even more beautiful with her clothes off—who is going to appear on the stage of some small theatre in Munich. The publicity men make up stories for the columns of the papers, you know, any kind of story at all, to get the name of a girl like that, and perhaps her photograph, into the papers. It helps sell tickets. Miss Mathia Merrifield, for that is her name, was said to be engaged to me. Her press agent thought it would be a swell idea to take a picture of us saying our goodbyes with the *Hindenburg* in the background. So we drove to the field and posed by the fence. A very touching scene, don't you think? Actually I am married and have three children in New York. It is just publicity. Surely you know something of publicity yourself, Captain."

Lehmann laughed. He said he did. "Mr. Kubis, escort Mr. Spah to his dog." Lehmann went back to the gondola to join his captains.

In his cabin Joseph Spah unpacked some dog food from his baggage, then rejoined Chief Steward Kubis in the little office. Through its back door a passageway went by the crew's quarters, then on to the lower gangway. From the ship's dark interior they could hear the drumming of the diesels quite clearly. Kubis led the way with a flashlight to guide Mr. Spah. It illuminated the lower gangway, which was no more than an aluminum plank painted blue in the immense black void of the ship's interior. "Passengers are never allowed back here unaccompanied," Kubis said.

"Ulla" was in a wicker basket almost at the stern. As Spah attempted to pick her up, the excited dog nipped at him. He almost stumbled backward with the dog in his arms. Kubis caught him, and steadied him. They settled the dog together, left food and water, then started back.

"What would happen if I had fallen?" asked Spah to the flashlight leading ahead of him.

"You would probably tear through the linen and then stop when you hit the Rhine. It would be a distance of about 700 feet below us, I'd guess. But then you might not hit the Rhine."

At the promenade windows Margaret Mather sat side saddle on the banquette, entranced by the magic below. The ship was droning along at her cruising speed of about 80 knots. The wind rushing past like a mountain torrent was the most noticeable sound in the lounge—the motors were way aft.

Beacons flashed below from hill to hill. They passed over hamlets and villages, "gleaming jewel like in the darkness," Miss Margaret thought, then came to a great spreading mass of lights, which someone said was Cologne, and suddenly they were looking down at the cathedral, "beautifully clear and dark amid the glow."

The *Hindenburg* seemed to be coasting. The engines had been stopped. Edward Douglas asked Steward Eugen Nunnenmacher the reason for the delay. Nunnenmacher said a mail sack was to be parachuted down for the city's postal authorities, each stamp canceled "Luftschiff Hindenburg," and each envelope stamped "The country that hopes to save itself will think only heroic, martial thoughts." Nunnenmacher thought perhaps it was a quote from Kant, or Hegel, or maybe it was Fichte.

Sure enough, a searchlight caught a parachute floating down 1,000 feet to the ground. Then the big ship picked up speed again. They could see people in the streets waving up at them. At about 10:00 P.M. a light supper of cold meats, salad, and Liebfrauenmilch was served.

Miss Margaret Mather sat at Captain Pruss' right at a long table where twenty men were seated. The Doehner family had a table of their own and the little boys, though obviously excited, were almost ready for bed. Couples had tables of their own in twos or fours. One odd couple was the drunk from the bus and a passenger whose name was Mr. Moritz Feibusch. The stewards had put them together because they were the only two Jews.

After putting away the lines and cables from launching, the crew had made for their bunks or their watch stations. In the very bow, by the nose cone, at the top of the stairs, Eric Spehl had coiled up the bow landing lines. First port, then starboard had been worked down in the classic seamen's style: free line in the right hand into the coil in his left hand, clockwise, both palms down. The lines were made up in their places on the shelf inside the bow.

Rigger Hans Freund had done the same thing at the top of the stairway where the lower horizontal fin joined the belly of the ship: port line, then starboard. Then he set the coils in their place at the bottom of the stairs, and went forward for coffee.

Chief Knorr would be on the first watch; followed by Freund, then Spehl; one watch always on, one standing by—but mostly drinking coffee and gossiping in the crew's mess, and one watch asleep in the bunk. When the watch changed, the off-coming watch got the bunk. Experienced men wasted no time talking, getting to sleep immediately—because in four hours they would be called again for stand-by.

Hamburg radioed DEKKA, the call letters of the *Hindenburg*, to warn of a squall line over the North Sea: thunder, lightning, turbulence. Willy Speck sent the message down to Captain Pruss. After greeting his passengers, and sampling the supper, and drinking a glass of cold mineral water, Pruss had hurried back to the gondola.

The political situation required them to avoid France (the French had even threatened anti-aircraft fire) and to detour around England. The course, therefore, was laid out down the Rhine to Holland, over the Ooster Schelde Estuary, out to sea over Flushing, then southwest in a zig through the English Channel past the white cliffs of Dover to starboard, and Folkstone Light, then to the North Atlantic.

The lights in the gondola were dimmed—almost like wartime. The lights of the compass and of the hydrogen pressure valves glowed a dull red—the least damaging glare to night vision.

They followed the Rhine first. Down below they could see sparks from a train's smokestack marking its course. The gondola searchlight picked the engine out from an altitude of about 800 feet. The train answered with a long hoot of its whistle.

Over Holland the crazy-quilt patchwork of the canals reflected rainbows when the light played on them. From the open windows it was possible to hear dogs barking below. Then they sighted the Channel— very rough waters. A big three-stacker was rolling scupper to scupper. The first scud of the approaching squall line obscured her from view.

Watch Officer Bauer read and reported the ship's own weather map. A strong thunderstorm front was moving fast from west to east. Captain Pruss ordered course north to skirt around it, but passage that way looked closed. They attempted to circle the front to the south by going over Belgium, but the big storm had spread out over the land there. Again they turned and headed north, turned into the black canyons of clouds, and steered for the back side of the front. Lightning played both port and starboard, but there was no creaking and groaning, no rolling as a ship would in the gale. Rain belted down on the linen cover. It sounded like surf.

On the back side of the front the *Hindenburg* gained the Channel. Bauer's maps showed a depression situated over Ireland with a projection of the depression to the south. Captain Pruss decided on a course WSW towards a point about 47.5 degrees north and 50 degrees west. There would be head winds. By then it was about 2:00 A.M. Frankfurt time.

Above them and forward Captain Lehmann had turned in. Behind them, except for three die-hards smoking and drinking in the bar, the passenger cabins of the great floating palace were dark.

# CHAPTER 5

# MEN OF GOOD WILL

"Two souls, alas! dwell in my heart together
The one seeks separation from the other."
—*Faust*, GOETHE

TUESDAY, May 4, 1937. Out over the Atlantic the sun rose at 5:12 Greenwich Mean Time. If the sky had not been overcast, Max Zabel (or any of the other navigators aboard the *Hindenburg*) could have calculated the sidereal time.

Behind them in the weather center the charts showed a trough—a small depression—extended from Ireland out over the middle ocean; the center of it being about 1010 millibars and at about 47 north and 38 west. By circling to the north of this small depression and its trough, they could possibly pick up easterly winds, and gain some of the time lost over the channel. In addition to reports from ships at sea, Chief Willy Speck and Radiomen Herbert Dowe, Franz Eichelmann, and Egon Schweikart monitored the radio broadcasts from land. There was another low coming from Quebec. New York had sunny, fair temperatures expected in the high seventies; London, showers, but clearing; Berlin, sunny, seventies.

Ludwig Felber, formerly rigger in the tutelage of Chief Knorr, was beginning his apprenticeship at the elevator wheel. Apprentice Navigator Eduard Boetius (and formerly helmsman) checked Felber's course, made drift calculations, recorded the weather and barometer, drew the radio fixes on the mid-Atlantic charts, determined and logged the mileage for the watch—Captain Sammt's watch. He sup-

posed that after breakfast the other captains would each visit the
gondola. Captain Wittemann really belonged on the *Graf Zeppelin*
where he was Captain von Schiller's relief officer. Captains Sammt
and Bauer would have their own commands just as soon as the Corporation could build them. When the LZ 130 and LZ 131 were completed they would need navigators like Eduard Boetius and helmsmen
like Ludwig Felber. For the moment, however, the Corporation had
too many captains, too many navigators and too many helmsmen. But
then in time, things would be better.

Miss Margaret Mather woke and rose. The bunk was furnished
with fine linen sheets and soft blankets. The flower vase still stood
beside her bed. She stared down at an angry sea, long streaks of white
foam trailed behind the grey shoulders of the waves.

Always the wretched sailor, she began to enjoy travel by Zeppelin
immensely. It was a gloomy day, but up above the Atlantic there
would be no need of the "handgrips" of ships; none of the vibration
of a fast liner's propeller shafts. She used the clouds on the horizon to
detect the slightest rolling. With the sea below like that, it must be
very windy.

And what comfort, she thought. She reminded herself that the
*Mayflower* pilgrims had slept on board shelves and rag piles inside a
bare hull. Nowadays, she mused, man measured his victories over nature by the hundreds of miles he could put between his dinner and his
breakfast. She admitted to herself that both man in general and Miss
Margaret Mather in particular were more interested in dinners, and
especially breakfasts, than sunrises and sunsets. Even if man had the
speed of the sun itself and could fly constantly in dawn's early light,
he would require the regulation number of breakfasts. She dressed
and made her way to the dining saloon.

Outside there was a veil of mist. Drops of rain traced paths aft on
the windows. They were sailing through some grey world which
drifted by without distinction. Nothing had definite angles or shapes.
But inside, in the dining saloon, a lively little world was droning west.
Stewards moved in and out of the yellow cones the lamps on the
tables cast. Cups rattled and silver clinked. There was the smell of

sausage, coffee, rolls, jams, and eggs. There were the quick, curious exchanges of passengers discovering each other.

Actually, Colonel Nelson Morris and Major J. Burtis Dolan were old friends. They had stayed up late in the bar, got up early to shower and "have a stroll." The showers were down on "B" deck. The shower nozzle looked big enough to rinse all the passengers in a single group. But Steward Severin Klein stood by to warn them that, regardless of how the soaping had progressed, the *wasser* shut off automatically when the indicator in the *badezimmer* showed *so*.

An airship must ration everything by weight, there was no margin for wastage anywhere. The chairs in the lounge or the table in the bar could be lifted with one finger; they were specially designed affairs of aluminum and canvas. But the sitting was as pleasant as in a fine club chair, and the shower was hot even if short.

Colonel Morris had convinced Major Dolan to take the *Hindenburg*. Dolan could surprise his wife and four children in Chicago by an early arrival. They would connect by plane from Newark. Quicker by a day than the Broadway Limited.

Morris had made the trip across before, and was a fund of information on the pleasures of the voyage. He was himself a flyer, though neither his rank of Lieutenant Colonel, nor Dolan's rank of Major, were "active" at the time. Their ranks were rewards of the Great War. Dolan imported perfume from Paris to Chicago. He was 47.

Colonel Morris had business interests in Chicago too. The Morris Meat Packing Company had merged into the P.D. Armour Company around the turn of the century. It was said that the Morris house in Chicago, Homewood, was a showplace.

Actually, Colonel Morris spent most of his time in Paris. His first wife had been Jeanne Aubert, the musical comedy star. He knew socially a great number of people in Paris, London, Rome and Berlin: people like Anna May Wong, the movie star; Sir Hubert and Lady Wilkins—he was the famous explorer and had introduced Morris to the pleasures of Zeppelins in 1929. Morris' second wife, Blanche Bilboa, was also well known on the Paris stage. She had not been able to make this trip to Chicago. As a matter of fact, she rarely got to Chicago. She had so many commitments. By flying both ways, Colonel Morris could return all the sooner. Major Dolan would be good company.

At breakfast Colonel Morris and Major Dolan did in a basket of rolls between them and several extra pots of coffee. There was no hurry. They discussed the great difficulties the bus strike had caused London with their fellow passenger, George Grant, London Assistant Office Manager of Hamburg-American Lines.

The city had been jammed when he had left: tourists preparing to have a glimpse of the coronation of George VI. Grant had seen the King take the barge trip down the Thames. "Couldn't move about the city, though, absolutely jammed."

The coronation was just a week away. Mrs. Simpson's divorce was final yesterday. "Ship's radio news had it. Edward, poor fellow, has appeared from his secret retreat in Austria and is said to be flying to meet her—though not in England, of course."

The three men examined the mural on the wall of the dining room. Twenty-one panels traced the history of exploration. George Grant believed airships would take over a great proportion of transatlantic trade in just a few years.

Colonel Morris noted that Dick Merrill had taken on a contract to fly newspictures of the coronation from London to New York, regardless of the weather! Major Dolan cited the news that flying boats were going to inaugurate a service to Bermuda before the summer was out.

All three agreed that the main use of airplanes was at war. In the past week the Franco forces had obliterated a Basque town—on market day—called Guernica, greatly aiding Franco's advance against the Loyalists in Bilbao. That's where planes were unmatched—as airborne artillery.

It was agreed the planes were actually flown by German pilots. At any rate, they appeared to be German planes. An exciting subject!

After breakfast they continued their discussions in the smoking room, while the steward supplied them with extra coffee. Too early for a decent drink. There was little else to do.


Colonel Erdmann wanted a chance to consult with Captain Lehmann alone. They agreed to meet in the officers' mess after breakfast. Over a coffee, Colonel Erdmann reviewed his fears.

He supposed that Captain Lehmann had received a copy of the

letter from Washington. He summarized the information he had on the "very dangerous passengers"—the Adelts, Joseph Spah and Douglas—they had on board. He omitted Feibusch because, well because it was too silly. Exactly how did Captain Lehmann think they should go about finding a saboteur, or a *Höllenmaschine*, aboard this Zeppelin?

Captain Lehmann tamped tobacco into his pipe: "Colonel, I have known Leonhard Adelt a good many years. He is my biographer. I have known Gertrud Adelt for four years now. They have had some troubles with the present regime, but a great many people have, you know."

He paused to perfect the seating of his tobacco in its bowl. Just as many other pipe smokers had found, he could use the pleasure of his habit to give other people time to think.

Something had suddenly occurred to Colonel Erdmann. "Is it all right to smoke here?"

"Yes, yes, of course. We are safe here. Would you prefer a cigar? No, well here are some matches to go with your cigarettes. It is a long walk back to the smoking saloon.

"Colonel, this Zeppelin is no different than the rest of life, nor any different than our experience in war. You and I are practical men. I think we must deal primarily with the probabilities. We cannot manage every eventuality. If we were to take fright at every possibility, we would not fly at all, is this not true?"

He had his pipe going on the first match. He drew down the first puffs with deliberation. The thing he had to do was to lay out all the facts for Colonel Erdmann.

"You know, Colonel, that the people in Berlin are not very pleased with our Dr. Eckener, but this does not make him a danger to our ships. At least no more dangerous than Mr. and Mrs. Adelt, or say, I am myself."

Captain Lehmann began to trace out the basic elements of the situation for his Luftwaffe companion. Certainly it was true, he agreed, that there had been threats against the Zeppelins. Zeppelin men had found threats to be a common occurrence. For some reason the shape of the airships, their presence in the sky over the great cities, attracted the attention of the unstable. Since the swastikas had been added, or perhaps because recently the new regime had upset quite a number of people, there had been quite an increase in the number of threats. But this information was available in newspapers or in rathskellers, and rumors of threats need not come from the S.S.

Zeppelins were great demonstrations of aeronautical progress. Since the very first days of the *Graf Zeppelin*, the men of the Luftschiffbau had been accustomed to envy as well as cheers. And they had a saying, based on their experience, that dogs barked at Zeppelins as well as the moon, and nothing could be done to stop them in either case.

Well, of course, they should take every precaution. Thanks to the procedures at Frankfurt, and those instituted on board, no one had on his person a match, a lighter, a flashbulb, a flashlight—because they contained dry cell batteries from which a bomb might be manufactured, except for a certain Luftwaffe colonel who now had his own matches, no?

Thanks to the cooperation of Berlin, Emil Stoeckle had already examined the mail with the special equipment, and there existed no possibility there. The passengers' baggage had been thoroughly checked. The freight manifest was skimpy for this trip. They were carrying two dogs, still and motion picture news films, airplane parts, publicity material for the Hamburg American Line in New York, tobacco leaf samples, and three fertile partridge eggs. All the freight had been checked as it was loaded. Even, said Captain Lehmann with an encouraging smile, the partridge eggs.

Well, one dog was consigned to a Mr. Fred Muller in Philadelphia. The other belonged to Mr. Spah. But he could assure Colonel Erdmann, having seen to the matter last night, that Mr. Spah would not visit his dog without being accompanied by a responsible crew member.

It was customary to take those passengers who might enjoy it for a tour of the ship. He had arranged for the ship's doctor, young Dr. Kurt Ruediger, to conduct the tour. He was an entirely reliable man, actually a *Sturmabteilung* (S.A.) man. Excellent not only in discipline, but very enthusiastic about Zeppelins.

Captain Lehmann was well aware that due to the political situation, Berlin was more anxious about the safety of Zeppelins than heretofore. However, reasonable men must keep in mind that causing a big commotion looking for a saboteur among the passengers would be almost as damaging to the reputation of the Zeppelins as the discovery of an actual bomb. It would be particularly damaging in the press, given the situation in Berlin, to make a fuss about what might turn out later to be a perfectly innocent passenger. As for the crew, Captain Lehmann could assure him that the men of the Zeppelin family were reliable.

Colonel Erdmann had to agree. But he was depressed. He realized that Berlin's information was the gossip of cooks—and he had no facts with which an exact conclusion could be arranged. Captain Lehmann was certainly reasonable, and should have been reassuring. Surely a vague mood of uneasiness was no fitting estimation of the situation for a trained German officer. The two men stood. Captain Lehmann said he'd have to get back to the gondola.

Colonel Erdmann rejoined a number of passengers at the windows of the promenade and watched the sea passing below. Perhaps, he thought, he was too anxious to end the long symposium. For seven years now at the secret airfields, at the Intelligence School at Halle, in the company of officers and friends—indeed on the radio and in the newspapers and on the streets there had been nothing but symposia. He knew from his experience of the men he had commanded that they were all (he included himself too) longing to come to some Damascus.

They were weary of textbook responsibilities. They had abandoned themselves to the faith of a new Germany, not all at once, but gradually. The talk of action was incessant, yet there really was no action. Now they were ready to move mountains. They needed to have at hand some concrete acts—something by which they could redeem themselves for their new enthusiasms. Heaven knows Germany's energies had been reawakened by the Berlin regime, but too much talk was getting to be a strain.

He was a mature enough man to realize that he was feeling sorry for himself, that he too had caught the fever, that now that he was aboard this Zeppelin and free for the moment from the daily excitements of the new politics, he was bored—they were all bored, and inventing, as a relief from all the talk, things which might happen. An event, any event, would be a relief.

Take his own case. What really had happened? The stupid Gestapo had collected some gossip from their usual unreliable sources. Then frightened by their own dreams they had managed to pass responsibility for the matter to the S.S., who in turn, to keep their political knives honed, had managed to pass the responsibility on to the Luftwaffe, all of which provided great excitement for all the schemers along the way. They could lie abed in the morning and dream of the moves they would make, the reports they could file, the postures they could take. Even if it were a requisition for a box of paper clips, it would be important, a matter of life and death. Their memoranda would require composition, dictation, copies made, countersigned, filed. Everything was important, nothing was unimportant lest its manager be unimportant too. The only trouble with that train of thought, he reminded himself, is that in this case if there really was going to be a bomb aboard this Zeppelin, it would be important. He wished he hadn't told Dorothea anything. He wished she hadn't come to see him off.

He was interrupted at that point by the pretty blue-eyed Mrs. Adelt. She joined him by the window. With a charming laugh she asked: "Herr Erdmann, you seem to have lost your best friend. Why so glum?"

Ashamed, he admitted in a low voice: "I feel strange on this ship."

Chief Heinrich Kubis was in his element. He unlocked the bookcases in the reading rooms. There were bound magazines, and novels. He sold writing paper and Hindenburg stamps. He explained how the passenger might post his letter from the library in a special tube which carried it directly by pneumatic pressure to the ship's own post office. The device always amazed the passengers. It really always delighted Kubis more. He had playing cards ready. He had chess and chinese checkers. At 11 o'clock he would serve bouillon, just like on the best ocean liners. Some of the passengers had said they were cold. He had summoned Chief Sauter who had found the fresh air vents wide open, closed them, and the situation was corrected.

Mr. Philip Mangone was remaining in his cabin. He was miserable with a cold. Chief Kubis had supplied him with an electric heater. The old couple, Mr. and Mrs. Ernst, sat side by side in the lounge staring through the windows, though in the weather they traveled there was nothing to see. They asked for blankets for their knees.

Stewardess Frau Emilie Imhoff, a good widow of 47, had been playing with the two Doehner boys on the floor of the dining saloon.
They were well-behaved, properly dressed German boys. The younger
one, who said his name was Werner, and that he was six, had a toy—
Mickey Mouse sat in a car which was wound up, then ran across the
floor. But it made sparks, and Chief Kubis confiscated it. He explained to the boys (and to Frau Imhoff): "We take no chances with
sparks on a Zeppelin."

Mr. Spah had wished to visit his dog again. Chief Kubis personally
accompanied the clown down the narrow catwalk to the stern. Mr.
Spah was astonished when he saw the inside of the great ship in the
daylight.

At night from the catwalk the interior seemed solidly enclosed, but
during the day, though still dark inside, the light shone through the
linen fabric stretched over the rings, girders, and struts. Mr. Spah
could see for himself that in the places where the catwalk had no
handrails, only the canvas covering stood between him and the sea.

"But it is truly dangerous!" said Mr. Spah.

"It certainly should not trouble a circus acrobat," Chief Kubis replied.

At the little freight room aft, Mr. Spah was surprised to find another dog beside his own in transit. With the daylight his Ulla
seemed more settled. "Ja, ja, mein liebchen, not yet a day in the air
and you are an old Zeppelin dog, eh? It's all right. Just two more
nights and we shall be in Douglaston and you shall have children to
play with."

On the way back, Mr. Spah said he would never send a dog by air
again. The poor dog had no way to run about, or relieve herself
cleanly. Mr. Kubis pointed out that conditions were no better on the
liners, and a two-day voyage was better than six days.

Before lunch, Joseph Spah joined a number of men in the bar. The
photographer, Karl Otto Clemens, was there. So were Moritz
Feibusch and William Leuchtenburg, Eric Knoescher—the importer
from Zeulenroda, and Otto Reichold from Vienna. There was a long
discussion of the Kentucky Derby coming up Saturday. War Admiral
was the listed favorite.

Colonel Morris and Major Dolan were developing strategy in
the Pacific. With the Washington Naval Treaty abandoned, Japan

was a threat to the Philippines. If the Philippines were threatened, the whole Pacific basin was in danger. The Panama Canal might be destroyed in a day by air. America would need a two-ocean Navy to protect both her coasts from the follies of Europe and the ambitions of Japan.

"America must be ready to stand on her own two sea legs," said Colonel Morris. He was a bit proud of that.

Joseph Spah said that reminded him of the story about the woman who had two suitors. Both were rich men, but the handsomer of the two had a wooden leg from the war. When she got pregnant, she confronted them both and said they must choose between them who was to play father to the child. The one with the wooden leg said that to be fair they should wait until the child was born. Then if it had a wooden leg, he would do his duty.

Major Dolan didn't see how that had much to do with war in the Pacific, but George Grant thought it was jolly good. They all went into lunch together.

A telegram was delivered from the radio room for Edward H. Douglas just before lunch. It wasn't in code—it just looked odd to Radio Watch Officer Dowe. It said: "AFTER YOU LEFT FIRST LOCAL UMPIRES SEARCHED YOUR DUGOUT STOP FOUND NO FOUL BALLS STOP BUT YOU'LL HAVE TO HOLDUP AT SECOND STOP WELCOME HOME REILLY."

He supposed that Reilly in New York was telling him the Gestapo had searched his office-apartment at 56 Neue Mainzer Strasse in Frankfurt and found nothing. He'd be staying home now, and wouldn't go back. Well that was the end of that.

His secretary was Jewish, though. The people from Dr. Goebbels' office downstairs had complained of her, but he had told them to go to hell. What would become of her now? She would have no American businessman to protect her. She was young and quite pretty too.

At lunch Moritz Feibusch explained to William G. Leuchtenburg that he had paid passage for two nephews from Berlin to San Francisco, and had arranged jobs for them in a tuna factory in Oakland.

Feibusch traveled to Germany each year to sell the products of California. He had a very wide acquaintance in Europe. He sold "fancy goods"—packages of preserves, dried prunes, raisins, sugared oranges and lemons—which German, Viennese, Hungarian, in fact many peoples, put up in pretty boxes as gifts in Christmas season. In the new cellophane boxes, the candied fruits were also very popular for the ship sailings and weddings. In what looked like a transparent hat box, they put all kinds of candied fruits and nuts. Tied with pink ribbons. Decorated with, maybe apple blossoms. $4.94. More substantial than flowers.

Feibusch and Leuchtenburg were sharing their table for two against the wall. Perhaps Leuchtenburg had an extra cocktail, maybe two, before lunch. He was listening to Feibusch's story of "fancy goods," but he seemed either pained or vacant. He certainly didn't eat much.

Feibusch explained he planned to bring his mother to San Francisco on his next round trip. The old woman had refused to leave "her Germany," the Germany of her husband, but in the past month the Government had passed an order that Jewish orphans and Jewish old people were not to be allowed to take up valuable space in German orphanages and German old people's homes. There were signs now, painted on the benches of the Kurfeurstendamm Strasse which read: "Nicht für Juden!"

Moritz Feibusch and his wife had no children. The old woman would get better care in San Francisco, which was a lovely city and a place Mr. Leuchtenburg should visit; his mother's Germany was gone now, anyway, and she should realize it. The arrangements were all made, he said. She could fly with him by Zeppelin because business was good in California. He was proud he could pay for such a flight. The papers had been difficult to get, but with a little money here and there in the right places, as it were, he would fetch her on his round trip in October, which was the time he sold his Easter goods, and brokered the winter tuna fish.

When they rose from lunch, they stopped in the passageway running across the ship between the dining saloon and the promenade lounge. In a niche at the head of the stairs a bust of Marshal von Hindenburg rode facing forward. And there was a big map of the Atlantic Ocean next to the ship's bulletin board. Every few hours a steward moved the little red flag which marked their progress westward.

They noticed the ship's clock had been set back two hours. The time they had spent at lunch must be passed through again. Steward Balla explained to them that the clock would be set back again before lunch tomorrow. In that way the total time difference between Germany and New York would be adjusted most comfortably.

Moritz Feibusch took that to be a lesson in philosophy: look, he said, no matter where the hands of the clock pointed, every man must live in his own allotted time.

William Leuchtenburg wanted to know whether the clocks would be set back before or after the noon opening of the bar.

"After," Balla replied, which seemed fair to both gentlemen.

At lunch, Leonhard and Gertrud Adelt had agreed to go in the first of two tours of the airship at four o'clock. Dr. Ruediger would be the guide. In the meantime they spent the two hours they had gained by the adjustment of the clocks side by side in their cabin.

They were sharing the one reading light in the lower bunk. It was too narrow for them both, but they arranged themselves for each other. In the comfort of their common touch, they could read slowly and with pleasure—in fact, without moving she could read a paragraph from his book, then return to her own. They were a most unusual couple. Not only were they in love with each other, they liked each other too. Both were journalists.

When Miss Gertrud Stolte had been an assistant editor on the Arts Desk of the Dresden paper, the Arts Editor had fallen sick and was absent for several months. She thought it a stroke of good fortune. She would cover art, the theatre, music and books herself, and show what she could do. But the publisher apparently thought she was too young, and a woman besides, and arranged on a temporary basis for Leonhard Adelt from Munich to fill in.

She was furious. Before he arrived she had visions of being under the thumb of a dry old man. She knew he was twenty years her senior. It turned out, however, that he was very handsome, very patient with her ambitions, charming, and besides he was a superb journalist. She admired his skill and his strength.

He found that not only did she have a quick tongue, but that instinct which a few women have, something which cannot be learned or imitated, something which must be wholly natural: absolutely perfect taste—a gift like perfect pitch. She was also very lively and certainly very pretty. Fortunately, he was already divorced and they could be married. If they had not had the sweetness of each other's company, it might have been a bitter time for two journalists.

Leonhard Adelt was well known in journalism. He had covered the Austrian front in the Great War, then been Munich's correspondent for Berlin's *Tageblatt*. After Hitler came to power, the Adelts were both in trouble, and the trouble was a most serious kind. Dachau's concentration camp had been opened by the S.A. for the "reeducation" of the prime targets of the regime: trade unionists, Catholic leaders, and journalists.

The Nazi party doctrine was explicit and detailed. Before the "Jewish question" could be approached, the influence of any possible opposition must first be eradicated. What was so chilling was that men like Wronsky could be a director of Lufthansa and a member of the party, while monks and editors were sent to camps because someday in the future they would object to the party court which would expel "a man of Jewish blood." The party was very logical, and far-sighted.

Not only were the Adelts journalists, they could be identified as Catholic intellectuals. They were known to be close friends of the Austrian Jew, Stefan Zweig, whose books were burned by the universities. And the danger to their independent minds came not only from the S.S., whose ranks included a great number of intellectuals, but precisely because when books were burned they were heaped on the fires by students, led by their professors. The Adelts were in danger from their peers. And the Adelts could not help but have differences with a nation whose gods were Wagnerian, and whose moral sophistications were drawn from Nietzsche.

"Freedom," their friends would quote Nietzsche, "means that the manly instincts that delight in war and victory have gained mastery over the other instincts—for example, over the instinct for 'happiness.' The man who has become free—and how much more the mind that has become free—spurns the contemptible sort of well-being dreamed of by shopkeepers, Christians, cows, women, Englishmen and other democrats."

The Adelts' friend, Stefan Zweig, moved to England. Leonhard Adelt became the aviation editor of the *Deutsche Allgemeine*. By dealing with technical subjects he could avoid the dangers of making uncomfortable distinctions which might anger the great newspapers' mass audiences, or instigate the critical jealousy of a "friend."

The Schriftleiter Decree of October 1933 established the press as "a public institution." Journalists were ruled to be semi-state officials, independent of their publishers or private interests. This, said Dr. Goebbels, was true freedom of the press because "it is better to serve the State than an employer." The decree obligated the working journalists to keep out of the press, among other things, anything likely "to weaken the strength of the German Reich at home or abroad, its unity, armament, culture, or economy, or to violate the religious feelings of others."

The list of subjects not to be reported grew to be incredibly long, but to reveal what was on the list was in itself treason, and the penalty for treason was beheading. It was said they shined a bright light into your eyes to blind and surprise in the moment before the axe descended.

Since the list of taboos was so long, the newspapers began to get dull. Dr. Goebbels complained that the party had no intention of creating "a lap-dog press." The formula was to be "monoform in will, but polyform in expressing that will." Newspapers were to be more courageous, and spurred on to be "brighter." The government's instructions on each day's news were issued at a daily press conference in the Propaganda Ministry. The editor in Dresden sent Gertrud Stolte-Adelt to Berlin to get some "brightness" into the Culture columns.

At the conference she attended, the day was spent specifying that reviews of motion pictures which starred Pola Negri were to be favorable, because she was of Aryan blood; but those of George M. Cohan were to be panned because he was a Jew. Gertrud Adelt laughed at their confusion with Cohan's Irish name. She refused to waste any more time at the Ministry's conferences. They lifted her press card, because, they said, "She obviously didn't use it." But without a press card, the law said, Gertrud Stolte could not work.

Leonhard Adelt got what work there was. He did small brochures on aviation. He did some translating from foreign languages. From Zweig he learned the way to escape the hypocritical bourgeois world was "flight into the world of adventure."

He began a collaboration with his old friend, Ernst Lehmann, on what would be issued as Captain Lehmann's autobiography. It would be published in the fall of 1937 in New York and London by Longmans, Green and Company. In Germany it was to be titled *Zeppelin, the Story of Lighter-than-air Craft.* Although the manuscripts of Lehmann's biography had been left at home, Adelt had with him on the *Hindenburg* a film script about Zeppelins which would be produced in Hollywood.

So even while Foreign Minister Ribbentrop was saying, "Intellectuals are a luxury—most of them parasites, anyway—we've put a stop to them before they carried their pernicious activities too far," the Adelts were surviving. And Leonhard Adelt would write a biography of Germany's greatest technical pride, the *Hindenburg* and its Captain.

Usually Captain Lehmann conducted the tours through the airship himself. With Captain Pruss now in command, perhaps he felt like a supernumerary. In any case, he was keeping to his cabin. In his stead, Dr. Ruediger assembled the first group at four o'clock in the promenade lounge. Everyone would have to put on sneakers first.

Steward Nunnenmacher had a box of various sizes. None of them quite fit, but it wouldn't matter. Bending over their laces in the first group were the Adelts, Mr. George Hirschfeld, Peter Belin, Dr. Birger Brinck, young Miss Doehner, and Joseph Spah.

Dr. Ruediger had only finished his internship at Bremen the year before. His ambition had been to travel—perhaps as a ship's doctor—before he had to settle down to practice. From his S.A. Yachting club, he had hit upon the idea of writing Captain Lehmann, noting their common interest in sailing, and suggesting himself as the first airship doctor. After a series of interviews, the Zeppelin men had accepted him and his enthusiasm for air travel had been part of their reward. He was taking over the tours because he said he was best qualified to supervise "health and education."

In Ruediger's tour group the first one to get his sneakers on was Joseph Spah. He stood up and stared down at them sticking out from under his trouser cuffs. The sneakers were far too large. They flopped at the end of his toes like a clown's. Spah met the occasion immediately. He improvised a short soft-shoe routine. The beginnings of a buck and wing ended with his ankles crossed as if he were

a ballerina at the end of a pas de deux—his fingers locked and swaying near the floor. Then he straightened to attention, transformed
into an imitation of Charlie Chaplin, and with Chaplin's walk stuck
two fingers of his left hand under his nose to make the moustache,
marched up to Dr. Ruediger, saluting with his right: "Sieg Heil, Herr
Doctor, Ready!"

It was a child's trick, all done in a twinkling. Everyone smiled and a
few even laughed. But there was an awkward moment before
Ruediger turned for the stairs. As Gertrud Adelt thought: These
days one could never feel certain of other persons even though this
great floating palace should have been a great place for happiness.

The tour passed through the doors of Steward Kubis' little office.
"This is the way to my dog," said Spah to sixteen-year-old Miss
Doehner. But her attention was already concentrated on the young
Yale graduate, Peter Belin. He held the compartment doors open, she
thought, for her as if she were a princess. But then she wondered,
had he really noticed her? What misery, she thought, if he were only
holding them gallantly for everyone.

They stopped first in the kitchen to examine the electric ranges.
There was a young cabin boy there, Werner Franz, only fourteen,
peeling potatoes. He served the officers' mess.

Chef Xavier Maier took a clipboard down from the wall and read
off the list of provisions. Besides fresh spinach, and a fine wine list,
the storage rooms of the *Hindenburg* upon leaving Frankfurt held
5,500 pounds of fresh meat and chicken, 220 pounds of fish, 330
pounds of delicatessen items—including caviar, 440 pounds of butter,
cheese and marmalade, 800 eggs. Of beverages besides the wine, there
were 55 gallons of mineral water and 33 gallons of milk.

They went on into the ship and passed the fuel and water tanks.
Dr. Ruediger explained the 25 tanks for the four Daimler engines
started the trip with 137,500 pounds of fuel. As the fuel was consumed, the ship became lighter. In fact, as the passengers consumed
the food and used some for their own energy (but wasted the rest),
the ship lost weight.

As the ship lost weight, its hydrogen increased its lift. The Captain
could "valve off hydrogen" to compensate for the lost fuels—human
and diesel—or choose to collect rain water for added ballast as they
flew along. The weather on this trip was perfect for collecting ballast.

The water ballast contained in the ship's tanks weighed 22,000 pounds. If the sun came out, dried the ship and heated the hydrogen, some gas would have to be valved to maintain the ship's trim. At night then, when it cooled, water ballast could be let out to increase the lift. Relatively minute amounts were used during any trip—perhaps 7% of the 7,000,000 cubic feet of hydrogen might be valved, and have to be replaced. But there were controls, which they could see in the command gondola, by which all the hydrogen and all the water could be dumped at once.

The group continued down the narrow lower walkway to the stern. When they passed the freight compartment in which Joseph Spah's dog was kept, he announced he would stop for a moment "to say hello."

Dr. Ruediger tried to explain to him that the tour group must stay together, those were his instructions.

"Well, good," said Spah, "then you can all visit my Ulla, but she is young and excitable so please don't frighten her."

Dr. Ruediger said Mr. Spah could come back later with a steward as an escort and visit with his dog then. The tour was scheduled to be finished at five o'clock, when he must take the next group. Wouldn't Mr. Spah please come along.

"Well, then go ahead," said Spah. "I shall catch up to you in a moment, goodness, even Zeppelins are run now like concentration camps, eh?"

That did it. Dr. Ruediger took the group on. He would be forced to report this. That Mr. Spah was insufferable. Ruediger was still flushed as they descended the two flights of stairs into the tail at Ring 62. He had mocked the Fuehrer too, for that's what it was, mockery.

Ruediger explained the emergency steering controls located there beneath the huge rudders. Everyone had a chance to look out the tail fin's windows and see the Atlantic only 800 feet below. In the afternoon's mist it had a milky white effect.

Then they climbed the stairs again, where Joseph Spah was waiting for them. Dr. Ruediger led the way up the ladder which led from the lower gangway to the middle gangway—or axial girder—at Ring 62, between Gas Cells IV and V.

When Ruediger was almost all the way up, he could hear Spah say to someone below him waiting his turn to ascend: "That Doctor better watch out. I will report him for cruelty to dogs, because he wouldn't let my dog have a visit from her best friend. How would that be?"

Then on the middle gangway, when they were all up, Spah discovered he could make his sneakers squeak by dragging them against the rubber sheeting which was its carpet. Ruediger pretended not to notice.

They walked along Indian file in a forest of wires and lines. The giant gas cells sagged and billowed in the drafts of the ship's interior like the wrinkled paunches of emaciated and very old elephants. When they came to the first of the lateral cross-walks leading out to the engine gondolas, Dr. Ruediger asked who would like to go across to gondola #3. Gertrud Adelt said she would, but when she came to the front she realized the little door led out to a gangway suspended over the sea. There was nothing but a thin guide rail to windward, and the wind was rushing by at 80 knots. She hesitated.

Someone in the group laughed, though perhaps it wasn't at her, but at their own fears. She unpinned her "leghorn" hat and handed it to her husband. Then she scrambled across the open space. At the engine gondola's door Mechanic Johnny Doerflein gathered her in.

Inside the nacelle she could look out a window to starboard as the ship sailed through the low rain clouds. The noise was almost unbearable, like the hammers of Hell, she said later. The trip back across the space left her trembling. Leonhard took her hand, until they had to go Indian file again to the bow.

Except for the windows in the upper skin through which the navigators took their star sights—and which cast large squares of diffused light down into the ship—the bow was an utterly silent, gloomy place. No motors aft could be heard. Because of the streamlining of the snout, not even the wind made any noise as it tumbled by. Everyone was pleased to descend the arc of the stairway which led again to the lower gangway. It had windows spaced along its length from which the crew at landings could look down. Stopping at its foot and looking back up its arch it looked like one of those paths up the side of a temple in one of Hollywood's jungle movies.

In twos and threes they descended into the gondola and saw the controls and wheels of the captains. Then up again and a look into the radio room, then aft on the port side of "B" deck through the officers' mess and the crew's mess, to arrive at the bottom of the main stairs. There they divided, some to go around the corner into the bar, and some up to "A" deck for tea. They figured they had covered about 600 yards for the round trip.

At about the same time the passengers were taking tea, Commander Charles E. Rosendahl was asking the Army at nearby Camp Dix for extra men. They were needed to aid the local fire departments struggling with a pesky fire northwest of the Naval Air Station. Smoke from the burning scrub oak and stunt pine was drifting in a black pall over the field. Rosendahl got his help after lunch.

Lunchtime in New Jersey was dinnertime in Frankfurt. The offices of the Zeppelin Corporation were closing for the night. Frau Beatrice Friederich appeared to ask about the progress of the *Hindenburg*. She was told that everything was perfectly normal.

The six o'clock news was broadcast into the lounge of the *Hindenburg*. It pleased George W. Hirschfeld: both in Europe and in New York cotton was up 9 to 12 points. There were few sellers. Unwanted rainfall in Mississippi and Alabama was said to have influenced sentiment on the exchanges. Texas was too dry. Cotton seemed to be coming back. Last month it had been down nearly $10 a bale, and George Hirschfeld often traded as much as 50,000 bales.

Big George Hirschfeld was 36, and except for the cut of his clothes, his perfectly clipped moustache, and his exquisite manners, he could have passed for the rangy Texas cotton man who would sometimes pass through the happier dreams of showgirls. Not only was he tall, dark, and handsome, but co-partner of the firm, Lentz & Hirschfeld, Cotton Brokers, Bremen.

In addition, he was Vice-President of the board of directors of Aktiengesellschaft für Warpsspinnerei und Staerkerei, Oldenburg; of Bremer Baumwoll Aktiengesellschaft, Bremen; a member of the board of directors of the Bankverein für Nordwest-Deutschland Aktiengesellschaft; of the Industrie und Handelskammer, as well as of the Wirtschaftskammer, Bremen.

George Hirschfeld had impeccable credentials. As showgirls knew, in the infinite reality of their dreams, cotton and money were interchangeable. A few bales of cotton, depending upon the market conditions, were the same thing as a Mercedes, as a box at Longchamps, as a pretty gold ring—and the exchange could always be made regardless of politics, irrespective of who held the reigns of power, and despite any ideas or theories of economics.

Cotton bales were not only a business, they were an art. Trading cotton had always led to a certain amount of confusion among theorists, for they always stumbled in the cane brakes of whether "art was a business," whether "good art was a crime," and such wanderings. Even more so when they tried to impose their theories in the swamps of whether "all business was a crime," and "cotton an art."

The first difficulty of the theorists was insurmountable: cotton was traded internationally. No matter what some theoretician argued its price ought to be, its price at any moment was, by definition, what it was. The price of cotton on any given day depended upon the rainfall next week in a place like Mississippi, an eventuality which was very difficult to legislate and impossible to administer, even for the most powerful of ministers of economics. For cotton brokers, as for artists, the world was disorderly; which was risky, but delightful.

Like money, the uses of cotton were intricate. The same showgirls who instantly understood its value, also used it for bras; priests wore it for surplices; spinning mills wove it; artists and printers colored it; men tied it at their collars; housewives set the evening meal on it. To the extent that Europe (or the United States, for that matter) could be said to be unified at all, it was unified on sheets of cotton—not on fields of war. But then cotton was necessary for tents and uniforms, for parachutes and gun rags.

Cotton grew in the American South (and the Old South had died for it); in Egypt (Pharaohs went to Isis wrapped in it); in the Ukraine (the commissars murdered tens of thousands for it); wherever sun and shade, skill and patience, and attention to detail might be combined. It was these artistic qualities for which the theoreticians had little respect.

Force, their argument ran, was the ingredient necessary to guarantee economic success. As if, with guns at their hip, committees of school teachers and postmasters could put some style into a canvas, or quality into a shirt. But sun and shade are indifferent to that kind of force.

The arrogance of these school teachers depended upon social theories constructed to support the notion that everyone can paint because every kindergarten child does; and that from the point-of-view of the child, his painting was as good as any other. The child, and his teacher, might lack what always raised the envy of their common view: credentials.

George Hirschfeld's credentials were inherited—an obnoxious notion to school teachers. His father had been a cotton broker too. His mother was born in Galveston, Texas. And at 23 George was sent to work for five years back at the cotton plantation in Hearne, Texas, on the Brazos River.

To trade cotton, "credentials," more than capital, were the essential element. "Credentials" won credit from bankers. "Credentials" meant the trader could distinguish between good cotton and poor cotton, between rain in Mississippi and Minnesota. "Credentials" were training, skill, trust, judgment and style: things which the new economic theorists lacked, and in their jealousy, discarded. They thought it was not necessary to have a Texas mother. They thought they could substitute several divisions of tanks to win the same thing.

In 1933 the little men of the party demanded some reward for their political victories. In Bremen, for example, they demanded seats on the Cotton Exchange and on the Board of Trade. The senior members of the Exchanges decided they needed "younger men" who could join the party, and keep the greedy "riff-raff" from taking over. The "younger men" could move up to seats on the Exchange. No good could come from upsetting the traditions of a Hanseatic town like Bremen. The seniors "wanted to keep control of their own institutions." George Hirschfeld joined the party May 1, 1933, Party Card #3075295, and moved up.

In Berlin, Dr. Hjalmar Schacht was the leading theoretician of the new regime. His theory required absolute control over every element in the national economy. He and his staff of economists could make Germany nearly self sufficient: Ersatz and substitute products were encouraged for those that were formerly imported. Certain sacrifices began to be necessary—restaurant menus had to be reduced to a few standard items—but the German people were found to be willing, and none that were unwilling could be found.

A chemist discovered how to make a fuel like gasoline; another showed how to make a synthetic rubber; and another proposed that hydrogen be converted into helium by a secret German process for the benefit of Zeppelins. If the task smacked a bit of alchemy, in most other cases the economic policies of Schacht seemed to work magically, for a while.

In 1929 American exports to Germany totaled a bit over 400 million gold dollars. Dr. Schacht reasoned that Germany did not need these things, and blocked them by tariff and currency regulations. By 1936 Germany's American imports had fallen by 75% to just over 100 million dollars. Partly as a consequence of Dr. Schacht's magic, and partly because American theorists now shared some of his ideas, German exports to the United States shrunk by a like amount: from 280 million gold dollars to about 80 million.

In a period of "miracle" recovery for Germany, trade was being choked off. But the autobahns were being built, and with so many factories making tanks, and planes and guns, who could have known that Germany was broke?

Dr. Schacht knew that he must win foreign exchange if Germany was to pay the bills. To do so Germany would have to sell pharmaceuticals, chemicals, machine tools, cameras, buttons, water heaters, Smyrna rugs, felt materials for making house slippers, and such. Germany offered to barter finished cotton goods from German textile mills for American raw cotton. Not having a Texas mother was an inconvenience; Dr. Schacht had to create his credentials from paper, and though they were unquestioned in Germany, there was no need to accept his word anywhere else.

Washington was very tough about it: they would sell cotton to Germany, but in addition Germany would have to take lard, of which Washington had a surplus. Eventually Dr. Schacht agreed: Germany would accept "cotton dunked in lard."

Lard could be dumped, even though in May 1937 it was down a penny on the Chicago market. The trouble was that university professors in economics often lacked the instincts, the credentials, to switch lard, for say, No. 4 Santos Coffee, and at the right time. The new theorists were visiting places of entertainment for which they lacked the style—as any showgirl could have told them after the first drink.

But George Hirschfeld had the style any working girl admired instantly. He was "quality," which finally the riff-raff had to admit. He

At 3:00 P.M., May 6, 1937, Manhattan had its last look at luxurious lighter-than-air transport. The May sun would soon be obscured by thunderstorms, and the scheduled landing delayed even later.

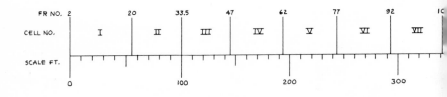

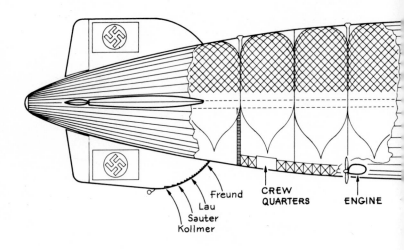

*Some crew positions at 7:21 P.M.*

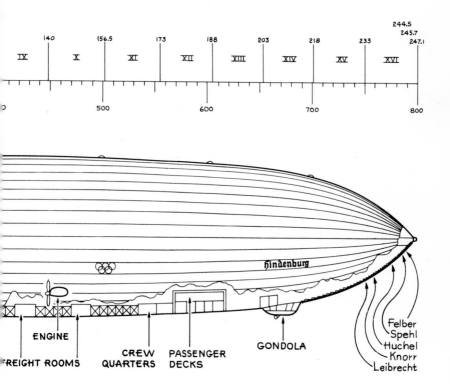

IX     X     XI     XII     XIII     XIV     XV     XVI

140    156.5    173    188    203    218    233    244.5   245.7   247.1

500     600     700     800

Hindenburg

ENGINE

FREIGHT ROOMS    CREW QUARTERS    PASSENGER DECKS    GONDOLA

Felber
Spehl
Huchel
Knorr
Leibrecht

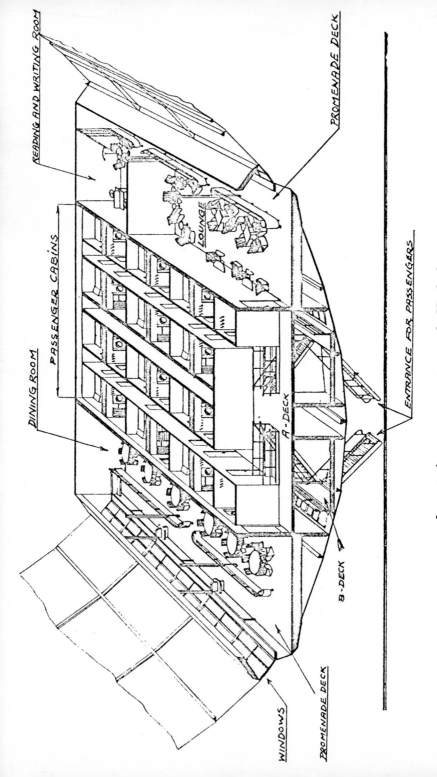

Layout of passenger quarters on the Hindenburg.

At 7:21 the landing lines dropped. The ship was silent as it was being winched down.

*Then more than 100 witnesses saw the fire glowing.*

*The second explosion was stunning. The* Hindenburg *began to sink tail first.*

The National Archives

*From the time the second explosion sounded until the bow crashed to the ground was only 34 seconds. Then they began to hear the screams over the roar of the inferno.*

The Zeppelin Museum

*The next morning soldiers guarded the wreck. Except for a shred of fabric on the tail and the eerie, twisted skeleton, there was nothing left.*

Working beneath the Zeppelin Corporation's swastika, U.S. Postal inspectors and Lufthansa officials catalogued personal effects salvaged from the wreckage. The film inside the camera case in the foreground was intact; thirty-five years later one could view scenes of the Hindenburg's last voyage.

As a board of inquiry investigated, Dr. Eckener was in the public eye one last time. On his right, in wing collar, was Dr. Dürr. Standing behind them, Commander Charles E. Rosendahl.

*Using a model he had built, insulated by three milk bottles and a bread board, and a generating contraption, Michael Fiore of Jersey City, N.J. illustrates the theory that static electricity had ignited the last great Zeppelin.*

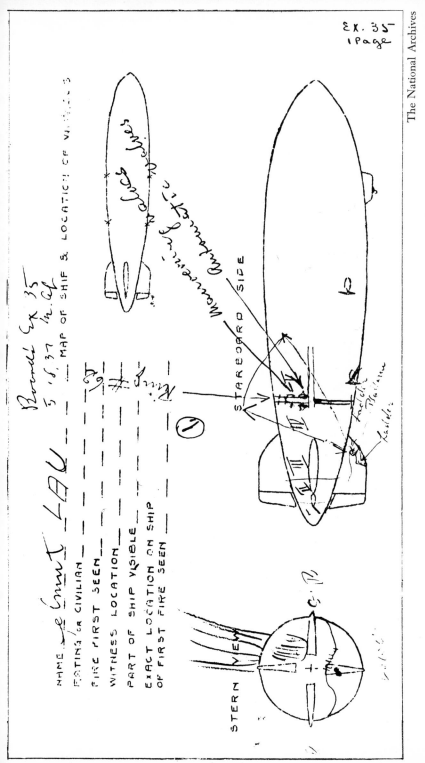

*Hundreds of eye-witnesses filled in diagrams similar to this at the inquiry. Helmsman Helmut Lau drew the ladders and platform from which he saw the fire before the explosion between Gas Cells IV and V.*

*Looking like a scene out of Nazi Germany, ceremonies for the German dead were held at Pier 86, at the foot of East 46th Street. Then the caskets were shipped home aboard the* Bremen.

*Captain Lehmann's casket here covered in lilies, was buried in Frankfurt in a common grave with the dead in his crew.*

Wide World Photos

*The* Hindenburg's *aluminum frame was trucked to Perth Amboy, then melted in Germany to become the frames for German aircraft used in World War II.*

was on his way to concluding the biggest cotton deal ever: 50,000 tons in one swap for Germany—and Germany wouldn't need to take the lard.

At the same time, in contrast to their narrow monomanias, he danced beautifully, had a cellar of fine wines, played tennis with gusto, and was full of choice gossip from every corner of the world.

The theorists were always culling events to find out what was "important." They could never understand that for the artist, or the cotton broker like George Hirschfeld, the Kentucky Derby was important, Wallis Simpson's scandalous affair with the King was important, the effort to close New York's burlesque theatres was important. George Hirschfeld's credentials came from his ability to judge light and shade, to buy futures based on his judgment of "confidence."

He loved the news every night and listened attentively to every detail. Before dinner on Tuesday night on the *Hindenburg* he heard that *Gone With the Wind* had won the Pulitzer prize; that the technicians in Hollywood's movie studios were on strike; that General Motors had declared a dollar a share dividend; that the Duke of Windsor had rejoined Mrs. Simpson at the Chateau de Cande, near Tours; that the Pope had insisted the Reich leave the Church alone; that the Reich was indignant about being charged for the bombing of Guernica.

Before dinner (which she always called "suppa," as they did in Boston), Miss Margaret Mather had arranged for Miss Irene Doehner to join her table. With the practice of her years as an effective godmother, Miss Margaret easily won the consent of Mr. and Mrs. Doehner to an offer of "a good deal of fun," which would be perfectly proper at the same time. The Doehner table would be reduced by the loss of their daughter, which excited the two younger boys.

With a net of somewhat the same reasons, Miss Margaret had gathered at her table the more attractive young men. For her they were honored to play the knight. By the time the stewards had cleared the *pâtés à la reine*, Herbert O'Laughlin had set aside the screen of his shyness and given a very enthusiastic portrait of his visit to Venice. Miss Margaret shared every sentence of his discovery, as if she too were learning about Venice for the first time. The warmth of her understanding was sufficient to carry O'Laughlin into a new interest in farm equipment when she turned to her right, and inquired of Clifford Osbun: "But your work must require you to travel all the time, doesn't it?"

Two tables away, Captain Lehmann had emerged from his duties forward and joined the table of his old friends, Mr. and Mrs. Adelt, Mr. and Mrs. John Pannes, and Dr. Birger Brinck.

Emma Pannes and her husband John were the most effective propaganda team Zeppelins could engage. He was Passenger Manager for Hamburg-American North German Lloyd Lines, and in America that company was agent for Zeppelin fares. Mrs. Pannes was originally Emma Romiser of Belleville, Illinois. Now their home was in Manhasset, Long Island. They had represented Hamburg-American and Zeppelins in Philadelphia, before he was appointed to the New York post.

He was about 60, and she about 45. They had a daughter, Natalie, now married and living in Chicago, and a son, Hilgard living in Manhasset, who would drive down to meet them when they arrived at Lakehurst.

They had left America the month before on the *Bremen* just so they could fly back on the *Hindenburg*. He loved every detail of flying and of Zeppelins, and he communicated his enthusiasm to passengers. They were "as American as apple pie." What was more important, however, was that husband and wife took such delight in each other's company, they were so sure and familiar with each other, they exuded a common charm which was more than double what each could have given alone. They rarely needed to turn their heads towards each other to express the common instincts of their love. Instead their heads, their eyes, their hearts always seemed to be beamed at some common objective: a pair of ducks always looking at the same ponds.

In their long marriage they had passed their personalities through each other. Emma Pannes could describe in detail the difficulties John had with some passenger's baggage, and he would enjoy her account immensely because it had more humor than his own.

Captain Lehmann enjoyed their company, partly because John and Emma Pannes always believed that with a little extra effort something could be arranged to make every task more pleasant. At dinner, before the roast beef, Emma Pannes had Lehmann describing his plans for Zeppelins twice the size of the *Hindenburg*.

With the roast beef Clifford Osbun remonstrated with Margaret Mather for drinking only water while they were passing over so much water. "At least, have a dash of wine with it," he urged.

Miss Margaret accepted a dash in her water from the fine red 1926 Beaune Cuvée de l'Abbaye he had ordered for the table. Across from them, with wide curious doe eyes, Irene Doehner described to young Peter Belin the pyramids of Mexico City, where her father had his chemical business.

Otto Clemens, his Leica opened wide to catch the last of the available light from the saloon's sloping windows, was snapping portraits. He moved from table to table. At his side was Joseph Spah. It had turned out that among Spah's hobbies was photography, and as he too recorded the voyage for posterity, he accepted the advice of Clemens on aperture and speed and angle. Spah was using a movie camera.

He did not see why the three German gentlemen, Erdmann, Witt, and Hinkelbein—Erdmann was the one who had been called Colonel on the loudspeaker when the ship sailed—why should they refuse to pose for him when they had consented to for Clemens?

At another table Major Dolan considered that even should transatlantic air service be inaugurated in the next few years, nothing could compare with the luxury of Zeppelins—a fine roast beef and a good red burgundy would always be a discount against the advantages of the airplane's speed.

"Not at all the point, though." Colonel Morris was thinking aloud. "Take this Guernica case. The whole advantage of airplanes was their speed."

He analyzed for Major Dolan the military element of surprise. Zeppelins were now useless in war; they were just fat targets. According to the B.B.C., the Germans did not cease the bombardment of the Spanish town for over three hours. The estimate was that more than 3,000 projectiles were dropped, many of them weighing 1,000 pounds. The airplanes came in waves, returned to reload, attacked again. Speed was the essential factor: in a given time the total load of bombs delivered—the "payload"—might even equal the payload of Zeppelins. "Provided the distances were relatively short, of course."

George Grant noted for them that H. G. Wells had envisioned the sort of thing the B.B.C. now reported: a guerrilla war in

Spain in which both sides attempted to destroy whole cities and their populations. He said that Mr. Churchill had been speaking regularly on the subject in the Commons, but no one seemed to be listening.

At still another table Rolf von Heidenstamm concurred with Hans Vinholt: steel was the product from which wars were forged; that no war was accidental, or precipitated any longer—production schedules leading to and from the forges had months, even years, scheduled on their calendars. The Swedish Naval officer and the Danish banker agreed that their southern neighbors were dancing on the edge of the abyss.

Mr. Rolf Anders, at their table, argued that Germany was only attempting to take her rightful place among the European nations. He was in the tea business and he could assure them that the most-favored-nation clauses regulating trade among the countries of the British Empire worked principally to the disadvantage of the German people. Things would have to be set aright in Europe by some means, but the German people, who had suffered so terribly before, had no desire for war now.

Mrs. Maria Kleeman was the only woman at their table. She agreed with Mr. Anders that no nation would really wish to start another war. But she had helped her husband in his business until he had died, and she had learned that these things sometimes took a little while to work out, and one shouldn't be too anxious to have everything perfect.

For her part she hoped for the best. In the meantime she was enjoying her first flight across the ocean. She was on her way to see her daughter and son-in-law in Andover, Massachusetts. Her daughter had become a real American now.

William Leuchtenburg and Moritz Feibusch shared their table against the wall again, and perhaps because Feibusch did not enjoy drinking himself, they had largely fallen silent. What was there to discuss?

Feibusch praised the food extravagantly. The ship's chef, Xavier Maier, had been at the Ritz in Paris. Wasn't that something? Leuchtenburg was unenthusiastic. Feibusch had to conduct his dialogues with himself.

So what if it was a German ship? They could still enjoy. If one began to collect injustices, then one would have to drink alone. Did it offend his dining partner that they had been put together and separated from the others? Then they should make the best of it. It was wrong to be Jewish? How could it be wrong to be the son of your mother?

Sure, there were those who thought they could be Jewish and at the same time avoid being strangers in the lands in which they lived, but sooner or later they would have to remember their mothers and their mothers' mothers.

Take his own case, for example. In his business he had to travel. He spoke French, German and English, but he hoped he always would remember how to think Jewish. Did this make him any less American? In San Francisco he had a partner in the fancy goods whose name was McDonald and there were many times he could cite when McDonald thought Irish. Was this so bad? In the opinion of one Moritz Feibusch it was good: good for their business, good for America, good in general. People should get along.

The Germans had gone crazy. The things he had seen! Over the doors of grocery and butcher shops, in the bakeries and dairies: "Jews not admitted." Hotels which would not give lodgings to a Jewish person. Signs outside of little towns which said: "Jews Strictly Forbidden in This Town," or "Jews Enter This Place at Their Own Risk." He had heard there was a road sign in the south of Germany which read: "Drive Carefully! Sharp Curve! Jews 75 Miles an Hour!" He had not seen it himself, but he believed they would do that.

He had heard that the radio could not play Mendelssohn. He knew that the best director in Germany, Max Reinhardt, had left. The owners of the *Frankfurter Zeitung* had been forced to sell. And what was the result? A dull paper, worse theatre, and no Mendelssohn to listen to. Although he did not care so much for Mendelssohn himself.

The laws had deprived Jews of citizenship, excluded them from public office, civil service, journalism, radio, farming, teaching, theatre, films, put them out of the stock exchange, and even though there were no laws that said so, they were being pushed from law, medicine, and science.

And what would be the result? Those with a little money, some learning, some position, would go to America. Germany's loss would be America's gain. The Germans would see someday: some Jewish boy would make them regret they had chased him away. And he consoled himself with the thought that such a revenge is a dish best eaten cold. It would take time, but that would be best.

In the meantime, he would plan the celebration he would give in Oakland when his mother arrived. He would ask all his friends to meet her: Irish, Italian, Jewish, even the one Japanese man he knew. His mother had never sat down at the table with a Japanese gentleman and he could bet she would say, "Moritz, these are all your friends?" And he would say yes.

Hitler had called the bishops "old fogies who are no longer good for anything." He had called priests and nuns, "cats and dogs who pass each other in the street"; he had said: "We will take away their children when they are 10 years old and bring them up." The children were to be drafted into the party, into the S.A., and the S.S.

Gertrud Adelt noted that the S.S. had been arresting 1,000 priests and nuns each week, charging them with "sexual crimes," and sending them away into oblivion. Soon there would be no one left to object to any crime.

Captain Lehmann appeared distracted. Emma Pannes changed the subject to Birger Brinck's interview with Governor Earle of Pennsylvania, scheduled for Thursday. Dr. Brinck explained the Governor would fly to Philadelphia for the interview, and then Brinck could sail again the same night on the *Hindenburg* to return to Sweden. The occasion of their talk was the 300th anniversary of the first Swedish immigrants to America. Earle was of Swedish descent.

The salad was excellent and followed by a fine Stilton cheese and then fruits. At Miss Margaret Mather's table Clifford Osbun described his adventure of the year before.

He had been en route to Puerto Rico by seaplane (Miss Margaret always called them "aquaplanes"), when its engines had failed. It crash landed in a rough sea. The pilot and copilot were injured. A motor launch presently arrived to rescue them. They abandoned the plane at sea, but then on the way to the harbor the launch's engine had exploded, and it began to burn.

They put on life jackets and had another swim. Fortunately, the burning launch marked their location until still another launch arrived to pick them up.

Irene Doehner said she thought Mr. Osbun was a very lucky man. Miss Margaret thought so too. Airplanes seemed too risky for passenger service. But she regretted that Zeppelins had no place for an orchestra so that the young people might dance.

With coffee, Birger Brinck described their tour that afternoon, how Gertrud Adelt had bravely crossed over to the engine gondola.

Captain Lehmann remarked: "Bravery most often depends on innocence. But to know the danger one faces and still march ahead to one's duty, that is the definition of courage!" But Gertrud Adelt thought he seemed so sad when he said it.

As the passengers drifted away from their places across the passageway into the lounge, Gertrud Adelt asked Captain Lehmann why the aluminum piano was no longer aboard. Everyone enjoyed it so much when he played.

He said that "it weighed 112 pounds." They expected 71 passengers on the return voyage—most of them on the way to the coronation of George VI at the last minute—and so "rather than leave a pretty lady behind," they had unloaded the piano.

He made his excuses then, said he had "duties forward."

Ernst A. Lehmann made his way forward, past the command gondola. He stopped in his cabin, took off his hat and his jacket, borrowed a sweater from Anton Wittemann, with whom he shared the cabin. He stared for a moment at the plans for the house in Zeppelinheim which he had left unrolled upon the bunk.

Once the sweater was pulled on, he picked up his accordion and made his way forward again, through the door marking the end of the officers' passageway. He closed it behind him, then climbed the stairs to the navigator's perch on the rigger's shelf by the nose cone. There were no lights, but he didn't need any.

He sat on the edge of the shelf, let his feet dangle down into the bow's cavern. He was sad in a way he had never known before. It was his son's death, in part. It was Marie's grief, in part. It was the estrangement that had been forced upon him from his old teacher and companion, Dr. Eckener, in part. It was his meetings with Colonel Erdmann—he had the sense that Erdmann, though he had not one hard fact, might be right. But what was there to do? The crew was alerted to be thorough in their inspections, but they usually were anyway. The first thing was to avoid silly panic.

He needed to think clearly. Instead he was in a maze, turning first this way, then that. For over a year now he had turned one corner after another to discover at almost every turning something so heroic he trembled in fear, or else something so monstrous he could not control the gorge of his anger. He settled his accordion across his knees and began to play, at first from his repertoire of *lieder*. No one in the ship would be able to hear him.

He drew on his experience as a navigator: "When in danger of shoals reverse the last best course to gain the freedom of the sea, then sail to sea until some fix can be drawn."

He had given his life to Zeppelins, and Heaven knows, they had rewarded him. He remembered writing to his mother and father after he had won his diploma in engineering at the Naval School at Kiel. He had told them he would never be happy as a civil servant. Though he was a licensed architect, "the more I think about it, I won't stay any longer in construction for the State than necessary. The whole civil service is too rigid."

He had described the "imaginary" caste spirit of the civil mind. "Any initiative except for the right behavior to one's superior has disappeared. The system, not the people, was responsible."

He was just 26 then. His father was a chemist in Ludwigshafen, his mother the daughter of a mayor—a real mayor, not the kind that had sprung up in recent years. He had told them: "Others may be lured by medals, uniforms, social standing, but these are all a burden to me. . . ." He had an overwhelming desire to accomplish things, and he thought he had subsequently had good luck.

Because he had loved sailing, and racing sailboats, he had met Dr. Eckener within the year. Sailing small boats was great training for sailing Zeppelins—both required the same experience with the elements of moving air, pressure systems, the northwest breezes of cold fronts, the ability to judge the wind velocity in a summer squall by its color. Dr. Eckener trained him in Zeppelins, and within a year he was the captain of the *Sachsen*.

During the war his luck had held. He had written his mother and father that they should not worry: "We are armed like a fort. We needn't fear the enemy airplanes. We'll shoot them down. From the ground, the shells cannot reach us. Don't worry. . . ." It was not quite true. All around him Zeppelins had gone down in flames. But it was true enough for him.

During those years he had come to love and respect many other men. He knew that many people liked his good manners, that his manners were attributes not of caste, but of some other noble derivation. Actually his manners were a result of preferring to exercise his kindness, because he had learned in the war that there were good men all around him, and he grew genuinely fond of them: men like Pruss, and Speck, and Lenz and Knorr. With them it was easy to have good manners. When Pruss had joined the party recently, Lehmann had withheld judgment of his old friend because he knew how much one had to love the quirks in one's own little family before one could love mankind.

The postwar years had been difficult because he saw in Germany so much suffering, such madness, because he saw men and women habituated to the manners of the jungle. He did not suffer much himself because his work had become so interesting. With his charm, his ability to learn languages, and his great patience he became, in effect, the Zeppelin Corporation's ambassador-at-large.

He had negotiated the Spanish-Buenos Aires Line, and the Swedish Line (that took six months in Sweden), both of which the Versailles Commission aborted. In 1921 he spent five months in America attempting to form an airship line between New York and Chicago. Although nothing had come of that, except good English and admiration for the gusto of Americans, in 1923 he had gone to Akron, Ohio, as Vice-President in charge of Engineering of the Goodyear Zeppelin Corporation.

His bombardier from the war, Baron von Gemmingen, had succeeded Graf Zeppelin as Director of the Zeppelin Corporation in 1917. Gemmingen died of cancer in 1923. When Dr. Eckener succeeded Gemmingen, Ernst Lehmann became "prokurist"—he could sign the company's checks. Eckener's strategy was sound: wait out the Allied Commission, keep the men together in so far as possible; sooner or later Germany would be able to build again. It didn't matter if the men worked in America or Friedrichshafen; they would still be working and learning.

On the LZ 126 Lehmann flew with Eckener to New York in October 1924, and stayed in Akron until 1927, returning to Friedrichshafen to build the *Graf Zeppelin*. Either with Eckener, or for him, he flew the *Graf Zeppelin* from 1928 until 1936. He supervised the continued training of the other captains: Pruss, Wittemann, von Schiller, Sammt and Bauer.

In 1935 the troubles began with Berlin. To build ships the size of the *Hindenburg* they needed money from the state. The new passenger corporation formed to conduct the transatlantic service had to have Christiansen, a party man, and a police chief, as a codirector. But Lehmann got along with him.

Then Berlin began to insist that all the Zeppelin men be "representatives of the party." In a way it was convenient that Pruss joined, and was next in line to command the *Hindenburg* anyway. But then within the ship, men like Chief Engineer Sauter, Watch Officer Walter Ziegler, and men way down the ranks, like Helmsman Helmut Lau, became vociferous members: always propagandizing, arguing for political ends, making reports to authorities in Berlin.

The politicalization of life in Germany was spreading like a plague. When organizations like the Zeppelin family became infected, discipline and morale began to suffer. No one was master in the house. Everyone began to serve their own cause. The sense of accomplishment which every man had once shared with every other within the Zeppelin family began to ebb in little riptides of discord.

When Dr. Eckener and his son Knud had been humiliated, he had found himself the Director. Now he had the medals, the uniforms, the rewards of responsibility. Men who had once been his friends now laughed too well at his own little jokes instead of their own. When he had played the piano before, for his friends or the passengers aboard the *Hindenburg*, he had enjoyed it just so long as each new melody was a discovery which he could share. Now if he should play, his audience would be forced to judge "a performance." The *Hindenburg* had become a symbol, and he was its keeper, and because of the times, he had lost the thread of adventure somewhere.

He had the advantage of travel, of knowing many men, of languages and their nuances, of having seen the flat plains of Ohio and the deserted wastes of Siberia. He could quote the commonplace about: "Bismarck made Germany great, but he made Germans small," but it was insufficient to explain the sleepwalkers he saw on every side these days.

They were extravagant in what they said, they were enthusiastic for a Greater Germany—whatever that was, they had given up themselves to certainties which they repeated over and over, in order, it would seem, to make them come true.

The result was that they had already bored themselves, and instead of adventure or accomplishment, they yearned for something to relieve them of their dreams, some game they might play, some real thunder to keep them awake. Instead of sleeping at night exhausted from the satisfactions of the day, they wanted to stay up, the way children do, to see what would happen next. They wanted to play with fate. He was forced to consider whether he carried the infection too.

He thought not. To the fever of ideas which flushed the cheeks and debilitated the virtues of most of his companions, he could oppose facts—marshalled from a lifetime's work as an engineer. It was a pity that they had inspectors of bridges and elevators, that they tested and tried every plane, every locomotive, and every airship before it could be certified for service, but there were no inspectors of social structures, or social engines.

It was a shame that Hitler had occupied the Rhineland: that no one seemed to realize what giants had been stirred into arming. To be fair, Chancellor Hitler had justification, because the Rhineland "belonged" to Germany as much as Manchester "belonged" to England. Hitler was only demanding a return to the rightful heirs of a portion of their inheritance. But Ernst Lehmann recalled the folk tale of the hero who drove his sleigh across the frozen Bodensee. The ice had cracked under his flying runners all the way across, but the speed of the horses carried them on. When the rider arrived safely at shore and stopped, he looked back at the danger he had traversed. In the folk tale, the hero died of fright on the spot.

Now when Ernst Lehmann heard the tales of bombing in Spain, he thought of the story. He was 51. Perhaps because he had finally been the father of a son, and perhaps because it was his son who died, he had begun, just from time to time, to wonder what his own death would be like. It made him uneasy in a way that the anti-aircraft batteries in the war over London had not. Then he had been afraid. Now he was resigned. He was not so much afraid of death as he was of the resignation.

Though Marie still trembled with grief over the loss of Luv, it did not seem to him that she was resigned. He had watched her fuss in her garden. She snipped the stems of fresh flowers and marched them to their vases. He would smell the flesh of her arms while she still slept, and it smelled sweet. Only a week ago he had spent at least an hour watching her from behind a book, while she snapped the ends off beans into a pot. Each bean was put in its place: snap-so; snap-so; snap-so; snap-so. And as he remembered her, his fingers stopped tracing melodies on the accordion's keyboard. (My, the songs had become sad ones, he realized.) He smiled to himself, and he rested.

At that moment, Max Zabel appeared through the door at the foot of the stairway 75 feet below. Zabel snapped on the guide lights. They were surprised to see each other.

"Time to try for a sight, my Captain." Zabel displayed his sextant as he climbed.

Lehmann rose and offered: "Give me your watch, Mr. Zabel, and if you see a star through those clouds, I'll mark your times for you."

They both peered through the windows in the bow, but they could see nothing except clouds approaching them at 80 knots, then scudding by. After about 10 minutes, Mr. Zabel excused himself, descended the stairs, then asked at the bottom if Captain Lehmann wanted the guide lights left on or off.

"Please leave them on, Mr. Zabel. I shall be following you in a moment. Good night, Zabel."

Well, Ernst A. Lehmann still had staggering tasks ahead of him. And he would not yet give up his faith in man as a rational being. Certain things were good for people, and certain things were bad, and he knew which was which. It was a matter of assembling the facts, then arranging them in their proper order, then putting them to analysis, and drawing from the analysis the best conclusion. If the world was crazy, he could remain cool and lucid. If he made a mistake, he would retain his ability to change his mind. If nations were determined to use some machines for wicked ends, he would put his skill and experience to work for good purposes. Then let history be the judge.

When Eckener kept insisting they must have American cooperation as the precondition of any regular transatlantic service, Lehmann had at first not wholly understood. Lehmann had seen the problem only in terms of payloads, schedules, terminal facilities, freight rates. Now he saw that once again, though characteristically plain-spoken and undiplomatic, Dr. Eckener was right. It was not the technical achievement that mattered, but the cooperation in effecting it.

Take the matter of hydrogen versus helium, for example. Dr. Eckener began from the premise that the Americans would not fly their ships without helium. Therefore, he said, German ships must also be equipped with helium.

Lehmann had differed with him. After all, the Germans were perfectly confident in their handling of hydrogen. They were trained in its use and the necessary precautions. Even in war, the hydrogen itself had never caused a problem—it was enemy attacks that brought ships down, not what sort of gas was used to lift them up. Further, hydrogen was far more efficient at lifting ships. Helium was frightfully expensive, even for Americans, who had always been forced to sail at night to avoid wasting their precious gas. As the airship got bigger, the cost of helium would make them almost prohibitive.

The *Hindenburg* took 7 million cubic feet of gas. At the current price of helium it would cost about $600,000 to inflate all her cells. Even if the American Congress passed the bill by which they would subsidize helium to a cost of $8 per thousand cubic feet (a tenth of the current price), the Zeppelin Corporation would have to carry 15 passengers more on each trip to make up the difference. These were but some of the facts.

Yet Dr. Eckener insisted the *Hindenburg* be designed to float on either gas—at considerable expense in construction. Why, argued Lehmann, should Germans bear the extra cost of construction for a gas which the Americans would not give them? And if the Americans did agree to give Germany the gas, the Germans would not want to use it.

Dr. Eckener was adamant. And blunt: "We must have the Americans."

The Americans wanted to build ships, but they would need German designers and German crews to train them. The Americans said, "we will give you the helium—which is much safer, if you will show us how to fly Zeppelins."

Dr. Eckener had agreed to it all. He gave them the plans, promised

them the instruction, agreed to use the helium in German ships—
everything. He was certainly a man of good will, which Berlin had not
understood.

Now Lehmann realized that when Eckener said, "Without the
Americans we have nothing," he meant that the technology of Zeppelins was useless without men of good will to plan them together, to
sail them together, to make a common work of their adventures.

When he got to New York on this trip he would pick up the
threads of Dr. Eckener's efforts last fall. He would visit the American
congressmen and businessmen. He would see if he could get the helium Germany didn't need for the Luftschiffbau. He picked up his accordion and started for his bunk.

On the way he stopped for a moment, descended the ladder into
the fuehrer gondola, and consulted with Captain Pruss on their progress. They had missed the north side of the low. They still had head
winds and bad weather ahead for another day. At 2300 hours GMT
(7:00 P.M. Eastern Daylight Saving Time) their position was only
49:02 north and 23:35 west, about 400 miles north of the Azores,
steering the great circle for Cape Race.

# CHAPTER 6

# ACTS OF GENIUS

"If I cannot influence the Gods,
I shall set all hell in motion."
—*Aeneid* VII, 312, VERGIL

WEDNESDAY, May 5, 1937. The sun rose at 7:18 Greenwich Mean Time, but no navigator could catch its upper limb or lower limb, since the *Hindenburg* still sailed on west through clouds.

For breakfast Chef Maier had baked fresh rolls. Joseph Leibrecht, said Helmut Lau, took more than his fair share. Leibrecht excused himself, and explained that he had the morning watch and needed a little something to keep body and soul together; that anyway he couldn't give them back now even if he wanted to; there seemed to be plenty of rolls for anyone; and was there some rule which Lau administered which required everyone to eat exactly the same number of rolls? "To each according to his needs," said Leibrecht, laughing. "Isn't that what the party says?"

"Yes, but you have the wrong party, Leibrecht. That's the Communist party. Anyway it's from each according to his abilities," said Lau.

"What in the world has ability to do with hot rolls?" Leibrecht laughed again at foolish Lau and went to his station at the electrical panels amidships. That Lau!

For his part, Lau had time to stay for a second cup of coffee at the table in the crew's mess. Breakfast rolls were not really the point. It just took a great deal more order than that fellow Leibrecht even suspected to make things go right. If the habit of disrespecting the quota on breakfast rolls were adopted by every man, there would be nothing but anarchy. Fortunately, anarchy was no longer the *leit motiv* of Germany.

Instead they had achieved the most bloodless revolution in the history of mankind. Industry, trade and agriculture marched together in the new order. Men had work and lawlessness had stopped. There had been some troubles with the S.A. people and the party had needed to eliminate some of them, but then nothing of importance could be achieved without some difficulty.

Helmut Lau regretted that his duties as an airshipman meant that he was almost always absent from the meetings of 5 Sturm 2 S.S. Standarte—his S.S. group. In the comradeship of his Standarte's meetings there were songs and ceremonies and lessons—lessons in history, geography, and philosophy; but not like those given from the pulpits of churches. Instead lessons with relevant meaning for the events of today: "The strongest and best organized states are those which should survive—the weaker political organisms must give way. . . ." and, "The history of the world is the world's court of justice . . ."; and "The state is the idea of spirit . . . it is conscious of its derivation from God."

Oh yes, membership in the S.S. had as one of its benefits the lessons of the university. They studied not only Hegel and Kant, but Fichte and Treitschke. They studied, not as the parasitic class egotists of the past, but because History was waiting for the German Volk. "Revolution was the sacrifice of temporal values in order to save eternal values."

The S.S. man must be "honest, decent, loyal and comradely to the members of his own blood." If he must be zealous in the performance of his duties, it was because the National Socialist Revolution demanded "unconditional liberation from the old social world of caste, class and family." The duties of the S.S. man were "officialdom, police work and teaching."

Hitler had been "ordained by the Karma of the Germanic peoples to save them. The Germanic Reich needed the Order of the S.S.—at least for the next few centuries."

Helmut Lau, helmsman of Zeppelins, missed the ceremonies of his S.S. Standarte: the lessons, the torches, the comradeship, the singing of the S.S. oath song—*Wenn alle untreu werden*. . . . On the other hand, it was the duty of every S.S. man to serve the State in his most appropriate capacity; and he was the only S.S. man in the service of Zeppelins.

From the electrical control panels Joseph Leibrecht reported the diesel driving the generators was not working smoothly: its r.p.m.'s were not keeping constant. Chief Sauter examined it and decided the fuel pump was not "working equally." He switched to the auxiliary diesel, and Leibrecht switched to the auxiliary generator simultaneously.

With the help of Richard Kollmer, Chief Sauter replaced the pump with a spare. Then they switched the system back to its original circuits. That was the thing with machines. If they were designed properly, their parts were interchangeable. If one component would not do its work equally, another could take its place. They were dependable.

Captain Pruss had ordered the ship inspected again from bow to stern. If the Captain's concern for security were excessive, it made no difference to Chief Knorr. He inspected the ship from bow to stern at all times anyway.

Young Spehl was on watch, Freund in his bunk. Chief Knorr said he would have a look at Gas Cells XVI to IX, and Spehl should have a look at those in the stern: from VIII to the tail. They could meet halfway and report.

Starting with the two cells in the bow, Chief Knorr felt each one with his hands for pressure, examined the cords against which the bags of gas strained, looked for chafing. Between each cell there was a flue leading to the top skin of the ship. On top there was a hatch, hinged at the forward end in such a way that as the ship drove ahead, the air current passing over the hatch would suck the still air (and any gas there might be in the interior of the ship) out into the atmosphere.

Chief Knorr scrambled up the sides of these flues like a chimney sweep. In them he had a vantage point from which he could see the straining top of each bag. From the middle walkway in the center of the ship, he could examine the bottom of the cells, which because of the coolness of the trip and the fact that the hydrogen pressed upwards, hung in loose folds.

It took about two hours to work up inside each of three flues, and then down again. Chief Knorr's inspection was thorough, of course. He met young Spehl at Ring 123.5, at the ladder in the fourth flue, between Cells VIII and IX. Together they inspected the maneuvering valves, and automatic valves, located in that flue. Spehl reported that all was well aft. The two men stood on the axial walkway and talked awhile.

The older man recalled the Olympics held the year before. Eric Spehl had been also aboard the *Hindenburg* when they had flown over Berlin, but Chief Knorr never missed a chance to impart another fatherly lesson.

It had been a dazzling scene. Against the background of a grey overcast sky 100,000 Germans filled the new stadium. They saw the greenest of lawns circled by a running track of red cinders. At one side was an orchestra, reinforced by the drums and bugles of a half-dozen military bands, and above them a chorus of a thousand, all in white.

Opposite the chorus was a pavilion in grey stone for the Fuehrer and his party, and below that a special section in wood for the ambassadors and officials of other nations. At the beginning of the ceremonies the *Hindenburg* flew over the stadium trailing a specially made Olympic flag 50 meters wide. The difficulty with the thing, Chief Knorr said, was in the design of the cross bar which was supposed to keep it flying horizontally.

From the towers at the top of the stadium, then descending down wide steps of the field, came a procession of uniformed, frock-coated and top-hatted officials, wearing around their necks the gold chains, the emblems of the International Olympic Committee. Walking at their head, between the two chief officials, in a simple khaki uniform, was the Fuehrer. Everyone recognized him immediately, and rose and greeted him with cheering and salutes. The bands played together a march from Wagner. After a little while he returned the salutes, but this only increased the cheering, which was truly deafening.

A little girl in blue, her fair hair bound by a chaplet of flowers, came forward and making a pretty German curtsey, gave him a bouquet of roses. He touched her hair and evidently spoke gently to her, then one of the notables led her up the steps to the dais. The assembly still remained standing and broke into another chorus of "Sieg Heils," which only ceased when the band struck up *Deutschland*

*Über Alles*, then into the *Horst Wessel* song, which most everybody sang too.

From the tallest and furthest tower of the stadium a deep note sounded from the Olympic bell—a bell on which was inscribed: "I summon the youth of the world."

As if in answer to the summons, there emerged from the archway forming the Marathon Gate below the staircase the Fuehrer had descended, the head of a long procession of athletes of the nations.

The Greeks, in modern blue coats and white flannel trousers, led the way, as was their right, having originated the games. Then the other nations in alphabetical order, with Germany as host last of all, following the United States.

They marched in a procession once around the arena, saluting the dais, each nation according to its custom, as they passed. Then turning across the field, they took their stand in columns great and small in front of the Fuehrer, each nation's flag at the head of its column.

Quite naturally in this long march there was much interest, signified by the volume of applause, in the type of salute each nation gave the dais. It was not always easy to determine because the Olympic and Party salutes are very similar. The Olympic salute being with the right arm extended sidewise, or nearly so, from the shoulder, and the Party salute much the same, but with the arm to the front. It seemed as if the nations were about equally divided between Olympic and Party methods of salute. The biggest applause was given to the French, who nevertheless gave the Olympic salute. The next biggest applause to the Austrians.

Every nation had uniforms of different colors. The Egyptians, for example, had red fezzes, and the team from Bermuda white pith helmets. Honors in marching went wholly to the German team who moved like a great machine. The march past the dais came to an end at last, and some 5,000 athletes from 52 nations stood ranged before the Fuehrer.

Then Dr. Lewald, organizer of the games, stepped forward. He said: "Only so long as sport isn't allowed to become an end in itself but, on the contrary, a moral duty, only so long as it isn't merely empty pleasure or the desire for thrills, but discipline and devotion to a higher ideal, dare it to be the object of such a festival." Then he asked the Fuehrer to declare the games open. Which the Fuehrer did.

The flags of the nations were run up the flagpoles surrounding the stadium. Trumpets sounded a loud fanfare. From a distance a battery of guns sounded a royal salute. And then the doors of several hundred covered cages (which had been standing unnoticed around the edge of the arena) were opened, and 3,000 white pigeons flew out!

The white-clad chorus began the singing of the Olympic hymn. At that, the *Hindenburg* was ordered to sail off, but it was, said Chief Knorr, a great day to remember.

Eric Spehl seemed to be paying attention, for he did truly enjoy the spectacle Chief Knorr had conjured up again, but Spehl's mind was fixed somewhere else.

"Come," said the older man, "your watch is almost up. We shall shake Freund into his duties." And they went down to the lower walkway, down into the community that lived along the walkway on the belly.

At 9:30 hours, Radio Officer Herbert Dowe copied this message from Mackay Radio and Radiomarine, and passed to the gondola below:

LOW CENTRAL MONTREAL 1008 SLIGHT EASTWARD MOVEMENT AND LITTLE DEVELOPMENT LAST 12 HOURS STOP CANADIAN HIGH ABOUT 1026 LATITUDE 53 LONGITUDE 87 SLOW DISINTEGRATION WITHOUT MUCH MOVEMENT FRONT OF LIGHT RAINS EXTENDS FROM MONTREAL TO ELKINS ADVANCED 300 MILES EASTWARD THROUGH NEW YORK AND 200 MILES EASTWARD THROUGH PENNSYLVANIA LAST 12 HOURS. WEATHER BUREAU.

Chief Radio Officer Willy Speck was off watch, and as an experienced man, catching his sleep even in the morning in his bunk. He woke sweating from a dream. He had seen his son of 12 playing with a group of young children—boys and girls together. They were at a game of "Cowboys and Indians." The little group had elected his son to be the captured cowboy, and they had tied him to a sapling. Then they heaped sticks and branches at his feet. Willy Speck was powerless to stop them. He watched them light the first twig. He saw the others catch fire. He saw the flames rising and his son twisting and the sapling swaying from the boy's efforts to escape. He had come awake then with a cry, and for a minute he needed to study the cabin around him to make sure of its details. Then he pulled himself together and went forward to the radio room to see how things were going.

In the library, Moritz Feibusch had bought 200 postcards from Steward Nunnenmacher. He had opened his address book which listed all his accounts and friends. He addressed the cards one by one and sent them into the tube which led to the ship's post office. The cards read: "Greetings from the maiden voyage of the Hindenburg—Moritz Feibusch."

William Leuchtenburg pointed out to him that the maiden voyage was last year—this was not the maiden voyage. But Feibusch was in high spirits:

"Well it is for me."

They would have to wait an extra three hours for lunch because the clocks had been set back again.

"You only live twice on a Zeppelin, eh?" said Feibusch.

William Leuchtenburg said he was going down to "B" deck to the bar. When Feibusch was ready he should join him.

After lunch Joseph Spah decided he needed more of a walk than the 100 feet of the promenade could provide. He decided to visit his dog at the stern, then climb the ladder as he had done with the tour yesterday, walk forward to the bow, then down the stairs to the lower gangway and aft again. He figured that if you counted the ups and downs his circuit would amount to about 600 yards, so three circuits would make a mile.

He needed the exercise. He was due to open his act in the new Radio City Music Hall in two weeks and he would need all his agility and strength. He felt cooped up. He went down to the office of Chief Steward Kubis on "B" deck to see how it was to be arranged. Kubis wasn't there. Joseph Spah found the door to the lower gangway aft unlocked, opened it and started off anyway. Kubis was right: it wasn't a very dangerous walk for a man who had spent his life as an acrobat on stage.

What he had always wished he could do was to be a comedian who told jokes. He did love jokes so. He loved them because in his world "a top banana" brought the best pay. The comedian held the acts together. The audiences liked the dancers, acrobats, jugglers and the dog acts well enough, but they would laugh at the comedian.

He loved jokes not just for the punch lines, not just for the effect a well-told story could produce, but for all the little details by which a really good comedian made his audience see the protagonists. When the King found the Bishop in bed with the Queen, the King wore his crown, sure enough, but also the purple robe with the ermine ruff. Then when the King stood on the balcony blessing the crowd (the punch line went something to the effect: because His Eminence was taking his part, the King must play Pope), that's when Joseph Spah blessed his audience with the magisterial authority of the greatest of Popes.

In jokes he could commit every crime. God could stutter, professors forget, marvelous accidents would arrive while his audience giggled in anticipation, virtue was punished and vice lost its sting, mothers were monsters and fathers fools, drunks were heroes accomplishing incredible feats, and the farmer's shotgun was loaded with nothing more than rock salt to protect the virtue of a daughter intent on nothing less than rape.

Instead, however, of being able to tell jokes, his act (because of its curious popularity) was always the same. Audiences loved it again and again, consequently theatre managers booked it again and again, and Joseph Spah did it so well that his life became a series of engagements in which he did the same thing again and again. He did it on stages in Europe; in Paris, Berlin, Stuttgart, Milan, and Munich. He did it in Ottawa, Montreal, Boston and Hollywood. He was flying back on the *Hindenburg* to do a month at the Radio City Music Hall at $400 per week, which in 1937 was not "top billing" only because the motion picture got that. His stage name was "Ben Dova" and his act was a simple one, but he didn't get one line to speak.

From behind the curtains at the right of the stage, the audience saw a circle spot on the head and shoulders of a man. The man was dressed in top hat, white tie and tails. The man stopped, the top hat was askew; it was obvious the playboy was drunk. He reeled ever so slightly—time enough to let the audience accept the first platform of reality.

Then the drunk advanced towards center stage, the center spots widened to take him all in, and the audience could see that he could hardly keep his legs under him. He stopped again.

The drunk began to search in his pockets. He was looking for something. Now the audience began to identify. From behind the blinding light of the spots, "Ben Dova" would begin to feel them too.

Together they looked into right pants pocket, left pants pocket, left coat pocket, pocket of the tails, ah! perhaps in the most obvious place of all, the breast pocket? Nope, not in the breast pocket.

At the very edge of their suspense, together they found it, right where it had been all along! A cigarette!

By then he had his first real laugh. He had begun to relieve them of reality. At about the same time the drunk on stage and the audience would realize together that now he needed a match. They knew this would be an even more difficult search. And so it was.

Once again at the moment when the search reached the outer edge of their suspense, the drunk and the audience would notice together a street lamp downstage—a gas street lamp. Now the drunk was resolute. He would climb the pole to get the fire he needed. He started to shinny up.

He slipped. They groaned on nights when "Ben Dova" really had them. He got two-thirds of the way to the top and came to the bottom again. Finally, he shinnied all the way to the top, where just as he was about to win the game, it turned out that the pole could not support his weight.

It began to sway back and forth, gently at first, but then in wild circles. The drunk looked down from his perch pleased. He was defying reason. He was mocking the rules of gravity. He swooped through the air, lit the cigarette from the wildly swinging flame, and took the satisfaction of one huge drag.

By then he had them. And they roared when he would almost slip. He was making anarchy of the rules of gravity. What man, or woman, or child, would not marvel then at the world turned upside down; who would not wonder that the powers of order could be suspended; that the mind could leap across rivers that engineers would not attempt; that good sense was gratuitous; that drunks were leaders and leaders drunks.

After the peak of the applause, when the enthusiasm was beginning to wane, but before the magic transubstantiation was finished being consumed, he would slide down, straight down, walk directly stage front. He took his bow quickly, still smoking his prop as if now it really was part of him, then let them see for just a moment the drunk's wobbly legs once again. He would almost always be off stage with the applause still ringing.

The life of "Ben Dova" and of Joseph Spah had become repetitious: a single act performed over and over forever. He used to say that if it weren't for his passion for golf, he'd go crazy on the road, like so many of them did with booze or women or drugs. He carried his golf clubs everywhere, and if in some God-forsaken town he could find no one to play with, he'd play a foursome himself, hitting each of four balls in turn. After all, he had a wife and three children to support back in Douglaston, and the act paid.

Yet this ship made him nervous. At least on a liner a walk took you somewhere. And there was deck tennis and shuffleboard and sometimes a swimming pool, and a gym.

On his very first circuit, he didn't encounter a soul. The interior of a Zeppelin going 80 knots over the ocean, with its strange shadows and odd frames and struts, with the light changing on the skin according to what unseen cloud passed outside, was certainly a strange place.

On his second circuit, as he approached the tail, he was stopped by Helmut Lau, turned about and marched straight back into Chief Kubis' office, who had reappeared from somewhere and began to make the most awful fuss. Chief Kubis said he would be forced to report this to the Captain immediately.

"You do that," said Joseph Spah.

In the galley Alfred Groetzinger spilled the soup for dinner on his foot, scalded himself, and Dr. Ruediger was summoned to treat his second patient.

Philip Mangone still stayed to his cabin, shivering beneath extra blankets and complaining of his cold.

The stewards reported that Newfoundland was in sight. Cameras and binoculars appeared, and all the passengers crowded to the promenade and dining saloon windows.

Gertrud Adelt was delighted when she spotted white dots which grew into icebergs. Captain Pruss ordered the ship to fly low and steer toward them. Gertrud Adelt remembered that twenty-five years ago the *Titanic* had sunk at night nearby. She was fascinated by the patterns of the pack ice.

For the *Hindenburg*, the sun came out for the first time. Margaret Mather saw the icebergs "with pools of vivid green in their depths and their forms spreading green under the pale water. Rainbows spread from everywhere," and she watched one grow around an iceberg "until it completed a perfect circle beneath the ship."

They saw the foothills and the limitless forests of the hinterlands, then Cape Race lighthouse, then the coast receded off into the distance as the ship headed southwest, and once again they floated without the sun in the grey fog over the invisible grey sea.

But with the landfall made, the boredom that had begun to infect every passenger began to lift. Everyone looked forward to dinner.

Before the offices of the Zeppelin Corporation had closed not only for the night, but for the next day as well because of the Ascension Day holiday, the last clerks on duty were surprised to be visited again by Frau Beatrice Friederich, who inquired of the ship's progress. They told her that the trip was routine, and that the ship was due to land at 6:00 A.M. New York time.

She wanted to know what time that would be in Frankfurt. They figured that would be one o'clock this morning in Frankfurt. "No, the office would certainly not be open."

Commander Charles E. Rosendahl was concerned about the fire northwest of the Naval Air Station. It was still burning, though it had now been reported in control.

He received a message from DEKKA (the call letters of the *Hindenburg*) to NEL (the call letters of the station) stating that because head winds had delayed the airship, landing would have to be postponed until 6:00 P.M. Thursday. It was signed by Pruss.

Which was not much help to Detective Arthur C. Johnson, Radio Announcer Herbert Morrison, or a number of other police, press, custom and immigration officials already at hand for the early morning arrival. Some of them went over to Toms River for dinner and a drink. They would just have to wait.

*     *     *

Cotton was still up on the six o'clock news, and George Hirschfeld pleased. The news also carried a report that a bomb had exploded on the Bordeaux-Marseilles express, killing one and injuring twenty others.

The bomb, apparently smuggled aboard the train, was tied to a coupling between two passenger coaches. Investigators said it was a combination explosive and incendiary machine.

It burst as the train hit sixty miles per hour, its maximum speed, and showered passengers with glass splinters. The dead passenger's body was so badly burned it could not be identified immediately.

The wounded passengers were in a hospital in Marseilles. They said the explosion shattered windows of their coach, which at once burst into flames.

Mrs. Emilie Bon, a first class passenger, was badly burned about the face. She said: "I had to fight my way through the flames to reach the vestibule. The other passengers were staggering along the corridor filled with smoke."

The train halted quickly, the passengers removed from all coaches, and the burning cars detached at Saint Martin, before the train was able to resume for Marseilles. The Reich's Ministry of Information cited the incident as further "proof" of anarchy.

Colonel Erdmann heard the news too, and from the promenade lounge he set off forward to find Captain Lehmann. On the way he gathered up Major Witt and Lieutenant Hinkelbein to accompany him. Now it was time to take some action.

Major Witt agreed. When they arrived in the officers' mess they sent cabin boy Werner Franz forward to Lehmann's cabin with an urgent message to fetch the Captain. While they waited Major Witt noted that after all the S.S. information had been amazingly accurate about the French railway bomb. He added that he had gathered two additional pieces of information.

First of all, he had been looking through the cablegrams in the radio room. It seemed to him that the spy Douglas had received a coded message. He had a copy with him. He produced it and passed it across to Colonel Erdmann. The way they were seated at the table Lt. Hinkelbein could read over the Colonel's shoulder. He laughed.

Erdmann wanted to know what he thought was so funny.

"Well, sir, that is not a very hard code to break. It is from American baseball slang. It means more or less just what it says. After Douglas had left his first base in Frankfurt, he would have to stop when he got to New York. The Umpires are the officials of their game, and the dugout probably means his office, or home, which has been searched by our Staatspolizei. It means the spy is going home. It also means that the Berlin Major was accurate again."

Colonel Erdmann paused a moment, then nodded: "What else, Major Witt?"

"The ship's Doctor, Ruediger, reported yesterday to the Captain that Mr. Spah absented himself from the tour conducted yesterday afternoon, in order to visit with his dog. The Doctor was unable to prevent this from happening, since the passenger appears to be uncontrollable. He was alone for perhaps ten minutes."

At that moment Captain Lehmann appeared. He apologized for the delay in his appearance. He had not been in his cabin, but visiting the command gondola. Lt. Hinkelbein admired his aviator's coat, a leather jacket of three-quarter length, lined with sheepskin. When they were all seated again, Captain Lehmann said: "What is it that is so urgent?"

Colonel Erdmann reviewed the S.S. information on the sabotage of the Paris-Marseilles express, and the radio news announcement of the event. He went on: "It has been reported to me that this Mr. Spah absented himself from his escort on the tour of the ship yesterday, and that this was reported to you, and that you have not informed me. I think it is time we did our duty, Captain."

Lehmann paused before replying. He was in a somewhat better mood than he had been at the beginning of the voyage: "I should be glad to do my duty, Colonel Erdmann, if you know exactly what that might be."

Colonel Erdmann thought he would drop the question of the Adelts, and of Feibusch, and he sensed that Douglas would be a bad place to begin, but Joseph Spah was someone they could do something about. He said he thought it the very essence of prudence to arrest, or detain Spah to his cabin until the *Hindenburg* had safely landed.

Lehmann took a moment to think. His pipe materials were forward in his cabin. He wished he'd stopped to get them: "I am bound to inform you that in addition Chief Steward Kubis has just recently reported to me that Mr. Spah was found wandering in the body of the ship this afternoon, unaccompanied. . . ."

"A second time! Then arrest him right now—that's reason enough."

". . . and I have been discussing just this matter not only with Chief Kubis, but with my captains forward. We have a number of duties to look forward to in New York, some technical and some diplomatic. We are considerably interested in forming a joint transatlantic service with the Americans. I do not think we can announce our arrival by arresting an American as a saboteur, not unless we have some exact facts to show that the ship is threatened. Do you have any such facts, Colonel?"

"I can cite to you the following reasons. First, he is not an American—he travels on a French passport, though in fact he is a German, a Strasbourger. It seems to me a German citizenship would be more logical. In any case, his confusion in citizenship papers is, in itself, reason for detention. Second, he is found wandering about the ship with who knows what intentions. He was forbidden to do so, even to visit his dog, which it seems to me was nothing but a convenient excuse to get access to the interior of the ship in the first place. Whatever his excuses, he has violated the law of this ship and your express commands, and that is reason enough for detention. Nothing need be explained about sabotage. After all, you can do as you please, Captain. No one need know about it.

"Third, and finally, we had express orders from Berlin to watch this man and protect your ship and your passengers from the dangers he might present. I don't think these are orders which should be lightly ignored."

Captain Lehmann studied the three Luftwaffe men. They were airmen like he was. They were the kind of men who had bombed that Spanish town, just as he had bombed London. Now they were talking as agents of Berlin, just as he had to admit he had become too, but Dr. Eckener had not.

The young Lieutenant, Hinkelbein, seemed a bit different somehow—he lacked their intensity, no it was not that, it was their earnestness: young Hinkelbein would be a great flyer. He knew he was lucky, that's what it was, so these decisions didn't matter very much. Lehmann looked at Colonel Erdmann, and speaking slowly, said:

"That Spah is a comedian. An artist. They don't make bombs, they make laughter. I do not wish to arrange things so that the laughter is directed at either me or my ship. People would know about it, quickly enough. Especially the Americans. He will not be arrested.

"Come now, Colonel. We all must gamble a little bit from time to time. Join me at dinner in an hour, and we shall have a bottle of wine together, and I shall make you some music afterwards to soothe your soul."

With their voyage due to end, with the coast of North America hidden below them in the fog, the charmed circles lingered around the lights of the supper tables. After dinner they followed Captain Lehmann across to the lounge so that the stewards could clear the tables.

He had brought his accordion aft, and at ten o'clock he was still performing for his passengers. Strauss, German and American folk songs, English ballads, came floating back to the crew's quarters where Eric Spehl was asleep. There were snatches of singing from time to time.

One of Spehl's bunkmates, Steward Nunnenmacher, stopped by to fetch a clean white jacket. His was stained. He would be busy for another hour yet, fetching brandies and white mints. Nunnenmacher heard Spehl groaning in a nightmare. He would have left the rigger alone except that the intensity of the nightmare was growing; Spehl's agonies were increasing towards a scream. Nunnenmacher shook him awake:

"What's wrong? What's wrong, Eric?"

Spehl blinked in the light. He looked at his watch. He wasn't due on duty until midnight—more than an hour. He examined the face of Nunnenmacher as he fished for the details of his dream. The steward's face was concerned, but not surprised. Spehl guessed that he had not revealed anything from his dream.

He rolled over to his right side, unlocked his hands from their clasp across his chest into his armpits, reached under his bunk for his ditty bag, pulled out a pack of cigarettes. Nunnenmacher was still watching him.

"You all right, Eric? Listen, you know it is forbidden to smoke here. You won't fall asleep again, eh?"

Spehl lit the cigarette anyway. As he shook out the match he looked for a place to hide it. He put it in the breast pocket of his coveralls, hung beside the bunk.

"I'm all right, thank you." His laugh was at something unsaid. "Just this once, Nunnenmacher." He waved the cigarette. "I assure you there's no danger from this."

"All right, all right," said the steward. "But just don't play the fool." He left to see to his passengers.

Spehl smoked perhaps half of the forbidden cigarette, then changed his mind. He snubbed it out against the side of the bunk, dusted off the mark. He swung his feet around and down, pulled on his duty coveralls, then his canvas shoes. He headed aft, away from the music, along the lower gangway towards the stairway in the tail. When he reached the landing between the first and second flights, he sat down. It would be quiet there. There were things he had to consider.

His nightmare had started them around in his head again. He wasn't as sure of himself as he had been Sunday night in Frankfurt. It was as if he were pushing open the door to the kind of little stone house he had seen from time to time near his home in the high Black Forest, the abandoned houses from some other age in which no one lived any longer, not even woodsmen; a house which contained spiral memories in its stone walls, crystals no one had ever seen.

When he was a boy he had been told by his grandmother to be careful because ghosts, outlaws with one eye, lived in houses like that. He'd looked for the ghosts, but he'd never seen one himself. Though he'd seen signs scratched in the hearths of the outlaw cabins which he could not decipher. Now he sensed he was crossing the threshold into one of those secret houses where everything would be different.

It was a strange feeling; sometimes feeling the freedom of childhood; sometimes giving way to tears like an old woman. He could not sleep when he should. Then when he should be awake, he was drowsy. He wondered if he would have to wait long for Beatrice. What if she did not come?

If this young man from Göschweiler was unsure of his Beatrice, it would only be fair to note that no one had ever been absolutely sure of the reports sent out from the silent wars and secret treaties made between any man and woman. Sure, the general outline of the story is known well enough: God had taken pity on Adam's loneliness and created woman as his companion. That ended boredom, even in Paradise. But since then the details have always been a bit fuzzy. In the dances since, generations of needs and satisfactions have been tested, selected, concorded. Anyone can see that, but it is not always clear exactly how it was done. In the process there have been a number of glorious misadventures, yet in the beginning of each of them, indeed in the beginning of all of them, who could have known? God himself didn't know.

Certainly the philosophers, philologists, psychiatrists, psychologists, pediatricians, paleontologists, archeologists, anthropologists, sociologists, all those scientists and poets, playwrights and painters, priests, popes and preachers have not provided much more than a collection of footnotes, some well-documented and some well-stated, for the beginnings of these affairs. As for the ends, or what went on between a man and a woman, no one really knows. It is lost in the dewy nights. What went on between Eric Spehl and Beatrice Friederich? What there exists for sure is a certain amount of partly reliable gossip.

Göschweiler, the town in which Eric Spehl was born, was extremely small, a tiny farm village with a population not exceeding 100, including those buried in the cemetery maintained on a slope of the village meadow. Spehl's father was buried there.

He had been a farmer, and Eric the youngest of the farmer's first four children—four boys. Not long after Eric had been born, his mother died. His father married again, this time to Eric's mother's sister, and five more children were born—two boys and three girls. Eric's stepmother was his aunt, though the arrangement was not uncommon in small farm villages at that time.

Their farm was not a large one. Typically the father hoped his two oldest sons would stay on the farm and work it. But as the younger boys reached 15, they had to leave. A small farm was not big enough to feed all of them.

When Eric Spehl reached 15, he traveled down from the Black Forest hills towards the Bodensee to Markdorf, where an apprenticeship as an upholsterer had been arranged for him. From 1927 until 1930 he worked and lived in a small shop, learned to run a sewing machine, learned to sew cotton, and linen and leather. Markdorf was not by any means a city, not even a very big town, but it was a great deal larger than Göschweiler, and Eric Spehl learned about cities still bigger than Markdorf.

He had been raised in the circumspection of a devoutly Catholic village. Moreover, he was naturally shy. As one of the "middle children" of a large brood, he was inadept at advancing himself. The quick tongues and self-assurance of the young women who worked in shops in Markdorf constantly amazed him. He did not know how to approach them. So at night, in the upholsterer's shop, he spent many hours listening to the radio.

When his three-year apprenticeship was up in 1930 he had heard a great deal of music, and in addition, a great deal of politics. He received his upholsterer's certificate, but by then the Depression had begun, and there was no work for him. He became an itinerant laborer, wandering to towns which promised work, living in miserable working class hostels when he could afford them, and returning to the farm when he was desperate.

He had just turned 21 when Hitler came to power in January 1933. In the tiny meadow town of Göschweiler there was general agreement that Herr Hitler might not be so bad. They had heard warnings from the priests, but priests could not give men work. It seemed as if no one could provide enough work for Germany. Perhaps the New Order would live up to its promises better than the previous governments had. Göschweiler voted for Herr Hitler.

When the new Reich instituted a labor corps, it was not clear in the village whether it was a compulsory service or a voluntary one. It happened to be compulsory, but it wouldn't have mattered. Eric Spehl went for the required year because there was no place else to go.

He didn't like it one bit. They were supposed to be rebuilding Germany, helping to build autobahns, starting new factories and such. Instead there was much marching, singing of patriotic songs, interminable speeches by men who had appointed themselves leaders, and not much work. When there was work, it was done with a spade as if they were convicts. The radio had pictured a more interesting world.

He returned to the farm in the fall of 1934 at harvest time. The tall blond boy was 22. His slender frame had lost the last of its baby fat. He was sinewy. The gentle laughter seemed to have gone too. The farm, and the village, were now too small a horizon for him. He helped with the harvest as willingly as ever, but he was quiet for long periods, almost withdrawn. He seemed to be trying to think of something.

One late October afternoon a younger stepsister went to the village church to put flowers beneath the statue of the Virgin. There she surprised Eric, sitting alone in a pew.

"For what are you praying, Eric?"

His reply had the tone of anger: "I'm not praying," but he quickly saw his vehemence had shocked her and that she might cry. She was only eight. He took her by the hand and together they put the flowers at the Virgin's statue. Then they had a drink of cider at the grey barn. He seemed gay again. Even though a quiet boy, he had always been happy. That's about all the family knew.

The very next week he heard there was work again in the Zeppelin factory in Friedrichshafen. And again he walked down to the Bodensee. His skill with a needle and with the sewing machine was demonstrable. He got the job as an apprentice rigger in the Luftschiffbau. Then Chief Knorr had selected him to sail on the *Hindenburg*. And then he met Beatrice Friederich.

The lover of Beatrice Friederich had been killed in Spain, but she was still to be seen in the company of many different men at the bars where politics and justice were discussed. What Eric Spehl was doing in one of those bars, no one knows. It was said that the first time they met at a table, he had been eager to talk to her all night, but that she had left early with another man.

It was said that she had returned another time alone—some said with nothing on her mind, while others said she was hunting for him. Both accounts might be true. Whatever the explanation, her apartment—the same one from which her artist had disappeared, and from which she had swept out that damn bartender one morning, and from which the lover had left for Spain—became a haven for young Eric Spehl.

There were those who said the rent he would eventually have to pay was beyond his means, but surely that was malicious envy on the part of the other women. She always had the attention of more men than they did, and they were jealous, that's all. As to the disasters which always seemed to befall her lovers, it should be noted that she always chose the more adventuresome kind of man, the kind who would test life's boundaries somehow, and it should be remembered that fate was cruel. Should she be judged because the men she loved tended to be experimental? Would it have been better if she had settled down and had babies by some safe, dull man, and they had sat there every evening in the kitchen listening to the clock tick, waiting until it was time to turn down the covers? Such a life would be not much more than a jail sentence.

Well maybe she'd have a baby with Eric Spehl after they got to America. He had taken up photography as a hobby, she encouraged him in it, and he began to think he was pretty good at it, which might be something to support them someday. She didn't know about the photography, but she could see that his confidence in himself was growing, and she liked the power she had to increase it little by little. In between the voyages of the *Hindenburg*, when she could have him with her at her apartment, it would not matter what time the clock said when she applied her magic touch.

When he was away on the tours of the Zeppelin, he imagined that no one else slept in the apartment except his Beatrice, which was true except for one or two exceptions which couldn't be helped. When he returned, she always made it seem like a holiday.

She began to introduce him to all kinds of men and women in Frankfurt from a world far different than any he had ever known. Even on the radio he had never heard such talk. And he found himself opening up a bit, as if she was necessary for his late flowering. To his surprise, the others listened.

For her, Eric Spehl had certain advantages. He was slim and strong and a very handsome display. But there was deep in his backbone— perhaps put there on the farm—something that she wanted to get her hands on.

She told him it must be his Catholicism, and teased him about it to see what he would say, or do. For a while every time she could, she gave him meat on Friday, then asked him whether he thought that really made any difference. The way he said he didn't think it did, gained her respect so she went back to buying fish for him on the Fridays when she could have him at home.

Because she always had a friend to see, or had won in bed what she knew and what she had, she had never listened too much to the radio.

But he always followed the news, and she began to learn from it too. She wanted to know what had happened to the lover she had lost in Spain. She didn't expect him back, it was rather that she thought it had been unjust, and the injustice must have some explanation. Perhaps the radio could provide the reasons.

At night as they lay together, he talked to her about what it was like on the farm; how he had got the job in Markdorf; about the year in Hitler's Youth Camps; how they built the Zeppelins. He tried to remember for her what he could of his mother, and he sketched a fairly acid picture of her sister, his stepmother. He talked about how his father had died, and about Chief Knorr on the *Hindenburg*.

She had been furious with him for his admiration of Knorr—she had all kinds of reasons, but it was something like the meat on Friday: after a while she let it go. The thing in his backbone was there all right, but she couldn't get at it that way.

Whether he was picking up a new set of ideas at the tables of her friends, who were always whispering about revolution, or whether the ideas were specifically his own, he couldn't tell. He didn't think much of most of the coffee house arguments. He had seen a great deal of the world, and he knew their ideas were all too small. Nevertheless he had to admit they made him begin to form ideas of his own which were very different from those he had when he left Göschweiler. On the long watches across the oceans when there was nothing to do, he had taken to reading all kinds of books.

Beatrice had books the artist had left behind. There were books for pennies on a stand down the street near her apartment; books thrown out for the junk dealer to sell.

He did not read according to any program, but more or less what came to hand—romantic novels; tracts on geography; mysterious arguments on economics which were illustrated profusely with charts and tables which fascinated him but which he could not understand; biographies of writers and philosophers of whom he had never heard, but whose lives seemed consistently more interesting than his own; detective stories; wild west novels.

In fact, he scavenged the whole great city dump of old ideas—which the censors of Dr. Goebbels' machine would have proscribed except that they were already consigned as "garbage." The attics of the neighbors were the libraries of Eric Spehl's curious education.

Of course, when the gossip made its rounds there were those who said that Beatrice Friederich was his school mistress, and she certainly must be given her due. Beatrice was his guide into a strangely fascinating new world. Probably more important in the end, however, was something he had noticed on the farm—for which, for a long time, he had not been able to account.

In every town and hamlet in Germany, and in Göschweiler, state officers collected the taxes from rich and poor alike for the support of the church—both for the Catholic Church and the "Evangelical" Lutheran Church, according to their registered populations. The prettiest building (and the costliest) in Göschweiler was the town's Catholic Church. The second prettiest (and second costliest) was the chapel set to the east of the walled cemetery.

Since the population of Göschweiler was about 60, neither of these handsome buildings could be described as if they were the hamlet's cathedrals, except in the relative sense. They were the centers of social congregation, the offices of birth, baptism, communion, marriage and of burial.

Every Sunday and on a great number of feast days the priests celebrated the Holy Mass, and read out the Epistles, the Gospels, and additional admonitions of their own. About the Epistles and Gospels Eric Spehl had no doubts. It was the supplementary lessons he began to question.

During his apprenticeship to the upholsterer in Markdorf, he had the radio every night as an alternative source of information. The sequence of his conversion began when he realized that the radio's lessons described a confused world, from which he deduced that the priests might be covering up the same things the Ministry of Propaganda was hiding.

He could see that if a crime were committed against the state, the criminal was sent to jail, but sometimes for no better reason than because the politicians wanted to put the criminal away, and they had had the power to do so. What was a terrible political crime in Munich, might be the reason to be elected Mayor of Berlin. Everyone had seen that happen.

Indeed, Herr Hitler had been jailed in Munich for advocating programs which had got him elected Chancellor, and now he had the power to put those in jail who had judged him a criminal. It was not a long jump to come to the next conclusion: all crimes were political, in a certain way. For example, if a starving man stole bread for his family from the bakery the judges could sentence because they had the power to do so. If the bakery adulterated the bread and so stole from all the poor, it would be a crime only when the poor had the power to sentence the bakers.

Eric Spehl tried out his thesis in the cafes to which Beatrice steered him, and it was accepted there without a doubt. Then more serious questions began to work cracks into the shale of his old faith. Didn't the priests administer very much the same thing as mayors? If he committed a sin for which the penance was three "Our Fathers," how serious was the sin if the punishment was so meaningless? Didn't it seem as if a priest was the town clerk for the Kingdom of God? Wasn't the authority of the best building in Göschweiler about the same authority as the former Kingdom of Württemberg? Didn't the Gospels themselves say that "the light" and "the Word" were within? Couldn't he see every day men who needed no more justification for breaking the law except that they wanted to, and they had the power to get away with it? And didn't he see priests who were first on this side of the law and then on the other, doing the same thing?

Did the priests who were being jailed by the Berlin Government have to say three "Our Fathers" for failing to pay their tax for the support of the community church? How could Berlin jail priests for which they raised taxes, except that they had the power to do so? Wasn't the argument an administrative one over spoils?

It was in the mood of these inchoate ideas that Eric Spehl met his Damascus on the radio. According to the radio reports, a twenty-year-old girl, Dolores Ibanruni, called "La Passionaria," was killed in the fighting in Spain. All the other girls in her battalion were killed or captured too, the radio said. None of the girls was older than their twenty-year-old leader.

"There's one thing you can be sure of, my Eric," said Beatrice. "The Spanish have not wasted a battalion of twenty-year-old girls by shooting them."

Just as St. Paul did, Eric Spehl began to talk about "judgment day," and have other apocalyptic visions. Even the radio he had trusted for so many years had begun to lie. But now he had other voices.

Then Beatrice's first husband had knocked on the door of the apartment in the early hours of the morning. The artist needed help very badly. The Gestapo had been at him for eight days. They had just let him go, but he did not know for how long he would be free. He needed money. He needed to get away, to run, but he was in no condition to even try. He cried constantly, but he had no tears for his sobbing. He kept asking for another drink of water.

Eric wondered if the water was simply fuel for the tears. Beatrice got salves and bandages by knocking on the doors of her neighbors.

The Gestapo had crushed his fingers in a vice, one by one. Where his nails should have been there was nothing but red pulp, oozing with yellow pus. At the knuckle on his left thumb the shattered bone showed through.

The martyr insisted he had to leave. They stuffed all the money they had into the breast pocket of his shirt. Eric turned the knobs of the door to the apartment, and the door to the street, so that he would not have to touch them. As he left he was still crying. He said to Eric: "God be in you." He didn't seem afraid.

It was that man's hands which were the central image in the nightmare of the farm boy from Göschweiler, the upholsterer from Markdorf, the sailmaker at Friedrichshafen, the rigger aboard the *Hindenburg*. Because of those hands Eric Spehl had decided for himself that "one act of genius was worth a lifetime of labor."

The bomb was perfectly safe. The only danger was old Knorr, but Spehl doubted that even the old rigger could find it. From the landing on the stairs in the tail, Spehl could almost see its position from where he was sitting. It was sewn into the bottom of Gas Cell IV. It had been there before they left Friedrichshafen. In order to activate it, he only needed to turn its timer, which was made from the kind used for enlargers. He had one of the same sort himself. They were very expensive.

When the time was right, he would cut into the folds of the gas cell with a knife. From the ladder leading up to the middle walkway he could reach over into the uninflated drooping part of the cell. Towards the end of the trip some hydrogen had always been valved off— perhaps as much as 15%, which meant that the bottoms of the cells were empty. The hydrogen forced itself up, straining against the top of its bag. The bottom of the bag hung in heavy folds, pressed in on itself by the pressure of the surrounding air.

He would cut into those drooping folds. It would then take only a moment to set the timer. The folds would hide the cut, and hide the bomb, as the timer marched around its dial in its appointed course. The dial had been rebuilt, its face scored by scratches which indicated half-hour intervals up to four hours.

No one need be hurt, but he could revenge the artist's hands, he could strike a blow at this symbol of the State. He could smash the machine the radio had praised so incessantly, and force it to tell the truth for once and admit its vulnerability. And he would earn the respect of Beatrice forever. He would wait until after the ship had landed, set the timer going, and then just walk off the American Navy base. The Americans maintained practically no security, and anyway, no one would stop a German Zeppelin man from leaving. He would change out of his uniform to the clothes Beatrice had helped to select. Then he would just take the bus to New York, and find a place to stay in Yorkville.

When the ship had been destroyed, he would not go back. They would think he was missing. They might think he was dead. Chief Knorr would probably grieve, but that couldn't be helped. Even if they suspected him, in the case that he was the only one missing, they would never find him in New York. No one needed any papers there. Their plan was that Beatrice would come by boat when it was safe.

He was excited by his prospects. All the rest of their life they would share a great secret. He would be the author of an event not one of those talkers in the cafes could claim. The only part that made him nervous was what if she could not come?

To aid him in the success of the plan he had designed in the pungent company of his Beatrice, he had around his neck a medal of the Blessed Virgin Mary, which he touched from time to time for luck.

# CHAPTER 7

# ASCENSION DAY

"I consider the foundation or the destruction of a religion essentially more important than the foundation or destruction of a State, let alone a party."

—*Mein Kampf*, ADOLF HITLER

THURSDAY, May 6, 1937. The sun rose at 5:49 A.M. and was due to set in Lakehurst, New Jersey at 7:55 Eastern Daylight Saving Time. Berlin reported 81 degrees, cloudy; Paris, 70, fair; London, 61, cloudy.

At dawn the *Hindenburg* was west of Yarmouth, at sea, on course for Boston about 350 miles away. During the night, she averaged 63 knots at an altitude of 700 feet in light rain, and a light head wind from the southwest.

Navigator Max Zabel had been able to get bearings from the lighthouses at White Head Island, Berry Head, Beaver Islands, Lipscomb Island, the lightship off Sambro Shoals, and the light on Little Hope Island. The log at 0400 gave their position off Cape Sable, 8 hours behind schedule.

The disturbance which was over southern Quebec had moved northeastward. Off Belle Isle, Newfoundland, the barometer had registered a low of 29.68. Another low which had been in the Mississippi Valley was moving rapidly eastward and at 8:00 P.M. last night had been centered over Maryland and central Pennsylvania. It carried a barometer low of 29.65. It was causing fresh southerly winds along the Middle Atlantic Coast and showers were expected with it.

At 8:45 A.M. Lakehurst copied from the *Hindenburg* the ship's 0800 position: 43.03 NORTH 67.35 WEST SPEED 35 MPH COURSE 255 HIGH 200 MTS.

At 9:35 A.M. the weather bureau sent its #8 which read: BROADCAST INCLUDES ALL AVAILABLE INFORMATION TO THAT TIME NEXT MESSAGE WILL INCLUDE REPORTS COLLECTED AT 1330 EST AND PROBABLE LANDING CONDITIONS WILL BE SENT FROM LAKEHURST ON REQUEST.

May 6 was forty days after Easter Sunday—the Day of Ascension, a holy day of obligation. Ascension Day does not always fall on May 6 because the Feast of Easter sometimes comes early in the spring and sometimes late.

The Gospel for the Mass of Ascension Day is taken from Mark. It is the one in which Jesus appears to the eleven at table and reproaches them for their incredulity and dullness, then tells them to go forth and proclaim the Good News to the whole of creation.

In Douglaston, New York, Mrs. Joseph Spah attended the seven o'clock Mass, taking Gilbert, 4, Marilyn, 2, and Richard, 1, with her. She planned to drive down to Lakehurst later that day to meet her man.

In Toms River, New Jersey, Detective Arthur C. Johnson, New York City Police Department, had a grand breakfast: two sets of two fried eggs and bacon, plus a side order of bacon, and plenty of coffee.

There was no sense in rushing over to the Naval Air Station because the *Hindenburg* was now not due until 6:00 P.M. Either six in the morning or six at night, that's the way they handled their schedules.

What with the usual landing folderol, he would probably miss "Amos 'n Andy" on WEAF at 7 o'clock, which he preferred to WJZ's "Easy Aces"; but he'd at least be able to get "The Answer Man" at 7:30, if there were no further delays. In the meantime, he had a long day's wait ahead of him.

He had time to read up on Zeppelins in the current issue of *Collier's* magazine. The May 8 issue had been on the newsstand since Tuesday. Publishers did that: put a date on their magazines a week ahead.

In *Collier's* the writer, W. B. Courtney, described a trip he had taken on the *Hindenburg* the year before. He described the ship and gave some of the history of Zeppelins.

Count Zeppelin, who thus broke all precedents for generals by amounting to something after he retired, was practical too; he began carrying passengers for money in his earliest models, long before the war and before airplanes did the same. German dirigibles since have flown nearly one million passengers without a fatality. And it is the firm conviction of this skeptical reporter, after close firsthand watching of their methods, that only a stroke of war or an unfathomable act of God will ever mar this German dirigible passenger safety record.

On the morning of May 6 Miss Margaret Mather awoke to announce she "had slept like a child." She awoke "with a feeling of well being and happiness," she said, "such as one rarely experiences after youth has passed."

At dawn no land was in sight and it was raining again. She ate breakfast, joked with the young men, her messmates, who "were always comparing my appetite with theirs." She packed her few things, wrote a card or two, and suddenly she realized they were flying over Boston.

North of Boston Lightship, Captain Pruss had taken the *Hindenburg* down to 600 feet, then to 500 feet. The morning fog was burning off. The airship appeared over the Customs House tower. The noonday crowds below at first had only heard the ship, but then they had their chance to gape. The sun finally had come out. In the harbor, ships tooted their whistles.

As they flew over Boston's suburbs Miss Margaret saw cars draw up by the roadside and their occupants leap out to gaze up. Airplanes came to circle about them and one or two accompanied them on the way. She thought it was delightful to look down on the gardens. "Yellow forsythia was in bloom, and some sort of trailing pink; the grass plots were vivid green," and she saw "apple trees in blossom and woods full of dogwood and young green leaves."

As the ship passed overhead it frightened the dogs, who rushed into their houses, or "stood their ground and barked long after the ship had passed." Margaret Mather could see the ship caused a great commotion in barnyards: "Especially among the chickens and pigs."

The pigs rushed desperately to and fro, "and seemed absolutely terrified, and the chickens fluttered and ran about in proverbial fashion. Cows and sheep did not notice as much."

They flew over Providence and she could recognize many villages, rivers, and bays. They crossed into the Sound over the Race, passed Plum Gut and Horton's Point on the Long Island side, and New London on the Connecticut shore. Peter Belin stood beside Miss Margaret. She thought him a charming lad, shared his enthusiasm for aviation, and did her best to sight his alma mater, Yale, as they passed New Haven.

Lunch was served early and everyone was quick about it, because they wanted to be free when they sighted New York. The course of the ship kept straight down Long Island Sound, from Stratford Shoals Light in Midsound to Execution Rocks at the Western end. Emma Pannes pointed out Manhasset Bay, where their home was. She said their son would drive from there to meet them at Lakehurst.

Everyone was excited. The passengers packed and collected their papers for their passport examinations. The stewards removed the bedclothes and piled them at the end of the corridors. Baggage was being piled up under the statue of Marshal Hindenburg in the passageway at the head of the stairs on "A" deck.

Captain Pruss had announced that the *Hindenburg* would refuel and reload in record time, then turn around to sail for Germany at midnight. He sent a message at 2:55 to NEL which read: RETURN OF LAUNDRY IS NOT NECESSARY STOP WILL SAIL AS SOON AS POSSIBLE PRUSS.

New York hove into sight. To Leonhard Adelt the skyscrapers below appeared "like a board full of nails." He thought the viaducts and highways looked as if they were in relief as in a model; the bridges appeared to swing across the rivers in a filagree of steel, and the Statue of Liberty seemed as small as a porcelain figure.

When the ship had passed over City Island, word was flashed ahead to Manhattan by telephone to be on watch for the *Hindenburg*. Captain Pruss steered for Times Square, passing directly over the sightseers on the West Side of Broadway. Leaving Times Square, the ship picked up an escort of airplanes, including a twin-motored Bernelli flown by Clyde Pangburn. *The New York Times* said Pangburn's big plane looked like an ant moving beside an elephant.

From windows, rooftops, sidewalks, fire escapes and other points of vantage, thousands craned their necks to see the *Hindenburg*. Bright sunshine made her swastikas gleam. Traffic stopped on many streets because drivers left their cars to gaze up. After rounding the Statue of Liberty, the ship crossed over Ebbet's Field in Brooklyn. The Dodgers were playing the Pittsburgh Pirates. The game paused for a moment to give the fans a chance to stare.

Captain Pruss turned north again, crossed over crowds on the steps of the Treasury building in Wall Street, then across town again. Leonhard Adelt said he could see the photographers on top of the Empire State Building, whose great silver peak had been originally designed as a dirigible mast, until it turned out that the terminal facilities at Lakehurst were less poetic but more practical.

Then over the Hudson, turning south to the lower bay, and New Jersey. Over the harbor, the *Hindenburg* was greeted by several sustained minutes of tooting and groaning from the stacks of the ships.

At 3:30 DEKKA radioed NEL: COURSE LAKEHURST PSE SEND WEATHER AR.

At 3:35 NEL replied: BROKEN CUMULUS CLOUDS SURFACE WIND SOUTHEAST ELEVEN KNOTS GUSTS TWENTY KNOTS SURFACE TEMPERATURE SEVENTY FOUR PRESSURE TWENTYNINESIXTYTHREE FALLING SLOWLY AR.

At 3:38 DEKKA sent: CREW DINNER WILL BE SERVED ON BOARD.

Captain Pruss planned to save time in the quick turnaround. Off to the west of the ship the captains in the gondola could see the black clouds of a summer thunderstorm gathering.

At 13 minutes to 4:00 P.M. NEL sent: GUSTS NOW TWENTY FIVE.

Shortly after 4:00 o'clock, the *Hindenburg* crossed over the Air Station at Lakehurst. Captain Pruss dropped a message with a weight attached. The message said: "Riding out the storm."

Though the *Hindenburg* was still in sunshine, the sky to the west did look ugly. Lightning played in towering cumulus. At the navigator's weather table they figured the front extended from the Hudson Valley at Bear Mountain down through a point west of Philadelphia. They could hear the roll of thunder.

Leonhard Adelt thought the storm looked like a pack of hungry wolves. He was disappointed they would not land immediately. As they crossed the field he could see automobiles parked around the edges of the field and people waving at the ship. He knew that among those waiting were two brothers whom he had not seen for thirty years.

Captain Pruss kept south for Atlantic City. Leonhard Adelt noted that he thought they were riding south along the storm wall.

Chief Kubis reminded Miss Margaret Mather the lightning was not at all dangerous, and that a Zeppelin can cruise about indefinitely above storms. Tea was served early and the Doehner boys looked charming in their Buster Brown suits. They were anxious to land too.

In the hangar Einar Thulin, New York correspondent of the Stockholm *Tidningen*, waited to meet Birger Brinck. There was a representative of the *Yale Daily News* there too, ready to phone the details of the ship's arrival to New Haven. Mr. and Mrs. Belin waited in their car to meet their son Peter. In the cloudbursts everyone took shelter.

Mrs. Evelyn (Joe called her "Vera") Spah got her three children into the car, but not before they were already soaked. While they waited, the windows of the car steamed with the humidity and the children were naturally restless. She had parked out beyond the fence. It was impossible to get any closer.

There was a sign there which read:

On Account of Brief Stay
of Airship *Hindenburg*
At this Port
The Public Cannot be
Permitted
At the Mooring Location
Or Aboard Ship

All Available Time in Port is Required
For Servicing and Preparation For
Return Voyage to Europe

AMERICAN ZEPPELIN TRANSPORT
General Agents

Captain Heinrich Bauer relieved Captain Albert Sammt as the duty watch officer at 4:00 P.M. After coming off watch Captain Sammt toured the middle gangway of the ship, then the lower gangway from stern to bow. He returned to the command gondola to report all was well.

Their course took them out over Toms River, then down along the beaches off the Jersey Coast. The beaches were bright white in the sun, but west of the ship it still looked like heavy going. They passed Seaside Heights, Barnegat Light, Beach Haven, got as far south as Little Egg Harbor, by Atlantic City.

At 5:12 NEL sent: THUNDERSTORM MOVING FROM WEST OVER STATION SURFACE TEMPERATURE 70 FALLING SURFACE WIND WEST SIXTEEN KNOTS GUSTS TWENTY ONE WIND SHIFTED FROM NORTH AT 1600 EST PRESSURE TWENTYNINESIXTYFOUR RISING.

At 5:35 P.M. Pruss queried: HOW IS VISIBILITY FROM LAKEHURST WESTWARD. The Naval Air Station replied: VISIBILITY WESTWARD EIGHT MILES UNSETTLED RECOMMEND DELAY LANDING UNTIL FURTHER WORD FROM STATION. ADVISE YOUR DECISION.

Captain Pruss answered: WE WILL WAIT YOUR REPORT THAT LANDING CONDITIONS ARE BETTER. And he signaled Steward Kubis to get some sandwiches ready for the passengers while they waited.

Sandwiches would not temper Colonel Erdmann's increasing displeasure with the delays. The leisurely crossing, looking at scenery, did not suit his Luftwaffe sense of timing. Despite Captain Lehmann's representations the night before, he had continued to worry. What in fact had he accomplished on this trip? He might just as well have been a passenger. And how exactly was he to accomplish anything on the subject of security with the notoriously undisciplined Americans? He decided to explain his problem and then ask their naval commander for a detachment of the American Marines. At least they were orderly.

Miss Margaret Mather hung at the sill of the promenade window. She watched the ship's progress over the scrub oak and sparse pine woods on the flat plains near the coast. She could see deer run from beneath the ship—in groups of twos and threes. She had wired her niece Peggy to meet her: Mrs. Louis A. Turner, the wife of a fine man, she thought, a physics professor at Princeton. She hoped that Peggy had got the wire in time. Peter Belin said his parents would meet him with a car. Miss Margaret told him she didn't care how long this cruising lasted, she felt foolish with happiness.

In the lounge Otto Clemens and Joseph Spah were taking their last moving pictures to record the flight. Spah seemed particularly restless. He kept moving from one side of the ship to the other, pacing back and forth. Lt. Hinkelbein, assigned the task by Colonel Erdmann, kept pace with Spah at what seemed a discreet distance. He heard Spah say to Chief Kubis: "When do we get down? I'm tired of this cruising around."

At 6:00 P.M. Chief Knorr relieved Eric Spehl on watch. Shortly before going off watch, Spehl cut the fabric of Gas Cell IV, deep down within the folds of the loose bag, and started the timer. He set it at 2 hours—that would be eight o'clock. He rearranged the folds of the drooping cell to hide the slice. Since the hydrogen was pressing up to the top of the cell, hardly any would leak at the bottom where he had made his cut—until the phosphorus burned away the fabric and the air began to pour in. Then the oxygen and hydrogen would meet and —poof!

Chief Knorr started his habitual inspection. When he put his hand on Gas Cell IV to feel its pressure, he thought it felt low. On his way forward he passed Kubis in the lower gangway and said he thought they might have a soft cell, so they shouldn't count on sailing at midnight, if it turned out they would need to make repairs.

In the command gondola, they read the message sent down from the radio room by Chief Willy Speck. At 6:12 NEL said: CONDITIONS NOW CONSIDERED SUITABLE FOR LANDING GROUND CREW IS READY PERIOD THUNDERSTORM OVER STATION CEILING 2000 FEET VISIBILITY FIVE MILES TO WESTWARD SURFACE TEMPERATURE 60 SURFACE WIND WESTNORTHWEST EIGHT KNOTS GUSTS TO 20 KNOTS SURFACE PRESSURE 29.68.

The captains presumed the message meant the thunderstorm would have cleared by the time they reached the field. They answered: OK.

At 6:22 Speck copied another from Lakehurst which read: RECOMMEND LANDING NOW COMMANDING OFFICER.

Radio Officer Herbert Dowe couldn't help but remark to Speck that they had been troubled by static since leaving Frankfurt, but now the air waves were absolutely clear—even though the storm was just clearing the station.

At 6:44 Captain Pruss wired Commander Rosendahl: COURSE LAKEHURST. He sent his position as FORKED RIVER. The *Hindenburg* turned for the field.

At the elevator wheel Eduard Boetius reported to Captain Bauer the ship was 3 to 4 degrees light in the bow and tail heavy.

Watch Officer Bauer explained to Boetius that as the *Hindenburg* poked through the rain squalls of the front, the wind drove the rain aft towards the tail, like water running down hill. But the moisture would evaporate back there soon—when they got to the other side of the front. They shouldn't valve to compensate, just wait a moment. They should be over the field in about 15 minutes.

The thundershowers had one advantage: Commander Rosendahl need not worry about the fire in the woods northwest of the field. It was out.

Commander Rosendahl had summoned the ground crew by steam whistle: 92 Navy men and 139 civilians. The mast detail had six men. Lieutenants Antrim and May would work atop the mast. Ten men would man the yaw guy capstans. Two men each on the yaw guy capstan cars.

The ship would drop its yaw guys first. Their bitter ends would be tied to waiting lines. Then taken up on capstan winches through single block leads. Each yaw guy coupling party was four men. The yaws would hold her steady until the main wire was let down from the bow.

The main wire coupling party took six men. They took the main wire in hand when it was on the ground and shackled it to a lead from the main wire winch on the mooring mast. The mast's diesel would crank her down.

Sixty-eight men were assigned to the forward landing lines party. The ship's crew would let spider lines down, each line with a toggle handle spliced into its end. The men on the ground took the toggles in hand, and kept the ship down by digging their heels in, if necessary. If the landing officer ordered, they could swing the ship; or steady her in a cross-wind. They were divided into two crews: port and starboard.

There was a similar crew of 43 men for the forward car; 37 assigned to the stern car; 46 assigned to stern landing lines. Five men were in the tractor crew for the stern railroad car on its circular track. There were one truck driver and a messenger assigned.

The men were lined up in two rows—port and starboard—parallel to the line the ship used in approaching the mast. The "landing line" was estimated to be dead into the wind. Upon the orders of the mooring officers, the bosuns lined the men up at their marks.

When the whistle had blown for stations, the men came from their houses around the field, from the barracks, from the Petty Officers Club. No sooner had they arrived at stations, than they were soaked by the passing squall. They were ordered into the hangar, then back to stations. It poured again, and again they were told to take shelter. Some tried to stay dry in the shelter of the mooring mast. At 6:45 they were called to stations again, but by then their whites were pretty much soaked through.

Civilian crewman Allen Hagaman had left his house with a ham sandwich in his hand when he heard the whistle. By 6:45 he still had it with him; it was too soggy to eat.

His daughter Sarah, 15, had also run from the house to catch the ride to the field. She wanted to see the big ship arrive. She had left her record player playing "The Dipsey Doodle." By 6:45 the needle was probably gone for good.

In the gondola Helmsman Kurt Schoenherr was steering approximately northeast from about Whitings to the south edge of the field. The chiefs reported to Captain Pruss at about 6:55.

Chief Radio Operator Willy Speck was about to order the trailing radio antennas wound up into the ship and the radios shut down.

Chief Lenz could report all generators, cables, transformers, circuit breakers were okay. Not even a fuse had needed to be replaced during the voyage.

Chief Sauter could report all engines okay.

Chief Knorr had already reported the apparent leak, or softness, in Gas Cell IV. They would have a look after landing.

In the dining saloon, Stewards Kubis and Nunnenmacher had just served sandwiches, then Nunnenmacher had cleared the silver sandwich tray to the pantry, and had set up a table for the customs and immigration men. Most of the passengers were at the open windows of either the dining saloon or the promenade on the port side. Someone said they were "getting an extended Zeppelin cruise at no extra cost."

George Grant had written one more entry in his diary: "The *Hindenburg* is likely to go to posterity as a forerunner of regular worldwide travel by airship."

Moritz Feibusch admitted to William Leuchtenburg he had not been able to finish addressing all his 200 postcards. He would have to finish on his way home to California.

The Doehner boys each had a teddy bear. Irene helped her mother by holding several pieces of small hand luggage.

A steam whistle aboard the *Hindenburg* summoned the ship's crew to landing stations just before 7:00.

Chief Engineer Sauter took his post in the stern at the bottom of the stairs in the lower vertical fin. From there he would man the telephone to the gondola. He could look out through the windows port and starboard to the ground. In the landing party at the station he commanded were Freund, to handle the stern yaw lines and drop the spiders; Lau, off duty as helmsman, to help Freund; and Kollmer, who would help let the main stern mooring cable down, then man the stern wheel.

Teams of mechanics were in each engine gondola. Schreibmueller and Bahnholzer in #1—starboard, aft; Fischer and Deutschle in #2—port, aft; Doerflein and Steeb in #3—starboard, forward; Bentele and Schaedler in #4—port forward. In addition, Schaeuble, Zettel and Ritter would stand by in the crosswalk forward.

The landing party in the bow was directed by Chief Knorr, who manned the phones from the window observation posts at the bottom of the stairs. He had Felber, Bernhard and Spehl up at the rim to work the main winch line and the nose cone connections. He could call for extra help if he needed from the off-duty watch in the crew's mess.

Jean Rosendahl had entertained her guests at the bridge table most of the afternoon. Between rubbers they had followed the reported positions of the *Hindenburg* all the way down from Westerly, R.I., over New York, and had seen it pass over the field. The Commanding Officer's wife had already had the table set for the dinner that evening which would honor Captains Lehmann and Pruss. There were fourteen places. The flowers were fresh and it was, all in all, a rather pretty table.

With Mr. F.W. von Meister, the American Zeppelin Company's representative, and Mr. von Meister's mother, with Mr. Farley and N.W. Hubbard, Jean Rosendahl was also out on the field, standing with her party of guests a little way back from the mooring mast, and her husband.

Herb Morrison had set up his sound man in a shack at the edge of the field. They had checked their equipment, and they were ready to record for the Prairie Farm Station. Morrison's cue sheets said there were 97 people on board, 36 of them passengers. When the ship had first passed over the field, he could see passengers at the open promenade windows, waving and laughing to their friends below.

Henry W. Roberts, Radio Editor of *Aero Digest*, Alice Rogers Hager of the *Washington Evening Star*, and C.B. Allen of the *New York Herald Tribune* were there. Standing with other gentlemen of the press were two girls who had managed their way past the gate. They said they were waiting to meet crewmen Franz Herzog and Franz Eichelmann.

From the gondola they could see the south fence of the field from about five miles out. There was still some overcast left behind the showers whose skirts were dragging off towards the Atlantic in the east. It was clearing in the west, but a light drizzle was still falling over Lakehurst. Twilight, under the overcast, was early.

They crossed the south fence at about 7:04; altitude, 200 meters— about 600 feet, making 73 knots, still steering northeast. They crossed directly over the landing circle, following the double track until it turned right for the hangar. The huge hangar doors were open. The old LZ 126, the *Los Angeles,* was berthed inside. There was room enough inside for the *Hindenburg* too. Captain Pruss had a look at the green blinker atop the hangar roof which blinked out "L"—dit-dah-dit-dit. On top of the Air Station's meteorological station a neon light sign gave the wind direction and velocity at the water tower. Pruss knew that it stood at 186 feet.

He had his ship's course altered to north, then northwest, then west. In a long arc the *Hindenburg* circled to the west of the station, then began to turn south to begin her approach. At 7:11 he ordered gas valved for 15 seconds, and her altitude began to drop to 180 meters. As she swung back towards the field, southeast, then east towards the hangar, he ordered "All engines idle, ahead." Then at 7:13 he had hydrogen valved from Cells XI to XVI, the forward cells, for 15 seconds because she was still tail heavy.

Over the field's west fence he turned her northeast again. Altitude was down to 120 meters. He ordered "Aft engines idle astern," then "aft engines full astern," then when he had slowed her enough, "Aft engines idle astern."

She was still heavy aft, and bow high. By telephone he ordered six men from the off-watch forward to the bow. The moment of their weight (900 pounds times about 400 feet) would be a total of about 180 tons. By stationing them in the bow, he would help trim his ship. It was 7:15.

Joseph Spah and Otto Clemens were still taking pictures. Most of the passengers were crowded at the starboard side windows, the promenade side, because from there, as the ship approached, they could see the hangar area. The stewards found places at the port side, in the dining saloon.

In his excitement, Spah had taken off his watch and laid it on the window sill. Leaning out the open window while winding up his Bell & Howell movie camera, he knocked the watch off into space. Spah asked Steward Kubis if Kubis thought they would be able to find it after they had landed. Kubis said, "sure." Lt. Hinkelbein thought it would be amusing if the watch still worked.

*          *          *

Watching from the observation windows cut like eyes into the snout of the bow, Eric Spehl waited at his landing station, ready with the main bow wire. He checked his watch. It said 7:15.

They had first crossed over the field at 4:00 and should have landed at 6:00. That's what the schedules said. He supposed the thunderstorms had held them up. Altogether they were now 13 hours late. But he didn't see why they couldn't have landed shortly after six. Now if his plan was still going to work, he had only 45 minutes to get off the base. At least they were finally landing, but he realized he was cutting it close.

From his perch he could look back down the arc of the stairs. Next to him he had Felber and Bernhard. The Captain had ordered six additional men forward for trim. He looked down at Huchel, then Biallas, Stoeckle, Flackus, and Mueller, then Chief Knorr at the phones, Joseph Leibrecht, the electrician, Kurt Bauer, an off-watch navigator, and Alfred Groezinger, the cook, who had burned his foot with soup.

With each man on his step, facing forward or trying to have a look out an observation window, they looked like acolytes at a very high Mass, each standing in line on the steps leading to the altar up on the rigger's rim.

From the windows they could see they were over the base housing.

As the *Hindenburg* approached its mast, a ray of sun broke through from the west, flashed on the windows of its gondola. On the ground Herb Morrison had started recording for his broadcast. The pencil reporters began their notes. "It was a great floating palace. . . . It looked like a silver whale. . . . It was a symbol of luxury and speed in transatlantic travel. . . . It was the latest in the line, even bigger ships were coming. . . . It was developed in war, Zeppelins had conducted the first raids against civilians . . . but now it was a symbol of peace and commerce. . . . It was the pride of Germany, the way Germany showed her new aggressive flag—the swastikas on her tail. . . . It was the wonder of awed millions in cities the world over. . . . It was landing."

On the steps of the BOQ Mess Hall, U.S. Navy Steward Joseph A. Kirkman had come out to have a look too. The ship passed directly over his head. As he watched, the ship let out water ballast, and he was doused in one blast of 1,100 pounds of water. He went to change his whites cursing.

At 7:19 Captain Pruss ordered "All engines full astern," and on a line heading just about south, the *Hindenburg* drifted to a dead stop just short of the mooring mast. Altitude was reported to be about 200 feet. At 7:20 he ordered: "Forward engines idle ahead; aft engines idle astern." If he needed a short burst to move her in any direction, his engines were ready.

Back under the stern Francis Hyland, line handler directly under the tail, stared up in an attempt to see whether his name still appeared on the port side of the ship. Last year he had written it there before the *Hindenburg* had sailed for Germany.

At 7:21 the forward starboard yaw line was dropped in a coil. Despite the wet sand, Captain Pruss noticed that as it hit, a cloud of dust came up. The port yaw line followed. The Navy men rushed in to take the lines in hand. They made them fast to the capstan lines.

During the approach Chief Steward Kubis had come from "B" deck up to "A" deck. He had checked down on "B" deck to see if there were any passengers left down there. From the dining saloon side he watched the yaw lines drop at 7:21. He would have much to do to get ready for a return sailing as soon as midnight. The clean linen in every cabin was the first task.

Colonel Erdmann, Major Witt, Lieutenant Hinkelbein and George W. Hirschfeld were in a group by the windows on the starboard side of "A" deck. It faced away from the hangar as the ship nosed into the wind toward the mast. When Colonel Erdmann saw the landing lines drop, he said, "Well, at least that's that part." Now for the American end of the problem. Lt. Hinkelbein observed to himself that as usual there was nothing to worry about.

If they had discussed it, Colonel Erdmann might have begun to agree. Although his instructions had specified that the greatest danger was on the American shore, he began to suspect that perhaps the S.S. had led him to play a fool, and that Captain Lehmann had shown the better judgment all along. Certainly, after close observation of Mr. Spah, the man seemed to be no more than what he pretended: a clown.

Gertrud Adelt was leaning against an open window on the dining saloon side. She too saw the lines drop at 7:21. She heard the motors go to idle, and become silent. She thought everything remarkably still, as if the whole world was holding its breath. She turned to her husband, she could not explain why, because she was suddenly afraid.

At the signal "landing stations," Hans Freund had gone to Ring 62 on the lower gangway, directly below the flue between Gas Cells IV and V. About three feet to starboard of the walkway there was a small hatch leading out through the belly of the ship. Through it, he would let out one of the stern spiders.

The spider was steel cable of about 60 feet, the steel end attached to the ship. Spliced into it were the fan of manila lines with the wooden handles at their tips for the ground crew. At the steel end, the spider was wound around a drum, and the drum could be let out, or taken in. Through the hatch hole, which was about a foot in diameter, he let out about 12 feet of the cable. At that point he could see they were about 100 feet above the ground.

He went aft to Ring 47, which is exactly at the point where the vertical fin faired into the hull. Through another hatch, he let out about three feet of cable, but then it jammed. The cable was stored in the lower fin, then hauled up the stairs inside the fin by a leader of manila line. The manila had caught in one of the strut wires beside the stairway. He called for Helmut Lau to clear it for him.

Lau's station was at 33.5 down the stairs in the fin. There was a window there, from which he could look out to starboard. The emergency elevator and steering controls were just ahead of him. He watched the variometer to check the descent of the ship. From the window he saw the starboard yaw line drop in a coil, and the dust puff up as it hit.

He saw the landing crew wait until both yaw lines hit the field, before they rushed in to hook them to the capstan lines. He could see that a light crosswind was pushing the ship to starboard, but that otherwise the ship had no movement forward. She hung still.

Freund was pulling the wire up the stairs for the line that runs out through the hatch at Ring 47. It snagged. Freund called for help to untangle it. To lead the line clear, Lau had to climb up the first flight of stairs. With one hand he got hold of the handrail that leads up the second flight, and with his free hand he led the cable clear. He watched it progress up the stairs on to the walkway. From the landing to the top of the stairs was about 30 feet.

Forty feet behind Freund's head, up where the axial or center walkway crossed the flue between Gas Cells IV and V, Lau saw a bright blue-white flash on the front bulkhead of Cell IV. He heard a *frump*, as if a big gas kitchen range were being lit—not a sharp detonation. Freund heard it too, and turned around to look.

The fire was a yellow-orange color at first. Its reflection on the cell wall was still small and flickering. They could see it burning inside the cell, and there was smoke with the red and yellow and orange. The fire was taking hold, but they still saw through the skin of the cell to the fire inside. Then the cell suddenly disappeared with the heat. The fire had got air, turned very bright, then rose in a ball more to the starboard side. Lau saw burning fabric beginning to rain down into the hull.

There was a tremendous second detonation as the flames burst through the top of the ship. It nearly threw Lau off the landing on which he was standing. It shook the whole fin left and right. He was still holding on with one hand.

Girders, molten aluminum, wires, struts, pieces of steel, and burning fabric were falling all around him. He tried to tuck in his head. It occurred to him he had forgotten his hat. He dove for the bottom of the tail to Chief Sauter's telephone position. Freund dove after him and landed on him. Sauter too was lying on the floor with his hands over his head, but he still had the phone in his right hand. They knew the stern was falling rapidly and would soon hit the ground.

In the command gondola they felt the ship lurch. Captain Lehmann asked Captain Pruss: "Is a rope broken?"

Pruss answered matter-of-factly: "No."

They saw a red glow spreading on the ground beneath them. Helmsman Schoenherr, feet still planted before his wheel, began to groan.

Watch Officer Ziegler said: "I better get the log book."

Lehmann and Pruss both looked down from first one side of the car, then the other. Lehmann said to Captain Bauer: "Drop the water ballast."

Heinrich Bauer attempted to execute the order by phone. There was no answer. He immediately tried the manual controls. He couldn't tell if anything happened.

In the bow Eric Spehl felt the tremor and heard the second explosion. Through his observation window he could see the red glow coming forward beneath the ship. The Navy men were frozen in their tracks like statues, their arms still reaching up on the lines to the ship. Then they dropped the lines and began to run. He looked at his watch: 7:25. It was too soon! Something must have gone wrong! Had he set the timer wrong? He couldn't think. Was his timing machine defective? Oh, Beatrice. . . .

Herb Morrison's recording for WLS, Chicago, had been going smoothly: "Here it comes, ladies and gentlemen, and what a sight it is, a thrilling one, a marvelous sight. . . . The sun is striking the windows of the observation deck on the westward side and sparkling like glittering jewels on the background of black velvet. . . . Oh, oh, oh . . . !"
"It's burst into flames. . . . Get out of the way, please, oh my, this is terrible, oh my, get out of the way, please! It is burning, bursting into flames and is falling. . . . Oh! This is one of the worst. . . . Oh! It's a terrific sight. . . . Oh! . . . and all the humanity! . . ."

On the promenade deck Otto Clemens was standing beside John Pannes. Clemens was leaning out the window, shooting pictures of the landing crew below. Through the lens he saw the Navy crew stiffen, then start to run. He looked up at John Pannes: "We'd better jump, Mr. Pannes."
Pannes said, "I think I'll go find Emma," and he turned for their cabin.

On the ground the Navy men had heard someone near the mooring mast yell: "Run for your lives." And they ran to get out from under the roaring fire above their heads. The linen-doped outer skin of the ship was just peeling away from its aluminum skeleton, as if a Japanese lantern had caught fire.
Next to the mooring mast, Jean Rosendahl began to scream for her husband. Commander Rosendahl had been up under the ship.

And then amid the roar of the flames, the screams, the confusion, everyone heard the fog-horn voice of Chief Bosun Bull Tobin: "STAND FAST!" They probably heard him over in Toms River.

Emil Stoeckle, traveling as a passenger and inspector of mail, had seen the landing lines drop. He went to his cabin to get a coat out of his suitcase. He was standing in the door of Cabin #44 on "A" deck when the ship lurched forward and began to tilt down at the stern. He was thrown against the wall.

He got up again, made his way to the staircase leading to "B" deck. Halfway down the stairs he could see through a window that the ship was still high above the ground. He sat down and waited. He could hear passengers running back and forth up on "A" deck. Some of them were yelling.

There was a terrific crash as the ship hit the ground. One of the windows burst from its frame. Stoeckle jumped through it, landing on his hands and knees. He got up and ran.

Henry W. Roberts, editor of *Aero Digest*, said the light from the burning ball of hydrogen was as bright as "a thousand, ten thousand magnesium flares," as bright as the sun at noon. As the seven million feet of hydrogen was consumed, a great ball of fire rose above the ship. As the burning hydrogen escaped its ruptured gas cells, it rose. As the huge burning ball of fire rose, a strange cloud formed around its diameter. It was sort of mushroom-shaped.

After putting the leftover sandwiches in the pantry dumbwaiter, Steward Nunnenmacher had gone to the middle windows of the dining saloon, on the port side.

The second explosion knocked him to his knees. He saw that he had fallen between the legs of a woman. He got up again and went to the windows. He hung on as the ship canted down by the stern. Chief Kubis jumped up on the sill and opened the window. He called to the others to keep the windows open. Nunnenmacher said to Kubis: "Jump!"

Kubis said: "No, I cannot, it is too high yet."

Others were jumping from the other windows. Finally Kubis jumped, and Nunnenmacher after him. Once on the ground, they ran for about 60 feet, then they stopped. Nunnenmacher took off his white jacket, which was burning, and threw it on the ground. They ran back towards the ship to help.

In the windows just aft of them, Max Henneberg and Fritz Deeg had waited until the ship hit the ground. It rose again a little way before settling down with a second crash. Then they jumped, and ran.

When they stopped, they looked back and saw that the flames were being driven by the wind towards the starboard side of the ship. They could run back to the windows of the port side. The dining saloon on "A" deck was now almost at ground level.

Fritz Deeg saw the two Doehner boys standing at the same window. They were hesitating. Behind them, their mother pushed them out. Deeg caught the hands of the first one and threw him. Deeg threw as if he were an Olympic hammer thrower. The boy sailed in an arc out of the fire zone. The second boy fell at his feet. The boy's hair was on fire. Deeg dragged him away.

Nunnenmacher called to the girl. She jumped into his outstretched arms. They both tumbled to the ground. She was on fire and it burned his hands. He tried to put out the fire in her hair and on her back. Captain Bauer appeared from somewhere and tried to help. Someone called: "Go away, the ship will sink down on you." They took the girl by her arms and started to drag her away. Her black flesh came off in their hands.

As they were dragging her from the ship, they passed Dr. Ruediger crawling on his hands and knees. They called to him, but he wouldn't answer. They didn't know that he had broken his leg. Nunnenmacher went back again and saw Mr. and Mrs. Ernst just coming out of the ship.

They were descending the main gangway just as if it were a normal disembarkation. The fire must have burned away the gangway lines which lowered it. Mr. and Mrs. Ernst walked down the stairs arm in arm. Nunnenmacher helped to support Mr. Ernst, who was about to break down. Men from the landing crew came up, and with two men on each side of the victims, they stumbled away.

At the fence Vera Spah screamed when she saw the ship burst into flames. She had Dickie in her arms. He began to scream too. She knelt down. She still had her rosary in her skirt pocket from this morning's Mass. She began to work the first three beads.

Gillie Spah was four. He kept saying over and over: "Please don't let my Daddy die. Please, God."

Werner Franz, cabin boy, age 14, had been in the officers' mess looking out the window. When he heard the explosion, he ran for the gangway. The steep tilt aft made him fall. Everything was on fire. Then a water tank burst just over his head, and he was drenched by two tons of water. He got up and jumped through the hatch in front of the smoking room. The water saved him.

Outside he met Mr. Kubis and Emil Stoeckle. They had Mrs. Doehner between them. She wanted to go back for her husband. They wouldn't let her. She had her two boys with her, but they wouldn't let her see her daughter. She asked: "Why not?" They wouldn't say.

Since he would have been one of the first men aboard, in the company of the Customs and Immigration men, Detective Arthur C. Johnson had been nearly under the ship. As soon as he realized what had happened, he knew it was his duty to get to a phone. They would need police, fire, ambulances, doctors. He started to run.

He was never too fast, and he hadn't gone far before he fell. He got up again, ran a short way, collided with some Navy man, went down again. He was aiming for the hangar, there'd be a pay phone in there. After another 50 yards, he was hit again. The place was a madhouse. Whoever had hit him should get fifteen yards for clipping. Within 60 feet of the hangar he tripped on the railroad tracks.

At the phone he dropped his nickel. He always carried extra nickels for emergencies. He finally got a connection. His call broadcast the alarm. Police, fire and ambulances would be on the way.

After the explosion, the fire had come forward into the dining saloon. Joseph Spah smashed at the window with his movie camera. The whole window fell out. Two men climbed out ahead of him. Spah followed them. The empty camera case on his shoulder fell to the ground below. He watched it go. It was a long way down.

All three men were hanging outside of the ship. Joseph Spah

thanked God that his act consisted of hanging on to a swinging lamp-post with one hand. One of the other men was slipping. He clutched at Spah's jacket, ripping off the lapel. Spah watched him drop, spread out, his legs kicking all the way down. It must have been over 100 feet. The man hit flat and his body seemed to bounce as it hit the sand. Spah hung on until he estimated the distance to be no more than 40 feet, then he let go. He remembered to keep his feet under him, and his knees bent. He rolled over after he hit, then brushed himself off, and limped away.

George Willens, who was at the field to fly on the return trip, recorded Joseph Spah's jump with his movie camera. He had never seen a jump like that to hard ground. He rushed up to Spah and intro-duced himself. "How on earth did you do it?"

"I don't know," said Spah. "Whew, am I lucky. Not a scratch!"

Later, in the hangar, when he had finally found Vera, she asked him why he was standing on one foot like a crane. She took him to the doctors.

August Deutschle and Adolf Fischer shared engine gondola #2 on the port side. At landing stations, Fischer manned the telegraph to the gondola. Deutschle was looking out the window at the hangar, watching the ground crew take up on the yaw lines when the second explosion knocked him down. He could see yellow flames shooting up from the ship by looking out the rear of the gondola through the prop. As the ship tilted aft, he was afraid for a moment he would slide out into the prop.

He pulled himself up on a stanchion, turned the throttle down, and fixed the propeller brake. The diesel chugged on for a while—which was characteristic of diesel engines—before it finally quit. He stayed in the car until it hit the ground. There was no fire in the car, just hissing and cracking.

After the crash, he tried to run from the ship, but engine car #2 was only about 90 feet from Ring 62, where the fire had been cen-tered. He had the feeling his back was on fire. He threw himself on the ground, and wriggled around to put it out. The sand was still wet and cool from the thunderstorms. But he couldn't stay where he was —the heat was too great.

He tried to get up and run again, but he couldn't even walk

anymore, so he wriggled on his belly, then on his back, to get away. While he was on his back, he saw Fischer pass him running towards the ship. Deutschle shouted at him: "Where are you going?"

Fischer stopped: "I thought you were still in the ship."

Fischer got some sailors to come and get Deutschle. They put him on a truck and took him away.

Herbert O'Laughlin had jumped, and made it clear. He ran to the hangar. He had to get a telegram through to his mother to tell her he was all right. The telephone operator told him she would send it free. As he turned away from the phone, someone asked him if he was all right. He said he was. He didn't have a scratch.

"Yes," they said, "but your face is all black."

Eduard Boetius had jumped out of the gondola. About 30 feet from the ship he saw Schaeuble lying on the ground unconscious. He dragged Schaeuble over to some sailors in the ground crew.

Then he joined Ziegler, Neilsen, Bauer and Deeg and together they climbed up into the port passenger quarters. They thought there were four passengers still in there. They saw the burning girl jump through the broken window.

Herbert Dowe had to get down the stairs from the radio room before he could get out the gondola window. All the drawers in the navigators' section had opened. All the maps and books were scattered on the floor. Once out the window, he was able to run only four or five paces before the framework of the ship collapsed over him.

He threw himself on the ground. The heat was intolerable. He started to burn on the head and face and hands. He crawled into the wet sand, trying to cover his hands and feet with sand. He couldn't remember if he had his shoes on, or not. He covered his head in sand, and waited for the outer cover of the Zeppelin to burn off.

Then he got up and ran. There was no cover now, just framework all aglow, steel wires and parts trailing like white vines. He stumbled clear.

George W. Hirschfeld was on the starboard side of "A" deck, the side towards which the wind was blowing. Colonel Erdmann, Major

Witt and Lt. Hinkelbein jumped through the window ahead of him. He saw Colonel Erdmann go down, felled by a red hot beam. He saw Hinkelbein zig-zagging to safety. He could not see Witt. Survival would be a matter of luck.

Hirschfeld landed on all fours—he figured it was about a twenty-five-foot jump. Parts of the framework and the ship's skin were burning on the ground around him. Hot wires were snaking through the air. Red hot glowing beams were falling ahead of him and behind him. He got up and started to zig-zag his way out. A burning wire snared his left foot, and he fell. He thought that was the end, but the air at the ground was cool and fresh because it was coming in from the outside to feed the rising flames. He managed to get his foot free again.

He jumped over some burning beams. He had to crawl under one beam and his face and hands began to burn. He had his Zeiss binoculars still in his right hand. He threw them away and patted out the fire on his face. He found he was finally free and fell down from shock. When he looked up, there was a man in coveralls standing there. He heard the screams of those trapped in the burning wires behind him. The man led him away.

Colonel Morris marched out of the collapsed frame, parting the white hot obstructing struts with his bare hands. His hands were flaming too. Major Dolan was going to follow him, but he never made it.

Some man found William Leuchtenburg in the dining saloon and led him down the stairs to "B" deck and then to safety. Leuchtenburg's eyes had been burned closed. At the bottom of the stairs, Leuchtenburg said he had to go back, he had forgotten his false teeth. The man said they could go back later.

Gertrud and Leonhard Adelt could not account for how they had jumped from the ship. They thought that maybe it was about 12 or 15 feet. They had to let go of each other's hands, to let Leonhard go ahead. He too bent the hot frames apart with his bare hands. He didn't feel any pain. They were in a sea of fire. It was like a dream. Their bodies had no weight. They floated like stars in space.

All at once Leonhard had the feeling that his wife was no longer at his side. He turned around to look, and flames seared his face. He saw her stretched out full length and motionless on the ground. He floated to her and pulled her upright. He gave her a push and saw her running again like a mechanical toy. The violence of his push threw him on his side. He lay on the oil-drenched, burning ground. He knew that this was dying, but it was such a feeling of well-being to stretch out and await death that the thought did not frighten him. Then he lifted his head to see if his wife was safe, and saw her, half blurred, still running through the vapors. That gave him a new start. He sprang up as if electrified, and hurled himself after the phantom of life.

Suddenly his scorched throat again breathed air. He stopped and looked back at the ship. It was blazing like a great torch. Something drew him toward it. He couldn't tell whether it was the feeling that he must try to save others, or that demon-like urge of self-destruction which drives the moth to the flame. His wife called to him, called more urgently, and ran back to him. She spoke to him. She took him by the hand; led him away.

On the port side, Peter Belin had been telling Margaret Mather how he had taken 80 photographs during the trip. They heard the dull muffled sound of an explosion. She saw a look of incredible consternation cross his face. The ship lurched, then took a steep tilt aft. She was hurled fifteen or twenty feet to the rear bulkhead wall of the dining saloon. She was pinned there against a projecting bench by several Germans who were thrown after her. The dining saloon furniture came crashing on top of them.

She couldn't breathe, and she thought to herself she would die, suffocated, but the men on top of her all sprang up, and she could sit up, with her back pressed against the bulkhead wall, and watch.

She saw the flames blow in, long tongues of flame, bright red, and she thought they were very beautiful.

The others were jumping up and down amid the flames. The lurching of the ship aft repeatedly threw them against the furniture and the railing, where they cut their hands and faces against the metal trimmings. They were streaming blood. She saw a number of men leap from the windows, but she just sat where she had fallen, holding the lapels of her coat over her face, feeling the flames light on her back, her hat, her hair. From time to time, she would beat out the flames on her coat and in her hair with her hands. She continued to watch the horrified faces of the others as they leaped up and down.

She saw a man detach himself from the leaping forms, and throw himself through the windows, arms and legs spread wide, with a terrible cry of "*Es ist das Ende.*" She saw Peter Belin jump. She thought: "Too bad, he was such a nice young man."

She sat there trying to protect her eyes. She thought it was like a scene from Dante's *Inferno.* She was just waiting. Then she heard a loud cry: "Come out, lady."

She looked and they were on the ground! Two or three men were peering in, beckoning and calling. She got up amazed. She looked for her handbag which had been jerked from her when she fell. "Aren't you coming?" called the man, and she ran to him over parts of the framework which were burning on the ground.

Once clear of the ship, George Grant rushed up to her with a cry of, "Thank God, you are safe." He helped her to a car and they drove to the infirmary.

At the moment the tail fin in the stern hit the ground, Chief Sauter seemed to regain consciousness. He dropped the phone he still held, and stood up. He was angry. How could this be happening? Someone had set fire to his church. It was sacrilege. Who would burn a church? But he went down again as the tail fin collapsed on its left side.

Helmut Lau saw Kollmer climbing out the entrance hatch to the fin. Sauter yelled to get out there. Freund stepped through first, then pulled Lau through. They both turned around to see Chief Sauter coming through. Blood was streaming down his face.

Lau got hold of him and pulled. Then all three ran. They stopped after a while and examined each other. Sauter's cut was on his head. Freund was burned on both hands and on his left cheek. Kollmer was limping. Lau was untouched.

They ran around the corner to the port side engine gondolas. The sailors would not let Chief Sauter go towards the ship. They could hear screaming inside it.

In the bow Joseph Leibrecht, electrician from Lindau, world traveler, boy trainer of birds, felt as much as heard the second explosion. At the top of the stairs he heard Huchel say: "Fire."

On the step next to him, the next one higher, he saw reflected in the face of Master Rigger Chief Knorr the rosy glow of Hell, and what he saw in the Chief's eyes made him close his own. He kept them tight shut. As the ship began its tilt aft, Leibrecht held on to the girder at his right with, at first, both hands, and then with his feet. He heard the other men begin to groan and then scream.

With the bow pointing higher and higher in the sky, the flames now funneled through the center of the ship. The axial walk was the filament for an immense blow-torch. With his eyes clenched shut, he did not see Huchel attempt to swing out of the ship on one of the yaw lines. Huchel was going to try to slide down. Instead he lost hold and dropped perhaps 150 feet to the ground flat on his back.

For some reason though, Leibrecht was acutely aware of the screams as the flames burned away the clinging hands of each man on the steps to the altar. First Spehl dropped like a partridge to be roasted in the inferno aft. Then Bernhard, then Felber, Biallas—each in his turn—Stoeckle, Mueller, and finally, right beside him, Chief Knorr. One by one, they let go and dropped behind him into the cauldron.

Somehow he knew he was the only one left, but he did not look, nor loosen his grip on sweet life. Through the lids of his eyes he could see Hell's fires dance. He was suddenly conscious of every beat of his own heart. He was amazed at how long each pulse took to sound. He could feel the flames working at his back, at the nape of his neck, and at his precious hands. He shifted his feet to make sure they had a good grip.

Curiously, what he really did see behind those clenched eyes was first of all a vision of the snow fields on Saentis and Churfirsten across his lake in Lindau. Then each beat of his heart brought some new vision, some new dream. The alpine snow fields faded and were replaced by a whale. He had never seen a whale before. The whale sounded, its flukes pointing up to the sky, disappeared into the sea. The sea was boiling. His heart beat again. A train went by. It did not stop. It must have been an express. How odd! There was no express to Bregenz. The white milky boiling sea disappeared. He dreamed he was a bird—one of those same song birds he had trapped and caged as a boy. But now he was the bird in the cage. A huge force, an unknown master, a cruel fuehrer, was swinging the cage around and around in circles. The bird had to hold his perch with his feet. He heard the church bell ring. It was six o'clock. Then the cage and the bird were tossed into the evening fire in a hearth. That was his house! His grandmother was in her chair by the hearth. She screamed. It was the high pitched scream of tearing metal.

His heart thumped again. Now he saw white again, but not the snow fields. It was the white of apple blossoms, endless orchards of them, unearthly ones stretching in meadows from time immemorial. He was flying over them, just above the branches, but at great speed. He could smell them.

Some child was running beneath the trees. He strained to see who the child was, but he could not. Was it his grandchild? He did not have any grandchild yet. His heart beat again. He was thirsty, God, he was thirsty. But he did not let go.

# CHAPTER 8

# AN ACT OF GOD

"Beneath the unclouded and mild azure sky . . . . the great
mass of death floats on and on, till lost in infinite perspectives.
. . . Nor is this the end. Desecrated as the body is, a vengeful
ghost survives and hovers over it to scare."
—*Moby Dick*, HERMAN MELVILLE

$F$RIDAY in New Jersey it was fair and pleasant. The sun set at 7:58
P.M., Eastern Daylight Saving Time.

Whether it was Friday or some other day, whether it was 1937 or
some other year, must have been a matter of complete indifference to
the imperturbable sun, whose unblinking gaze swept west as always
over the ancient seas and shifting mountains of the turning earth.
"There go the ships; there play the Leviathans in the sea." It was May
and countless possibilities still remained.

By Friday, newsreels of the disaster were playing the neighborhood
theatres, and it was at least a week before the crowd began to turn
their attention to other disasters, other deaths, other loves.

When the second explosion sounded, the newsreel photographers
had swung their cameras up at the burning ship.

As one of them ground on, he kept saying, "Oh my God, Oh my
God. . . ." But he kept his camera to his eye.

By counting the number of frames exposed and dividing by the
speed of the camera, it was possible to calculate: from the time of the
second detonation until the time the ship's frame lay settled on the
ground, a total of only 34 seconds elapsed. The oil fires burned on for
hours. So did the Duraluminum rings, girders, struts, tension wires,

stairs, tables, navigation equipment, pots, bar tools, wine racks, landing lines, and such.

There were some witnesses who had compared the force of the explosion the day before to the brightness of the sun, another example of mindless vanity. The hydrogen fire-ball boiling up from the *Hindenburg* was perhaps 400 feet in diameter; whereas that of the sun is estimated to be 11,404,800 times as large.

Nevertheless, in Friday's dawn, except for a half-burned swastika still showing on its dislocated tail, and the eerie, twisted skeleton of a beached whale, its aluminum rib cage still glowing, there was nothing left.

When the news reached Germany Friday morning, there were more than a dozen women at the doors of the offices of the Zeppelin Corporation before it opened. When the doors had been unlocked, and the lights switched on, and the clerks had barricaded themselves behind the counter, they did their best to answer what questions they could. On Friday morning they didn't know much.

Beatrice Friederich demanded that the insurance she held on her man be paid immediately. A clerk answered her: "But how do you know he's dead? We have no list of who is dead, or missing, or in the hospitals yet."

In the confusion at Lakehurst, from the terrible stench of burned flesh, the moans and shrieks of pain of the night before, there were still stories to tell.

Mrs. Spah had got her husband into the emergency dispensary set up on the field. A doctor examined him: "You have fractured your heel."

"After all the falls I've taken," said Joe Spah, "this is the way I finally break something!"

Because he spoke German, a nurse asked him to come to the next room. There was a young crewman there who wanted to send a message to Germany. The man was horribly burned. Joseph Spah copied down the address, and the message. It read: "I live." But Joseph Spah never sent it, because the young man, Eric Spehl, had immediately died.

\*        \*        \*

After Miss Margaret Mather had been escorted down the stairs from "A" deck and led clear, George Grant had insisted she go to the infirmary. Instead she wanted to find her niece Peggy, who Miss Margaret knew would be looking for her: "But I'm not asking you to go out of your way. Put me down at the nearest point. I'm not hurt!"

One of the crewmen said: "Look at your hands, lady."

It made her sick when she looked at them. She looked at the heavy winter coat she had on. It was all full of holes, like lace, she thought. She had been trying to keep her hands off it, so that she would not smudge it with oil. She had lost one shoe.

In the infirmary she sat with one shoe on, perched on the edge of a table, her legs swinging down, too short to reach the floor. She was amazed she didn't have the slightest feeling of pain. That was a great consolation to her. She had always worried so about Jeanne d'Arc and the martyrs who were burned at the stake. Now she believed that in their state of exultation, they probably hadn't felt a thing.

Facing her on another table, Captain Lehmann sat quietly with a large piece of gauze in one hand and a bottle of Picric acid in the other, swabbing at his burns. From time to time they passed the Picric acid back and forth to each other. When she had seen him aboard ship, he had always looked alert but genial, with keen blue eyes. Now his face was grave in stoic silence. He would nod from time to time as the rescue squads carried his men past on stretchers, or on boards.

His clothes were practically all burned off, and the hair on his head was gone. From the front he didn't look that badly, but those who had seen his back said he really didn't have any—the charred flesh was falling off in chunks. When Miss Margaret would reach for the bottle, he would hand it to her with grave courtesy, wait patiently until she had wet her hands, and receive it back with a murmured "Danke schoen."

She thought it was a strange, quiet interlude, almost as though they were having tea together. From time to time he would look out the window, and repeat: "I don't understand." He died at about 2:30 that morning.

She could not bear the smells, or the cries and weeping. She went outside and walked up and down in the light rain, and watched the remains of the ship burning. Her family had assumed that everyone in the Hindenburg had perished. No one could have survived a fire like that. They had left. Miss Margaret kept asking people to call her family for her.

Eventually they offered to take her anywhere she wanted to go in an ambulance. She said she would like to be taken to Princeton. She rode on the ambulance's stretcher with two Navy men beside her, and two up front. They regaled her with tales of the horrors they had just seen, but they were very kind, trying to avoid bumps in the road and stopping often to ask directions. They finally left her at her niece's house. From there Miss Margaret could call the family doctor and call her brother in Washington's Crossing. Her family were over there lamenting her death.

Gertrud Adelt said her first thought when she and her husband were clear of the ship was not for the people, but as she looked back, for the beautiful ship that was gone.

They were led to a car which would take them to the infirmary. It was a big car and there would be room for many in it. But in the back seat, Mrs. Doehner held her two badly burned sons in her arms. She looked like a lioness with her cubs. Her face was alabaster white. She kept saying over and over: "There's no room, there's no room in here."

The infirmary smelled terrible: alcohol, lysol, burned flesh. There were quiet bodies just laid out on the floor like mummies. A nurse came up to Gertrud Adelt with a morphine syringe.

"I don't want it," Mrs. Adelt said. "No one will know who I belong to."

There was a young man lying on the floor in the rags of his blue coveralls. He looked up at Gertrud Adelt and asked: "Do I have to die?"

Her own voice seemed so loud to her, and so light: "All people in this room will live."

She bent down to pull off his shoes. Someone had knit his socks by hand for him. He said he wanted to make his confession. She got a priest for him. The priest's violet stole was just thrown around his neck, and it hung down over the young man's face. It was the face of an angel, and it was peaceful as he died.

Her brother-in-law took them away from the Air Station's infirmary, and got them through the cordon surrounding the field.

Thousands of the curious jammed the roads to have a look. The Adelts drove off into New Jersey. They had to get away. They were astonished, disturbed, and they didn't know how badly burned they both really were. Leonhard began to complain he was suffocating. The smoke from the burning oil must have got to his lungs.

They stopped at a Juvenile Home for the Disturbed. A doctor—half asleep—received them. Leonhard's scalp was burned to the bone. They left him and drove on. Gertrud was received at a hospital in her brother-in-law's home town. When she finally woke up the next morning, she said the first thing she saw was a chestnut tree. She watched it for a long time.

Two reporters and a photographer found her in the hospital. With them she went back to the Naval Air Station where she saw the skeleton of the ship in the sand. She said it had no meaning to her anymore: "It was just a pile of iron parts."

A Navy officer escorted her into the hangar to see the *Los Angeles*. In the contrasting shadow of the hangar, darkness swam up before her eyes. She felt herself vanishing. Did she faint?

A few weeks later they visited the Metropolitan Museum of Art where they saw a painting they were surprised to learn had been done sometime before the disaster. It showed a burning Zeppelin in the sky over New York. It was, she thought, a barbaric painting. The passengers were coming down from the ship comfortably hanging from parachutes, but their teeth were bared in either a strange smile, or a grimace. It was hard to say which.

Elsa Ernst survived the *Hindenburg*, but she was 62 then. She shared a hospital room with her husband at Paul Kimball Hospital. He died May 15.

George Grant survived, and so did Hans Vinholt, Rolf von Heidenstamm, Philip Mangone, Colonel Morris, William Leuchtenburg, Mrs. Marie Kleeman, and Clifford Osbun.

The photographer Karl Otto Clemens survived, went to his cousin's house in Ridgefield, New Jersey. He just sat there at the piano for three days, lighting one cigarette after another, playing Chopin.

George W. Hirschfeld survived the glowing beams and wires that trapped Colonel Fritz Erdmann. He still lives in Bremen and could still pass for a big cotton man from Texas. Major Franz Hugo Witt made it clear too. Some say he died in a plane over Russia in the war; others say his name appeared on the lists of the East German Air Force, but no one is sure if the name represents the same Major Witt. Lieutenant Hinkelbein lived through the *Hindenburg* disaster and the war. He was always lucky. He died in Koblenz in the sixties as a retired Colonel.

Peter Belin, once clear of the ship from his jump, went back to help the injured to the base infirmary. Maybe an hour, maybe two hours passed. His mother and father searched for him in the confusion at the field. He was not on any of the "injured" lists. They assumed he must be among the "missing," out there in the glowing skeleton. They went to their car, and started to ease out of the parking lot for home.

By then Peter Belin had realized they must be searching for him. He ran for the parking lot to find their car. He saw it just as it was leaving. He gave the family whistle. They still didn't stop. He chased the car, jumped onto its running board, and stuck his head in the window. His mother was sure he was a ghost. She fainted.

Peter Belin maintained his interest in flying, joined the Navy Air Corps, retired as a Captain, thirty years later.

Of the 36 passengers, 13 died on the field, in the infirmary, or at the nearby hospitals: Ernst Rudolf Anders, Birger Brinck, Herman Doehner (the father), Miss Irene Doehner, "Major" Dolan, Edward Douglas, Otto Ernst, Moritz Feibusch, Eric Knoescher, Mr. and Mrs. John Pannes, Otto Reichold, and Colonel Erdmann.

Chief Ludwig Knorr died in the fire, along with 16 others in the crew who died on the field or in the infirmary and consequently were listed "Dead on Arrival": Biallas, Dimmler, Eichelmann, Huchel, Frau Imhoff, Flackus, Moser, Mueller, Reisacher, Scheef, Schlapp, Schreibmueller, Schulze, Alfred Stoeckle, and Eric Spehl. Three more crewmen died in Paul Kimball Hospital in Lakewood, New Jersey: Bahnholzer, Felber, and Captain Lehmann.

Bernhard died in Fitkin Memorial Hospital in Neptune, New Jersey. Chief Radio Officer Willy Speck was moved from Paul Kimball Hospital to Presbyterian Hospital in New York on Friday night, but he died Saturday morning anyway. Captain Pruss had gone back into the burning ship to save Speck, and was horribly scarred for the rest of his life. After six months of plastic surgery at Presbyterian Hospital, he returned to Germany. He died of pneumonia in 1960.

Navy crewman Allen Hagaman tripped on the landing circle's rails and fell. The ship's burning frame crashed on him. He was identified by his wedding ring the next day. Leonard Jacobsen, another in the Navy crew, was hit by an auto on the field, and had to be taken to Paul Kimball Hospital, but he lived.

Chief Engineer Rudolf Sauter was not badly injured at Lakehurst. He served as an engineer through the war, then afterwards opened department stores. He died peacefully in Frankfurt in his sixties.

Chief Philip Lenz survived. In 1971 he was still Chief Electrician at the Luftschiffbau in Friedrichshafen on the Bodensee.

Of the 61 crew members, 22 died. One ground crewman died, which including the 13 passengers dead, made a total of 36 dead.

Immediately after the disaster in Lakehurst, the Department of Commerce appointed a commission to investigate the cause of the explosion. The Germans joined the American Commission as "observers." Dr. Hugo Eckener came, and so did Ludwig Dürr, among others.

For a month witnesses were questioned, experts gave testimony, and evidence was introduced. A number of interesting theories were heard: a rocket fired by an experimenter from Connecticut's Berkshires had been the cause, its inventor claimed, but his fantasy was a little ahead of its time; a radio beam aimed from near the field; a loose propeller had flung itself into the belly of the ship—a sort of mechanical ceremonial suicide.

German and American airmen and scientists, technicians, chemists and physicists discussed "ball lightning," "a demon proton," "static electricity," and "St. Elmo's fire."

All agreed there was no probable way these conjuries could ignite the hydrogen *inside* the ship, where hundreds of witnesses had seen its start; nor would St. Elmo's fire cause two explosions of the sort all agreed had taken place.

The difficulty was that the Americans had agreed among themselves they "would not consider sabotage." Their reasoning was quite sensible at the time. They thought it would be better to avoid "the implications of a nasty international incident, especially on our shores." They settled for St. Elmo's fire, among the "most probable causes," although no one could cite an instance in the history of air or sea voyage in which St. Elmo's fire had caused an explosion.

Commander Rosendahl wrote Mr. South Trimble, the Commission's solicitor, enclosing the confidential memorandum which the German Technical Commission prepared at the request of the board on the subject of sabotage.

"As you will recall, the arrangements with the German Commission in this regard were that the memorandum would *not* be included in the record and would in every respect be considered confidential and solely for the use of the Board in considering the possible sabotage."

But the secret German memoranda were not much help either. The Americans did not know that General Goering had instructed the German Commission to "discover nothing." No mortal means was to be accorded the honor of destroying a key symbol of the Reich.

"It was," said the Luftwaffe chief, "an act of God."

# EPILOGUE

Apparently not satisfied with the progress that had been made up until 1937, the Central Committees, Reichstags, Diets, Parliaments, Assemblies, Congresses and their Presidents, Prime Ministers, Emperors, Duces, Secretaries, Generalissimos, and Fuehrers, and their representatives, devoted themselves to getting the world at war again.

There were charges and counter-charges, of course, but on the whole it could be said that it was a war democratically conducted by all participants. Everywhere the people were even more enthusiastic to redress their grievances than before, and with the aid of a good deal of ingenuity and a number of new technical devices, the total casualty figures were estimated to reach something like 40 million, perhaps 50 million. Or was it 60 million?

After the war, Germans were charged and found guilty of genocide because they had deliberately murdered six million Jews. To be fair, it must be said on their behalf they murdered at least that many others who weren't Jews at all. To the lasting credit of the United Nations, the Allies killed without regard to race, color, or creed. With an admirable sense of justice, they destroyed in seconds whole cities at a time.

Coincidentally, Adolf Hitler committed suicide in his bunker eight years to the day after the *Hindenburg* went down. There is no significance to the cojunction of the dates. If his suicide for the sake of his people could not exactly be described as a *beau geste*, it was by definition an *acte gratuit*. But it is such musings which cause philosophers to fall into dispute. Most scholars agree the application of Nietzschean principles to the State on so grand a scale was no more than a meander in the course of history, only possible under the special conditions which obtained at that time, and not likely to be repeated in the logic of evolution. However, the Iron Law, which surely applies, has recently eluded definition.

The last act of the *Hindenburg* brought to an end the long line of Zeppelin development. The experience, the ambitions, the dreams of the men of the Luftschiffbau, the successors of Graf Zeppelin, were played out.

Just as there would never be any more cavalry charges, the Zeppelins had no function—they were archaic, rather curious machines, somewhat like a huge toy, anachronistic in an age of guided missiles and flame throwers, a meander in the lazy river of technology.

The *Graf Zeppelin* was grounded upon its arrival from Rio on May 8, 1937. The next year, the *Graf Zeppelin II* flew around the coast of England repeatedly to test the radar defenses of that island of blood, sweat and tears. Mr. Winston Churchill complained of its intentions in the House of Commons, but that was the last notoriety in the final chapters of the "crazy old count's invention." Zeppelins were the wrong technological choice; they were the wrong variation.

The scrap from the burned-out wreck in New Jersey was sold for $4,000, then shipped back to Germany to be reforged into airplanes. The other two ships—the old and new *Graf Zeppelins*—were melted down to become fighters and bombers in 1940. Thereafter, when Zeppelins bombed London, they had to do so as aluminum ghosts.

Who knows? Perhaps they did. Beyond the lightning, wisdom is hid in the depths of darkness and understanding veiled in secrecy.

There were various accounts about what Frau Friederich did when she heard Eric Spehl was dead. One version was that she immediately went to Vienna. At the time of the Anschluss, she was forced to move on to Hungary, and then to Russia. Another version is that she went to Switzerland. Another version is that the Gestapo arrested her and held her for eight days, then released her.

Another account is that she was for a while the girl friend of Helmut Lau, who escaped the disaster and was decorated and promoted to Lieutenant by the S.S. for his heroism in saving passengers at Lakehurst.

Beatrice Friederich is not her real name, although the initials would
be more or less the same. Helmut Lau says he doesn't remember her
real name; doesn't particularly remember "Frau Friederich" at all, as
a matter of fact. He says, "There were many girls in those days." He
doesn't know if she really ever existed. He doesn't care to speculate if
it would be still possible to find her in Frankfurt. "In any case," he
says, "she'll never talk."

It is said, however, that Eleanor Pruss, the widow of Captain Pruss,
will cross to the other side of the street in Frankfurt to avoid meeting
her.

Curiously, the Gestapo did arrest Mathia Merrifield, the stripper
with whom Joseph Spah had posed for the publicity shots at the
Frankfurt airfield. The Gestapo held Mathia for a week. They told
her that Joseph Spah, who they insisted was her boy friend, had died
in the disaster at Lakehurst, and that she might as well confess what
she knew about him.

She figured it wouldn't matter very much if he was dead anyway, so
she told them what they wanted to hear, and they let her go. Of
course when she found out that Joe Spah was still alive, she wrote him
a letter to apologize. Vera Spah gave her husband some advice about
getting mixed up with the wrong kind of women. He told her again it
was "just publicity."

On the way home from Lakehurst in the car, Mr. and Mrs. Spah
had told their children that Ulla, the dog they had hoped for, had
been saved. It was, they said, a miracle. Within a few days the parents
produced a dog whose name was indeed Ulla, which the children did
love.

As the children grew they hung on Ulla's neck to learn to walk,
they took her to their bedrooms in the house in Douglaston for "company," they hugged her from time to time, and swatted her sometimes
too. What they really knew about the disaster they had seen was immaterial. The two boys, Gilbert and Richard, followed their father
into show business, and after a while there was a successor to "Ben
Dova," whose name was "Gil Dova," playing Miami Beach.

But no one could ever match Joseph Spah as the drunk on the lamp-
post. He was to play it thousands of times more. He learned to play it
on roller skates and on ice skates, and he played it the old, flat-footed

way in theatres, movie houses, hotels, and the big nightclubs. He didn't stop until the heel he had fractured in 1937 crippled him with arthritis.

Even then, thirty-four years later when he was 67, he could still hobble up out of a chair in his living room in Douglaston, and while Vera watched, cock his head, start his hands searching through his pockets for a cigarette, and the drunk would appear: the same irrational, determined, obsessed fool that had caught the imagination of his audiences, delighted them, made them explode with laughter at the truths they recognized. It was exactly as Captain Lehmann had said: Artists don't make bombs because they make jokes.

Every year until the war, and then afterwards again, Miss Margaret Mather flew back and forth to Rome. Summers were spent on Cape Cod. She always said she would never hesitate to fly on a Zeppelin again. It would perhaps be a bit boring for a young person because there was no movie and no dancing, just peace, which young people generally don't like too much, but for her it was the best way to travel.

She lived on another thirty-one years. By then she had godchildren all over the world. She cared for those who were happy, and for those who divorced, for those who fell sick and for those who perhaps had lost their mind a little.

They could all tell stories about her: how she had still run after trolleys at eighty; how she still sailed in the "S" class boats at Quisset; how she had escaped a taxi crash with stitches in her head, and then been furious that she had missed half her Friday concert; how she liked to do over her apartment at the top of the Spanish Steps. You could see St. Peter's from there, you know. She died in Rome at 98.

In 1937 the Adelts took the *Europa* back to Bremen. On the way, when the ship stopped in England, they hoped they could talk awhile with their friend Stefan Zweig. But he was afraid to come aboard, because the Nazis might grab him. It was not a good time.

Gertrud Adelt had a brother who was a Jesuit priest. By the end of 1937, the Nazis had closed or taken control of all the Catholic Schools. He had to leave. He went to Japan to teach at a high school there, in a city called Hiroshima.

When the war finally came, the Adelts were in Berlin. They had a young son by then, and as the raids increased in intensity, as block after block was reduced to rubble, they thought it would be wiser to move. They went down to Dresden because there were no targets of any military value there.

On the evening of February 13, 1945, in the fire storm that sucked even the oxygen from the center of town, they were able to get out of the house. But while she held their son, Leonhard Adelt went back into the house to get a manuscript. The house collapsed on him. So it goes.

She survived and their son survived. Her brother in Hiroshima was up on the hill that morning, and he survived. She moved to Hamburg, where she collected again the few things they had left in their apartment in Berlin, including a sugar teaspoon with the swastika on it, the sun sign, except that theirs was backwards—the way the Indians make it.

Her house is surrounded with the flowering rhododendrons for which Hamburg is famous. She says she compromised with her vanity for her big blue eyes a few years ago—when she was sixty-five, and bought some glasses. Now she realizes that she had gone through life seeing as if it were colored from the palette of the French Impressionists, a little indistinct when you are up close. She revels in her new, more acute vision.

Chief Steward Heinrich Kubis lives in Augsburg, on Ritter von Steinerstrasse. Kubis' son died when he was 57. Chief Kubis keeps house with his widowed daughter-in-law.

He tells a curious story about Marie Lehmann. Officers and crewmen of the *Hindenburg* were buried together in a ceremony at a common grave in Frankfurt. Mrs. Lehmann went to Frankfurt and had her husband dug up. She had him cremated, brought the urn of ashes home to a house she had rented near Munich. She put the urn in her garden, beside the urn which contained the ashes of their son, Luv.

Within two years she was engaged to be married to a man who had been the friend of both Captain Lehmann and his wife. That man died just before they could be married. She had him cremated, and set the third urn in the garden.

During the war, her son from her first marriage was killed in Russia. Somehow she was able to struggle through the bureaucracy of governments and armies. She got his body back to Munich. When his ashes were in an urn, she set it beside the others. The neighbors complained that she had no permit for a cemetery, and she was forced to move to another house she kept with a widowed daughter on the Starnberger See, near Munich.

Kubis' story is probably an exaggeration. He also says that after the disaster at Lakehurst, the Zeppelin Corporation gathered up what they could from the burned-out skeleton of the ship, toted it to their offices in New York, and spread it out on the floor. In little piles were blackened rings, false teeth, burned papers, scorched cases of leather, and a crystal necklace in which the reds and blues had melted into one. All the little baggage with which people travel.

Oh, yes. He can remember it all. His once blond hair has turned grey, and thinned, but the blue eyes are still quick. He has coffee and cakes to offer, and a fine cigar. On his dining room wall he still has the picture of the *Graf Zeppelin* over Rio made from butterfly wings.

He can tell you that no German, no member of the old Zeppelin family, would have ever sabotaged the *Hindenburg*. Every Zeppelin man who knows anything at all agrees with him, he says. He is unequivocal. In his opinion it was that acrobat, the only passenger with access, that artist, what's his name.

Joseph Leibrecht was the only man in the bow section to survive. His forearms and hands are hideously scarred, his left hand cramped like a claw, but it works well enough for an electrician.

Sitting in his garden in Lindau, he plays with his grandson Freddie, who is only two. The child helps to fill the space left empty when Leibrecht's wife died. Leibrecht figures he'll probably get along awhile longer by eating and drinking and sleeping—pretty much as other men do.

From his bedroom he can name every white-topped mountain he can see across the Bodensee: there is Hoher Kasten, there is Churfirsten, there is Saentis. Along the tracks behind the house, trains pass going East to Bregenz, or West to Friedrichshafen. He no longer takes the train to the Luftschiffbau to work because he is retired now, but the days don't seem long—there's a lot to do around the house. He can keep time from the church tower, which rings the hours for him.

There are apple orchards across the tracks, in the gulley and up the side of the hill between his house and the lake. Behind him every farm has acres and acres of them. He can smell the blooms in May and the fruits in fall. Their branches are spotted with cockbirds singing promises, singing of treaties made, territories won, defeats suffered. They promise their loves—well, they promise protection on the one hand, time enough to work out the possibilities, and adventure on the other. It is an ambiguous song. In May they sing of fulfillments yet to come.

# ACKNOWLEDGMENTS

When I began my investigative reporting on the story of the last flight of the *Hindenburg*, I feared an event thirty-five years in the past might have the details of its circumstances blurred by time. For reasons which are not clear to me even now, however, the *Hindenburg* disaster seemed to sear the memory of everyone even remotely connected with it. Scores of people turned up who had, they believed, some connection with what had made headlines. In most cases their involvement was tenuous. But among those directly involved, memories were extraordinarily sharp, the details and circumstances stored up in perfect order.

Let one example stand for the rest. After the *Hindenburg* went down, Heinz Wronsky, the general passenger agent for the Hamburg-American Line, went to work for General Motors in Russelheim. When the war came he served as the famous navigator for fleets of Heinkel bombers in the Battle of Britain. Then he was shot down, crashed on the French coast. He recovered from his injuries on furlough and flew again in tactical air support at the Battle of Stalingrad. Towards the end of the war he was taken prisoner. His home was destroyed by American bombers, but he survived. In fact, he had to survive again and again.

He has memories, of course, about the Battle of Britain, of Stalingrad, of poking through the debris of his home, but they are memories on some grand scale—he was a small actor in an immense play of events. About the *Hindenburg*, on the other hand, he can remember the most astonishing details: what Dr. Eckener said when

Minister Goebbels called him to Berlin; how they designed the flag
for the Zeppelin Company; what was written on Douglas Fairbanks'
slippers; how Lady Ashley's perfume affected him. Exactly why he
should remember more about the *Hindenburg* than he remembers
about Stalingrad or the Battle of Britain is, I think, mysterious. Yet
Heinz Wronsky was typical of most subjects I interviewed.

Besides the copious personal details remembered by participants, I
discovered the last flight of the *Hindenburg* may well have been the
most completely documented, reported, and analyzed disaster on record. Since the Zeppelin *Hindenburg* was *the* glamorous method of
air travel at the time, and since it had such a spectacular end, I should
not have been surprised to find plenty of source material. Yet still
there were surprises.

The National Archives of the United States hold roughly 21 linear
feet of materials on the *Hindenburg* disaster alone. The Department
of Commerce, under Secretary Daniel C. Roper, appointed a Board of
Inquiry which held its sessions for over six months. The members of
the board were Mr. South Trimble, Jr., as solicitor; Major R. W.
Schroeder, Assistant Director of the Bureau of Air Commerce; and
Mr. Denis Mulligan, Chief of Regulation and Enforcement Division,
Bureau of Air Commerce.

A great number of technical advisors were appointed to assist the
board, among them Commander Rosendahl; Colonel Rush Lincoln
for the War Department; Colonel Harold E. Hartney, technical advisor to the Senate Committee on Commerce; and Mr. Grover Loe-
ning, aeronautical advisor to the United States Maritime Commission—appointed by the commission's chief, Mr. Joseph P. Kennedy.
All of these gentlemen kept notes, submitted memoranda, maintained files of correspondence.

Ninety-seven witnesses were heard in official testimony. The log
and radio logs, charts plotting the final days of the flight in minute detail, weather maps, and the personal escape stories of those who survived were all dutifully recorded and form part of this book. The
official transcripts run to some 1,200 pages, plus a number of exhibits
and indices. Yet the official transcripts comprise less than half the materials now in hand at the National Archives. The other half of the
material has been accumulated over the years, and it was the additional materials which often proved to be most fascinating.

Among these materials were letters forwarded from the Secretaries of Commerce and Interior reminding Solicitor South Trimble, Jr., that "a finding of sabotage might be cause for an international incident, especially on these shores." But while the Board of Inquiry did its best to avoid the discovery of sabotage in its public hearings, almost every dirigible man (including Captain Pruss, Captain Bauer, Designer Dürr, Commander Rosendahl, and many others) in private agreed that sabotage was the cause. Over the weeks while the Board of Inquiry conducted meetings during the day, both the German advisors and the American commissioners and advisors held meetings at night to discuss, off the record, the inescapable evidence of sabotage before them.

I might never have known about these evening sessions had I not found among the additional materials the diary of Mr. Denis Mulligan, in which he meticulously kept the minutes of the off-the-record meetings. His papers have made their way to the National Archives.

So also have the memoranda of the German advisors, Staff Engineer Friedrich Hoffman, Professor Guenther Bock, and Professor Max Dieckmann. In 1937 there were only two copies of an English translation of their findings, prepared at the request of the board, on the subject of sabotage. No one at the U.S. Naval Station except Commander Rosendahl and the translator had seen it. It too eventually made its way to the National Archives.

So also did the letters warning the German Ambassador of the impending disaster—to which Major Hufschmidt referred in his meeting with Colonel Erdmann. There, also, is a description of the materials from which the bomb was made—analyzed from the remains collected at the site by Detective George McCartney of the Bomb Squad of the New York Police Department.

In sum, the job of investigative reporting was not a burden at all because, for example, I could read the eye-witness account of the bomb's explosion inside the ship given in public testimony by Helmut Lau (the description in this book is taken almost verbatim from the transcript) and then turn to the private diaries, papers and correspondence and see how the bomb was made. Instead of being unable to discover sufficient details, I soon had too many from a combination of officially recorded evidence and unofficial, but now available, materials. In May 1971 I took to Germany some 50 kilos of excess baggage—all of it notes.

In Germany there are a number of subjects and situations which are still painful, or delicate. Although most of the libraries were sacked or destroyed, and materials which would be assumed to be easily accessible in the United States just don't exist, a number of special libraries contain incredibly detailed information. It is possible, for example, to learn the pelvic measurements in centimeters of Major Hufschmidt's wife. Obviously that kind of information is irrelevant to this story, but perusal of such a file before conducting an interview is a great aid to a reporter. Until 1945 Germany maintained active files on 30 million people. Every telephone conversation, even an innocuous call to the butcher, was meticulously recorded from 1933 to 1945.

I used *The New York Times* on microfilm at the U.C.L.A. Library. Besides its biographies, besides its complete file on the story of the Zeppelins, besides the daily record of major events in 1936 and 1937, *The Times* was my source for all kinds of details: for example, Joseph Leibrecht's car crash in Elizabeth, New Jersey in 1936 had been solemnly recorded in a three-liner; the passenger lists of every crossing; menus and wine lists; the vote count aboard the *Hindenburg* in the Rhineland election; the complete record of the contest between Joseph Goebbels and Dr. Eckener. Curiously, many of the dispatches upon which I depended most heavily were cabled from Berlin by Mr. Louis P. Lochner, the Associated Press bureau chief, who was one of my boyhood heroes.

This is all by way of saying this book has had hundreds of collaborators, contributors, and without exaggeration, thousands of citeable sources. I am indebted to them all.

Obviously none of these collaborators can be held responsible for errors, which are solely mine. In some cases I pieced together anecdotes or materials from several sources. In other cases I heard conflicting stories about who said what or did this or that, and I had to choose among them. What might be the wrong version of a conversation is often the most useful in clearing up exactly what the right version comprised.

I might have footnoted contributions as I went along, which is the proper and scholarly way of doing things. For example, I was told two similar but different versions of the accidental burning of Chief Willy

Speck's son, by Heinrich Kubis and Gertrud Adelt. A third person, Heinrich Bauer, insisted it never happened at all. Footnotes are designed to accommodate such situations, but instead of wracking the reader with endless citations, I tried to draw what I thought were the most reasonable conclusions, based upon the available evidence.

In a number of cases it was necessary to avoid breaching confidences, or causing people who had been no more than generous to become accessories to my conclusions. It was in this sense that I changed the name of Beatrice Friederich. Despite Helmut Lau's vagueness, she did indeed live near Frankfurt.

I made one other change of fact. The telegram signed "Reilly," represented as sent to Edward Douglas, was sent instead directly to my father, James D. Mooney, who was the General Motors director to whom Douglas reported in Frankfurt.

To James D. Mooney I am indebted specifically for his papers of the period, some of which are in the Yale library, and which include the history of the negotiations between Great Britain, Germany, and the United States for which he often served as a courageous messenger. For example, the details of the cotton barter deal, "dunked with lard," which George W. Hirschfeld was en route to New York to execute, came from James D. Mooney's minutes of his meetings with Dr. Schacht and with the United States State Department representatives.

More important, his constant urging to "see if you can find out what happened in the thirties," led me to do more study of this period through the years than I would naturally have been inclined to. He always taught that economic and political conditions do not change very much; "the showgirls just get a different kind of boy friend." In a way this book should have been dedicated to him. By the understanding we have finally reached, I have dedicated it instead to his grandsons, which I know would have made him laugh.

In addition to my debts to Mr. James Walker and his staff at the National Archives, to the special libraries of Germany, to the immense record of *The New York Times*, I owe a number of special debts. The list which follows is in no special order, omits some contributions deliberately and probably others unfortunately. To those below and to those I have omitted, I thank you.

From the reportorial skills of Leonhard and Gertrud Adelt I have drawn my own portrait of Ernst A. Lehmann, much of the history of the Luftschiffbau, nearly all the quotes about "the miracles of Echterdingen," Captain Lehmann's analyses and descriptions of bombing London, the scene in which Dorothea Erdmann returns to the ship to say goodbye to her husband again, a large part of the dinner table conversations, and portraits of their fellow passengers and many other vignettes.

Lehmann's autobiography, *Zeppelin*, Longmans, Green and Co., London, New York, Toronto, 1937, was written "in collaboration with Leonhard Adelt," who also described "The Last Trip of the *Hindenburg*" for *The Reader's Digest*, November 1937. Leonhard Adelt also wrote an appreciation of Ernst A. Lehmann, *Der Luftschiffkapitan in Krieg und Frieden* for Mettenetco, Verlagsanstalt, Berlin, 1937, which Gertrud Adelt was kind enough to give me.

Gertrud Stolte Adelt wrote *Die Katastrophe von Lakehurst*, Pfeiffer Verlag, Munchen, 1964, which I used. But then she told me story after story of the *Hindenburg*, its passengers and crew, and of Germany; and besides was marvelously hospitable at her home in Hamburg. To both Gertrud Adelt, and posthumously to her husband, Leonhard Adelt, two incredibly courageous people, my thanks.

Miss Margaret Mather wrote "I was on the *Hindenburg*," for *Harper's Magazine*, November 1937. In 1956 she also made a recording of her impressions for the benefit of her family. Mr. Robert Montgomery acted as interviewer. Mr. and Mrs. Louis A. Turner were kind enough to give me the recording, and in addition to provide the story of Peggy Mather Turner's aunt—Miss Margaret.

Mr. and Mrs. George W. Hirschfeld rearranged their schedules, and took in a stranger who stayed on and on, like the man who came to dinner. George Hirschfeld had saved every clipping he could get of the disaster; and in addition he had 16 mm. movies taken on board during the final trip, which he gave me and which must have been recovered from the cameras of either Clemens or Spah, or both.

Mr. and Mrs. Klaus Pruss were invariably hospitable. Klaus Pruss, the son of Captain Pruss, is the United Press International Bureau Chief in Frankfurt. He has kept up on the records of the story of the *Hindenburg* as his avocation. He knew exactly what would help, including the latest address and phone number of everyone possibly connected with Zeppelins.

Mr. and Mrs. Joseph Spah told their own story, with the kind of anecdote and detailed delight in life which makes a reporter's work a pleasure. Joe Spah retold the jokes he told in the *Hindenburg* bar, mimed those passengers who had caught his fancy, provided many of the details on Moritz Feibusch and on William Leuchtenburg, and was at the deathbed of Eric Spehl.

Mrs. Maria Spehl is the only member of that family still alive in Göschweiler. Despite her insistence that Eric Spehl was not the kind of boy to do such a thing, despite her annoyance at the story of his adventure which had appeared from time to time in the German press, she was courteous, kind and patient. She provided the details of Eric Spehl's childhood, without which much of his later actions might have seemed puzzling.

Mr. Wellington (Bill) Long, United Press International chief correspondent for Germany, not only had addresses and phone numbers of scores of leads in his head at all times, but took patient hours to explain difficulties, get translations, taught me history, gave me books to read, arranged difficult interviews, and steered me to sources, all as if he had nothing else to do, and in an unusual spirit of delight in someone else's story. Bill Long is one of the great professionals.

For accounts of the early history of Zeppelins, of aircraft, and of the *Hindenburg*, I am indebted to a long list of writers, but particularly to: Beril Becker, *Dreams and Realities of the Conquests of the Skies*, Atheneum, New York, 1967; Ken Dallison, *When Zeppelins Flew*, Time-Life Books, New York, 1969; Basil Clarke, *The History of Airships*, Herbert Jenkins, London, 1961; A.A. Hoehling, *Who Destroyed the Hindenburg?*, Little, Brown and Company, Boston, 1962; Dale M. Titler, *Wings of Mystery*, Dodd, Mead & Company, New York, 1966; and John Toland, *Ships in the Sky*, Henry Holt and Company, New York, 1957.

I have also drawn from: R.W. Cooper, *The Nuremberg Trial*, Penguin Books, London, 1947; Winston S. Churchill, *The Gathering Storm*, Houghton Mifflin Company, Boston, 1948; Joachim C. Fest, *The Face of the Third Reich*, Pantheon Books, New York, 1970; G.M. Gilbert, *Nuremberg Diary*, New American Library, New York, 1961; Ernst Hanfstaengl, *Unheard Witness*, J.B. Lippincott Company, Philadelphia, 1957; Friedrich Nietzsche, *The Anti-Christ*, Penguin Classics Edition; Friedrich Reck-Malleczewen, *The Diary of a*

*Man in Despair*, The Macmillan Company, New York, 1970; William L. Shirer, *The Rise and Fall of the Third Reich*, Simon and Schuster, New York, 1960; Albert Speer, *Inside the Third Reich*, The Macmillan Company, 1970; Edmund A. Walsh, S.J., *Total Power*, Doubleday & Company, Inc., Garden City, 1948; and Stefan Zweig, *The World of Yesterday*, Viking Press, 1943.

I owe a very special debt to Dr. Richard L. Bauer, Chief Archivist, United States Mission, Berlin, and to his staff, especially Dr. Werner Pix, not only for maintaining records from the Third Reich, but for the courtesy and advice which a visitor found he needed. Otherwise mountains of material would have been unintelligible.

My thanks to those who told stories, or provided other aids including: Alfred Wright, Dr. Anton LaVey, Admiral E.N. Eller, Admiral Charles E. Rosendahl, Marianne von Adelmann, "Leppo," Dr. Hans Scharpf, Mrs. Maria Spehl, Heinrich Kubis, Wolfgang Merz, Baron Rudiger von Wechmar, Dr. Kurt Ruediger, Max Zabel, Captain Hans von Schiller, Heinz Wronsky, Brigette Falbe, Mr. and Mrs. Helmut Lau, Eric Helligardt, Wolfgang Senghaas, Philip Lenz, Captain Heinrich Bauer, and Joseph Leibrecht.

Finally, my thanks to the Virginia Center for the Creative Arts, and to Mrs. J. Churchill Newcomb; to Elizabeth C. Greenleaf, who typed; to Margot Shields, researcher and "chief correspondent," to my brothers Alan and John; and to Thomas Lipscomb, editor in chief at Dodd, Mead, whose idea it was.

MICHAEL MACDONALD MOONEY

*East Hampton*
September, 1971